The Atkinson Family

IMPRINT IN HIGHER EDUCATION

The Atkinson Family Foundation has endowed this imprint to

illuminate the role of higher education in contemporary society.

The publisher and the University of California Press Foundation gratefully acknowledge the generous support of the Atkinson Family Foundation Imprint in Higher Education.

What Can I Get Out of This?

What Can I Get Out of This?

TEACHING AND LEARNING IN A
CLASSROOM FULL OF SKEPTICS

Carlo Rotella

UNIVERSITY OF CALIFORNIA PRESS

University of California Press
Oakland, California

Library of Congress Cataloging-in-Publication Data

Names: Rotella, Carlo, author.
Title: What can I get out of this? : teaching and learning in a classroom
    full of skeptics / Carlo Rotella.
Description: Oakland, California : University of California Press, [2025] |
    Includes bibliographical references and index.
Identifiers: LCCN 2024058428 (print) | LCCN 2024058429 (ebook) |
    ISBN 9780520416550 (cloth) | ISBN 9780520416567 (paperback) |
    ISBN 9780520416574 (ebook)
Subjects: LCSH: College teaching—Massachusetts—Boston—21st
    century—Case studies. | American literature—History and criticism.
Classification: LCC LB2331 .R633 2025 (print) | LCC LB2331 (ebook) |
    DDC 813/.54090071174461—dc23/eng/20250213
LC record available at https://lccn.loc.gov/2024058428
LC ebook record available at https://lccn.loc.gov/2024058429

Manufactured in the United States of America

GPSR Authorized Representative: Easy Access System Europe,
Mustamäe tee 50, 10621 Tallinn, Estonia, gpsr.requests@easproject
.com

34   33   32   31   30   29   28   27   26   25
10   9   8   7   6   5   4   3   2

For Pilar Vives Rotella, teacher of many lessons

No l'apaguis

Contents

1 A Quick Look Inside Our Heads Before We Begin

The first day of class always has an immemorial feel to it, an air of familiar routines eternally renewed. Getting myself in order in my office in the minutes before class began, I made sure I had my handouts—copies of the syllabus and a one-page sheet on the basics of literary form—and ran over in my mind what we were going to get done today. There wasn't all that much to keep straight: hand out the copies, go over the syllabus, make sure everybody talks, and if there's time, we can do an exercise or two to start everyone thinking about form and meaning. I was also, mostly below the level of conscious intent, getting into character. That character was me, basically, but a little more energetic and visibly interested in things; slightly upgraded in self-presentation (black pants that weren't jeans, dark blue button-down collared shirt, a fresh shave); and a lot more willing to take over and run the show, rather than sitting off to one side and observing as my instincts incline me to do.

Time to lower my idle. I took three progressively slower deep breaths, then one forceful one in and out, then one more very slow deep one, thinking about nothing but moving my diaphragm with glacial intention, feeling my heartbeat and my breathing slow to the point that it seemed like I had all the time in the world to decide when to take the next lungful of air.

Talking to a roomful of people can be daunting, no matter how often you do it. Sometimes before class, in addition to the two-minute breathing routine, I find myself reminding myself that I love school the way I love playing music or basketball and that teaching is both my job and one of the principal ways I belong to a community. Plus, because I don't have *that* many years left, I should choose to do what I do until I can't do it anymore. So, sitting at my desk in my office, I reminded myself that fear is the mother of courage and humor and invention and other useful impulses. I reminded myself, too, that school is school, forever and always, no matter what else is going on in the world outside the classroom, and school is one of my things. Along with writing, teaching is my craft, my profession. I'd be in real trouble if in a few minutes I had to go out there in front of everybody and do something I love that I'm not all that good at, like play Western swing with hot-picking pros or cover a 6-6 guy with blazing moves to the basket, but I've worked much more diligently at the craft of teaching than on developing my guitar- or ball-playing chops. All I had to do was lead a bunch of at least semiwilling people in figuring out together how some books work and how both what's in those books and the process of analytically getting at it would be of value to them in and beyond the classroom. I could probably do that.

It was almost noon on Tuesday, January 14, 2020, the start of spring semester. I picked up the stack of copies and a manila folder holding my notes and a printout of the class roster with thumbnail photographs of the students and walked out of my office and down two flights of stairs to room 209, Stokes Hall South.

.   .   .   .   .

Meanwhile, in 209, a cathedral hush prevailed among the thirty-four young people sitting in rows and waiting for me to arrive so class could begin. There were a couple of murmured conversations between students who already knew each other, but most were staring into space or at their phones. There was something familiar, even reassuring, about this uncomfortable anticipatory quiet. It was the second semester of their freshman year, so the students weren't as freaked out as they had been at the first meeting of fall semester classes, but being nervous on the first day of class is an eternal feature of school. Will the group chemistry, the vibe, turn out to be good or bad? Will I learn something worthwhile here? Will I be revealed as an idiot and humiliated? What if the teacher proves to be a bore, a maniac, a jerk?

Also, there was a certain amount of resistance in the room to the course that was about to begin, a required freshman literature course known as Lit Core, which, for most students at Boston College, is their first and last college-level encounter with literature. Students could choose which of the many different sections of Lit Core they took—and usually did so based on how it fit into their schedule, not on the subject matter or teacher of that particular section—but not whether they took Lit Core at all. Most of those present would rather have been taking some other course they chose for themselves that was more closely related to their eventual major, and they envied the handful of fellow freshmen who used AP scores to place out of Lit Core. The initial reaction of most of the students awaiting me in Stokes 209 to the prospect of taking Lit Core had been *Can I get out of this?* It was going to be part of my job to show them that this was the wrong question and that the right question featured one more word: *What can I get out of this?*

At bottom, Lit Core is about how, together and alone, we extract meaning from—and impose meaning on—the world around us. This is a subject you should encounter at some point in your time on campus, whether you want to or not. Making it difficult to duck this encounter is part of the value of Lit Core, and, more generally, of the distribution requirements of a core curriculum that obliges students to at least dip a toe in many disciplines. Students—often egged on by their parents—would typically rather be using college to prepare intensively for a particular career, like training full-time in a sport as preparation for playing that sport professionally, but they will graduate into a working world where the games and the rules keep changing, and they need to be ready for everything and anything. So I was going to make the students ante up and care about Lit Core, at least enough to do a creditable job in it. Still, I had some sympathy for the way they felt—especially since, similar to them, I would rather be teaching something else. The other courses I teach are typically smaller and full of students who have genuinely chosen to be there, which makes those courses easier and more fun to teach. Lit Core can be a slog, but it's also the sternest test of teaching chops that I regularly face—which makes it good for me, too.

Beyond the fact that students had to be there and therefore needed to be convinced that this course mattered to them, I also had to reckon with their inbuilt skepticism about what we would be doing in it. I don't think that my fellow professors necessarily appreciate how suspicious freshmen taking their first college-level literature course can be of the whole enterprise of interpreting fiction. Such skepticism about the meanings that teachers claim can be found in books pervades the culture at large, despite the plain fact that all of us go around interpreting the meaning of things pretty much nonstop. People are perfectly happy to close-read their aunt's cryptic comment about their cousin's shirt, their friend's car accident, the state of their neighbor's yard, the coded autobiography in the lyrics of a Taylor Swift breakup song, the horned beast and seven seals in the Book of Revelation, you name it. But, weirdly, the same people can get hinky when you turn the interpretive lens on novels or short stories you read in English class, even though works of literature are expressly made to carry meaning. (Poetry often gets a pass, perhaps because its compressed language and its tendency to foreground features other than plot seem to persuade many readers that interpretation is necessary.) So teaching a required freshman literature class obliges me not only to cover the material but also to show students that what we're doing is a real thing, a craft that can be mastered and is related in kind to the interpretation we all do as we go about our daily business.

Fewer than a third of the students in the room had entered college already enthusiastically on board when it came to interpreting literature. Some of these, like Stella and Luke and Dan, had an ingrained love of figuring out what things mean that went all the way back and extended beyond literature into law, architecture, music, whatever you got. Others had been converted along the way. Dave, for instance, had run across an excellent English teacher in high school who changed his point of view. Prior to that class, Dave had maintained a defiant attitude of confidence that those who claimed to be finding anything in a work of fiction beyond plot and character were reading too much into it. But that teacher had brought him around to the idea of paying close attention not only to what happens in a book but to how it's said and to discerning patterns in the *what* and *how* that reveal an organizing logic, a deeper intent.

But most of those present began from a position of significant doubt about the principles and process of extracting meaning from a text. Some had never encountered close reading before, having had high-school English classes that stuck to plot, character, and theme. Others had encountered it in crude form—red means danger, the bird symbolizes hope—and been rightfully unimpressed. Others had encountered it in more advanced form but saw the process as a mysterious black box rather than a learnable craft. Most of them would come around to some degree once we got into the work of the semester and once they'd had a chance to hear their peers and me offer observations and readings that struck them as plausibly persuasive. But, even so, they approached interpretation from somewhere between highly guarded curiosity and a suspicion of "reading into" the text—that is, forcing onto it an overstretched, flimsily supported interpretation that doesn't hold up to reasoned scrutiny.

Among the suspicious was Liz, who responded with anxiety and resistance when others saw things in a book that she didn't see. Part of her envied other students their insights, and part of her reflexively, and perhaps defensively, dismissed what they said as bullshit. A dutiful student wired to do well and give her teachers what they asked of her, she worried that she would be called on and have nothing to say because she thought the conversation was bullshit, and she couldn't ever say that to a teacher. That's where she started from, anyway, but discussing a book in class could gradually overcome her initial response and win her over. As others offered their thoughts, she would begin to take some notes, consider those ideas, and move from instinctively rejecting them to evaluating and even accepting them. Liz would go on to take two more classes with me and major in English, but she still tended to begin from a worry that others were seeing meanings that she wasn't seeing, and her first instinct was to suspect that those meanings weren't really, provably, there.

Others had trouble with the principle that there wasn't a single best interpretation, that we would have to be satisfied with assessing the strength or weakness of the argument for any given reading, and that a near infinity of readings was possible. Eva was one of these. She saw herself as good at logical things, like math, and less good at what she regarded as the more abstract subjects of literature and history, where it bothered her that there wasn't a single correct answer. Free-flowing discussion of multiple and even contradictory kinds of meaning frustrated her. It worked the same way outside of class—if, for instance, she encountered a song with ambiguous lyrics and she couldn't figure out to her own satisfaction the meaning of that song. She needed to know exactly what the singer meant, what meaning the songwriter had placed in the song so that a listener could extract it whole. In high school, she rejected out of hand the entire premise of the interpretation of fiction. Authors were just saying what they wanted to say, whatever meaning you might want to find in a book was right there on the surface, and that was all there was to it. She found it ridiculous to drag out the details in the search for something hidden. Over the course of our semester together, she would slowly adjust her attitude to accept the principle that a reader could find and argue for meaning in the text that the author didn't intentionally put in there like an Easter egg, but she started from a position of flat denial.

Count me among the skeptics, as well as among the converted. I frequently find myself unconvinced by a fellow scholar's reading of a text or bored and depressed by an overly stretchy lecture or conference paper and the self-inflating vagueness of the Q and A that follows. Yes, I'm utterly sold on the basic principles: form expresses meaning, interpretation is a craft that can be learned and taught and done better or worse, and how and what things mean is often their most important trait. Is the most important aspect of your job the raw salary number or what the work you do, and how you do it, says about you? But that doesn't mean I'm sold on literary criticism across the board. I find a lot of what I encounter at the office to be weakly argued, unconvincing, hamstrung by the need to seem formidable—for lack of a more precise word, bullshit. I need to spend a lot of time outside of academia altogether, but when I am in school, I tend to prefer my discipline at the retail level. I consistently value the nuts-and-bolts attention to texts that happens in a Lit Core class, for instance, more highly than what happens on the upper end of scholarship as performed by fellow professors, where I find that I'm much more likely to feel that I'm getting empty calories dressed up as advanced cuisine. I don't read all that much literary criticism, much preferring to read the actual literature itself, or history, social science, journalism.

I try to make sure that my skepticism about literary criticism inclines me not toward contempt but toward assessing the arguments I encounter on their merits. How clear and logical is the chain of assertions? How solid is the evidence? Am I being asked to make too many adequately theorized leaps of faith? These are the same questions I ask of students' papers, and these are the questions I urge them to ask of their own drafts, just as I ask these questions of my own drafts. In class discussions, I urge students to be alert for that shaky feeling that comes over you when you're not convinced by what we're saying, either because it's unclear or because it's not well-founded in the evidence of the text. It should feel as if we're proceeding on solid ground, or maybe up a rock face from one well-considered handhold to the next, so you should speak up and sound the alarm if you start getting the feeling that we're cantilevered out over open space on wobbly footing. Remember, in class we're all roped together, and as a group, we should respond to that feeling by trying to sharpen our thinking and looking for more or better evidence to support it. We're not just talking about our feelings or trying to sound sophisticated. We're trying to make good arguments or, to shift the metaphor, to lay pipe that doesn't leak. Dara—who told me later that part of the way she came around to interpretation during our semester together was learning to look for metaphors, figurative language, and other features of form— would underline the previous sentence.

·   ·   ·   ·   ·

I'm not like the others. In one way or another, most of those waiting for me in Stokes 209 were thinking that, and during the semester most of us in the room would feel this way on multiple occasions. Allie, the capable and soulful teaching assistant for this course, was the only graduate student and several years older than the other students. I was the only professor, and also the only person present who had been alive at the time of the first moon landing and the assassination of Martin Luther King Jr., the emergence of classic rock and soul and punk and disco and hip-hop and metal, the urban crisis and the oil crisis and stagflation and the wars in Vietnam and Bosnia and Kuwait . . . the only one who had seen firsthand a sizable chunk of what my daughters call "the 1900s."

There were other obvious differences. Stella and Arun were Asian; Dalha, Peter, David, and Nina were Asian American. Dan and Dara were

Latinos. Wilson, who had attended private schools on Long Island before moving temporarily to Michigan at the age of sixteen to live with a billet family while playing for the US national hockey team's under-eighteen squad, was long used to being the only black kid in the room or on the ice.

Then there were differences that you couldn't see so easily. Stella, Arun, and Matteo weren't American citizens, though only Matteo had an accent strong enough that you might suspect as much when he spoke. Kathi had a heart problem that had almost killed her in high school, and Ryan had beaten Hodgkins lymphoma. Dan had digestive trouble so severe that it qualified in the university's estimation as a disability. Jenny's father had died only a couple of years before. Stella and Eli and Liz thought of the study of literature as their strong suit, their academic specialty, and were considering majoring in English, but there were more who thought of it as their academic weakness. The parents of something like half the students in the room were divorced, in some cases recently and bitterly, and those for whom the damage was still raw tended to assume that everybody else came from an oppressively happy, whole, normative family.

Several people in the room, though they typically dressed and acted similarly to their peers and thus couldn't recognize each other as members of the same group, were acutely aware that they didn't come from money and assumed that just about everybody else did. They included Colleen, Dan, Peter, Luke, Susannah, and a few more. Susannah was probably the most solidly middle-class of this subset, yet even she felt that a significant class divide separated her from most of her affluent peers at BC. Her mother was a technology specialist in a public school, and her father worked at a bank; together they made enough to sustain a comfortable life in Gorham, Maine, but not anywhere near enough to put three kids through the kind of exclusive colleges they were strong enough students to get into. Susannah, the middle child, had worked at a restaurant all through high school to earn her own living expenses for college, which she managed herself, and even with financial aid, her parents had had to take out a second mortgage on their house. She came to college expecting that what she considered the BC template wouldn't fit her, and she was acutely aware that a lot of her fellow students—not everyone, but enough to make her feel like an outsider—fit what she saw as that mold: a well-to-do family, private or fancy suburban public high school, expensive clothes and vacations, a cushioned existence. It put a chip on her shoulder to see how these people were used to getting what they wanted, to see how unthinkingly selfish they could be. It seemed so intuitive and easy for them to be at college, and she herself felt the insidious pull of that attitude. Everything about BC seemed smooth and lubricated by privilege, just going to class and being with her friends and going out and having fun. Then, when she went home for a visit, she would be reminded of what real life was like when her friends would tell her they weren't going out because they couldn't spend anything until next month. Money was tighter, life was tighter, back home. Her mother, a BC alum, had warned her that there would be culture shock, but Susannah hadn't really been ready for those around her comparing notes on winter break getaways to Rome and Cancun, endemic Canada Goose and Lululemon, and peers who thought nothing of having a credit card connected to their parents' bank account. It took some getting used to, and she felt she would never get all the way used to it.

Then there were the usual freshman worries that almost all students feel to some degree. The most common is that everybody else went to an impossibly sophisticated high school where grotesquely brilliant and attractive students strolled down the halls discussing quantum physics and reverse enthymemes, and sooner or later it would be revealed that you're a troglodyte who slipped into this university by mistake. When the letter arrived informing Elizabeth that she had been admitted to BC, her disbelieving mother said they must have sent it to the wrong house. Her mother's reaction actually made sense to Elizabeth, who believed she didn't have the grades or the scores to compete. She saw herself as a pretty good student for her high school, but when she got to college, she decided that she belonged at the lower end of the spectrum. She concluded that by sheer luck she must have written just exactly the essay—something about women and empowerment—the admissions people wanted to see.

Another common worry was that everybody else is making best friends at college and you're not, or at best, you're only just starting to find a few people who might possibly turn out to be okay. There were actually some friend groups in the class: Wilson and Phil were hockey teammates; Paul and Dave were pals, as were Ryan and Lawrence; Charlotte and Kathi were close and had begun to form a friend group that included Liz and

Bill. But still, most of those present felt lonely—a little or a lot—and worried that their experience of college wasn't measuring up to the ideal of social joy, intellectual discovery, and caterpillar-to-butterfly personal transformation they had been led to expect. Boston College's vastly oversimplified reputation as an aggressively normal school filled with nice, well-rounded, well-adjusted suburban kids who want to grow up to be their nice, well-rounded, well-adjusted suburban parents only increased the general tendency to feel unlike the others. The norm in Stokes South 209 was to feel like a misfit.

.   .   .   .   .

Among the small minority of students in the room who would have no trouble speaking up in this or any class were Dave, a future captain of the fencing team, who admitted to loving the sound of his own voice and had to put his own limit on the number of times he raised his hand; Eli, who had triumphed over a childhood speech impediment by taking up debate and improv in high school to inure himself to the fear of speaking in front of others; Wilson, a future captain of the hockey team, who saw himself as a leader and pushed himself accordingly; Marguerite, who had a talent for finding things interesting; Dan, nervous but hellbent, who could not envision a scenario in which he didn't max out on his participation grade, and anyway couldn't go seventy-five minutes without crossing swords with somebody over something; and Stella, who, like a poker player holding killer hole cards, would sit back for a bit first to survey the table and let the pot build up, then make her move. But most of the students were worried that speaking up in class would be difficult for them. That was especially the case for such a large class, thirty-three being the outer limit for one that I run primarily as a discussion.

Why was raising their hand and speaking up difficult for so many of them? Above all else, they didn't want to say something wrong or ignorant that would cause others to conclude that they were stupid and didn't belong at BC. Actually, students rarely say something in an English class that's just plain wrong, and rarely does anyone conclude that anyone else is stupid. Vain, self-absorbed, deluded, annoying, odd, yes, but not stupid. Furthermore, as a veteran teacher, I have, in fact, said countless verifiably stupid things in class over the years and lived to tell the tale, so I had the enormous advantage of knowing that saying something stupid wasn't the end of the world and that most people don't even notice when you do it. That's especially true for students who say something that embarrasses them, since even when fellow students remember what the professor said, they tend not to remember which other student said what.

Many of the students were also worried that their nervousness would cause them to stumble and grow incoherent, which would lead to their being adjudged pathetic and—once more—stupid. Factor in, also, impostor syndrome, skepticism about interpretation, the common belief that English was not their strong subject, bad experiences in high-school English classes, good experiences in cozy high-school English classes among kids they knew well that felt irrecoverably far away now that they were among intimidating strangers, and the fear that they would somehow indicate by mispronunciation or errant word choice or in some other subtle way that they didn't belong. A majority also felt—mistakenly, since they were in the majority—that they were abnormally shy about talking in class and assumed that participation came easily and naturally to the others. On this first day, too, before we'd had a chance to start building a community or get into an analytical groove, talking in class still qualified as public speaking; and many people fear public speaking, a perennial leader among phobias, some so acutely that it becomes incapacitating panic. Electronic isolation and the related rising incidence of anxiety disorders make this all worse, of course.

In a few minutes the students in room 209 would hear me say that speaking up in this class was expected and, in fact, necessary in order to earn even a moderately good grade, which only increased their nervousness. But my postsemester interviews with them made clear that this policy had also given them greater incentive to overcome their discomfort and give it a try; it also led to more of them doing more of the reading so that they would know what they were talking about and not sound like an idiot when they did bring themselves to speak up. I didn't feel good about putting more pressure on students or about the sense of low-grade dread that many of them admitted to feeling in Lit Core class until they had spoken a few times and gotten into the swing of things. I was, in effect, using their academic anxiety as a counter to their fear of speaking in class, I realize, but I believe that the benefits of engagement far outweigh the costs of discomfort.

Several students told me later that they felt I was speaking directly to them on the first day of class when I described the racing heart, burning ears, sudden sweat, and fears of a brain short-out that come with the realization that you have something to say; and they appreciated hearing that I had learned the hard way that if you don't force yourself to talk at the beginning of the semester, it will rapidly become too late. Kathi and Colleen, in particular, were half-paralyzed by the fear of talking in class, but both resolved to give it a try even if it did terrify them. That resolve proved not to be enough on its own. They both would have trouble finding their way into class discussions and fall silent, and eventually I had to cook up a plan with each of them to get them involved. For many other students, the prospect of speaking up was not quite so daunting, and they would succeed in pushing themselves to do it.

They would have different approaches to how they went about it. Some jotted down in advance ideas for specific things they might say in class. Others listened carefully to classmates and waited for an opportunity to jump in and build on what somebody else had just said. The latter was the most common approach, a reminder that students in a literature class run as a discussion may get analytical equipment and useful background from the professor, but they get most of their interpretive ideas about the text from other students. Some put up their hand as soon as they had a rough idea of what they might talk about and worked it out on the fly, but most planned out their comments in more or less detail. The planners tended to focus almost entirely on how they would start and where they would go from there, but only a few, like Dave and Stella, devoted much thought to where they would stop, which gave their contributions a distinctive conciseness and roundedness. I was a little surprised to learn how many students rehearsed a comment word for word before putting up their hand, and that cleared up a mystery for me. I had always wondered why it happens sometimes in class that a student will say something and then another student will say pretty much the exact same thing, as if the first student hadn't spoken. When that happens, we all experience a silent little hitch, as if we'd seen the black cat that indicates a déjà vu hiccup in the

Matrix, and then go on. Now I have a better idea of why that happens, at least in some instances. Yes, sometimes it happens just because the second student has something to say and is going to say it—and rack up class participation credit for saying it—even if it has already been said, but sometimes the repetition glitch happens because the second student stopped listening in order to concentrate on rehearsing a comment and therefore didn't even hear the first student.

Figuring out how to get into class discussions was part of the process of learning to college—in the sense that people in prison talk about "learning to jail"—in which all the students in Lit Core were engaged. Freshman year is a shock to the system for most students who have moved away from home for the first time because it's their first taste of being fully in charge of their own affairs—not just academic work but also living arrangements, eating, sleeping, dealing with money, having fun, making friends, figuring out what you want to do with yourself and who you're going to be. By spring semester, some of the initial frenzy had worn off, and they were starting to feel for a sustainable rhythm. Many had stopped going around with their freshman hall like a herd of llamas and begun to fall in with a chosen friend group that felt like it might last. Some had realized that it's more fun and easier in the long run if you stop drinking before you throw up. Many had begun to feel for a more efficient academic rhythm, which entailed everything from figuring out good times and places to work to identifying what Dan called "the big-ticket items on a syllabus" and apportioning your effort accordingly.

Being at a relatively early stage of learning to college also helped explain why many of these students were in my class at all. Some of them had chosen this section of Lit Core, which featured books exploring the theme of the misfit, because they thought that misfits would be an interesting topic, or hated this topic less than the others, but most had chosen it because it fit into their schedules. None had chosen it because I was teaching it. More experienced college students learn to check up on whoever's teaching a course, and many of them move during their college careers toward taking the professor rather than the course. After all, a great professor teaching a syllabus of minimal initial interest to you will probably lead to a surprisingly good experience, while a terrible professor teaching a subject you find fascinating will almost certainly lead to a frustratingly bad experience. But freshmen usually aren't thinking that way yet because they're still learning to college.

.   .   .   .   .

I walked into Stokes South 209 and went to the front of the room, where there was a table on which I could set the room's portable lectern. I put my stuff on the table, bent from the knees to pick up the lectern from the floor, put it on the table, and put the folder holding my notes on it. I always try to execute the lectern-lifting routine smoothly, with no visible effort. It would be embarrassing to struggle with it, or to allow the minimal strain of picking it up to somehow cause me to grunt or make some even more embarrassing involuntary noise. The nightmarish scenarios seem endless, yet of course nobody but me notices or cares how I pick up the lectern. The students, thirty-two freshmen and one sophomore, were seated in rows before me. They were expectant, nervous, and they hadn't had anywhere near as much practice at hiding it as I had. Having reached the midpoint of what I like to think of as forty-seventh grade, I was closing in on a hundred semesters as either student or teacher. That's a lot of first days of class.

The classroom had windows that opened, a door that closed, heating, chalkboards, the lectern and table for me, and five rows of chairs with attached desk arms for the students. That was pretty much all I needed from it. Except for the occasional session devoted to working on paper-writing chops, during which I would project paragraphs from student papers on the classroom screen from my laptop, we wouldn't be taking much advantage of the room's advanced technological capabilities this semester. The way I teach it, Lit Core is as basic as you can get: humans pay close attention to books and one another.

.   .   .   .   .

I am going to tell the story of one semester in one classroom where on Tuesdays and Thursdays from noon to 1:15 a community of thirty-five people gathered to wrestle with a series of formidable books. I will mostly follow the syllabus and the sequence of events of the semester, though I'll jump ahead now and then in the chapters in which I profile individual students. The semester in question, spring 2020, started out like any other, but the arrival of the Covid pandemic halfway through it and the subsequent shutdown of campuses and move to Zoom forced everyone to think long and hard about what's essential about school. So this is a book about teaching and learning, and it's also about the tension between the seemingly detached timelessness of what we do in class—stepping away from the rush of daily life to read good books and sharpen our analytical chops by finding meaning in them—and the ways in which the outside world impinges on the classroom and inflects the thinking and experience of everyone in it.

For all the heatedness of the national conversation about higher education these days, there's relatively little substantive public discussion about what actually happens in college classrooms: what lessons we learn, how we learn them, how they sink in or don't, how we process what happens in school and go about connecting it to our thinking and feeling lives beyond school. That's what matters most about the classroom, and I wanted to convey not only my experience of it but also the experiences of others in the room. So—starting about eighteen months after the semester ended, which was for most of these students the fall of their junior year—I interviewed almost all of the students who took the course in the spring semester of 2020, and I'm drawing on those interviews when I tell you what they thought and said. (I have changed the students' names, one of the choices I explain in the afterword.) My decision to organize the syllabus around the literary theme of the misfit colored students' reflections on the semester. They had a lot to say about fitting in and standing out, getting with the program and making their own way through the world of ideas and the world at large.

Giving them—and myself—a chance to reflect on that eventful spring of 2020 was the best way I could think of to try to understand what happened when we converged on Stokes South 209 for half a semester to engage with literature, then dispersed in a wild scramble to our various homes and other pandemic redoubts, then reconvened on Zoom for the rest of the semester, then went off on our separate trajectories. Because so much of the debate about the purpose and value of college, the humanities, and the study of literature is uninterested in teaching and learning or abstract to the point of uselessness, I thought it might be useful to tell you what some actual humans at college actually did with literature.

The closing of campuses and the move to Zoom forced us all to think in particular about the value and meaning of what happens in the classroom, which gave this book a strong bias in that direction. I realize, of course, that writing, which mostly happens outside the classroom, is one of the core competencies that a college education should develop. Writing is the work that means the most to me (even more than teaching). I teach writing in all my courses; I also teach nonfiction writing courses that tend to attract students who want to write for a living, and I certainly believe that teaching writing is one of the essential functions of English departments, but that's a subject for another book.

So is the rise of AI. As a writing tool, in its current form it's a high-end autocomplete function that students who are unintentionally practicing to be replaceable by AI typically use to produce mediocre work with little effort, and its drum-machine prose is usually short on soul and surprise (except when it hallucinates, which makes for the wrong kind of surprise). As in the case of drum machines, which were supposed to make human drummers obsolete until it became clear that you can use one much more effectively if you're a competent drummer, you're going to get a lot more out of AI as a writing tool if you're a competent writer. But I recognize that people will find new ways to use AI as a writing tool as it continues to develop and that it will affect what teachers and students do in at least some ways—which include encouraging teachers to put less weight on papers and more on what happens in class. Looking back, the semester chronicled in this book was one of the last before ChatGPT and such came along to make academic life even more complicated than it already was. That development may be a worthy subject in its own right, but it's one for another day and another author. And, like Zoom, AI is another supposedly game-changing emergent technology that has the ironic effect of helping us see what's unique and irreplaceable about face-to-face discussion in the classroom.

At least in courses built around discussion, what happens in the classroom is increasingly the one academic feature of college above all others that students and their families are paying for—that is, they're paying for the admissions process that produced the other students in the room, the hiring and promotion process that produced the teacher, and the possibilities for substantive exchange within that community. What happens in the classroom feels, on the one hand, timelessly special and separate from everything else in life and, on the other hand, deeply connected to everything else in life. In Stokes South 209—and then, much less effectively, on Zoom—we were engaged in the business of figuring out how meaning flows through texts, lives, the world. That's part of the essential work of being human that we all do at all times and in all kinds of places, not just in a college classroom.

2 The First Day

Time to get down to first-day business. I had handed around copies of the syllabus when I came in and given the students time to look it over while I took attendance and started trying to learn everyone's name. Going over the syllabus, I explained that in Lit Core, we work on the fundamental skill of extracting meaning from language, and we do that by making interpretive arguments—together in class discussions, individually in writing—about the elaborately worked language of literature. There was nothing cutting-edge about what we were going to do, and I hadn't tried to pick the most important novels and short stories for us to read. I had just picked works about misfits that were resonantly expressive enough to reward the effort to interpret them. There were a couple of dozen sections of Lit Core offered that semester, each with its own theme and reading list, often chosen expressly to appeal to freshmen. I thought misfits would make a compelling subject for a bunch of teenagers trying to figure out who they were and into what scenes, institutions, stories, networks, or personas they might want to fit or not fit themselves.

Our developing encounter with the literature would provide one of the throughlines that gave the semester shape and momentum. We would start with Stuart Dybek's dreamlike Chicago neighborhood stories in

Childhood and Other Neighborhoods, some of them written when he was the same age as the students in the class. In those first weeks, we would also read some chapters from a textbook on analyzing literature, just to make sure we put a basic set of interpretive tools in our shared kit. We would move on to Edith Wharton's novel *The House of Mirth,* a classic realist tale of an entrepreneurial beauty who must marry to keep her place in turn-of-the-century New York's high society but can't bring herself to choose among the available options. Like a lot of misfits, she's caught between working the system and the notion that there has to be something more than working the system. Then would come Junot Díaz's *The Brief Wondrous Life of Oscar Wao,* which, despite its college setting, would be a stretch for many students, who would have to reckon with Spanglish, Elvish, and an unreliable narrator who might not be telling us everything we should know about his heroically abject frenemy, Oscar. We'd move on to Annie Proulx's sweeping, music-filled novel *Accordion Crimes,* in which generations of oddballs struggle to make a way and fashion something lasting in the creolized slurry of American identities. Finally, we'd close with a pair of stylistically opposed first-person treatments of the counterculture of the 1960s and early 1970s: Joan Didion's coolly detached essay "Slouching Towards Bethlehem" and Hunter S. Thompson's overheated novelistic gonzo memoir *Fear and Loathing in Las Vegas.*

Leading the group as they practiced their analytical skills by working through a range of genres and writing styles and the roster of misfits and the social orders to which they were misfitted, I would be something like a trainer bringing along a young fighter. Designing and teaching a Lit Core syllabus is like having your prospect spar with an opponent who can take a punch, then an opponent with a stiff jab, then a swarmer, then an elusive counterpuncher, and so on, all part of a graduated process of habituating the prospect to facing different kinds of problems and styles. (I have spent a fair amount of time in the fight world, so in what follows, expect the occasional boxing analogy. Also, for similar reasons, music analogies.)

I went over some of the mechanics of the course. The written work would include three five-page papers, and after you got the first one back from me, you could rewrite it for a fresh grade if you wanted to, though you would be required to meet with Allie or me to discuss the revision before you did it. There would also be a take-home final featuring big fuzzy questions designed so that the essays you wrote in response to them would have to sharpen the question to make it answerable, then range across the semester's reading to assemble examples to support the argument of your response. You would barely have to study at all for the final if you had kept up during the semester, and writing it up would be no big deal. If you hadn't kept up, it would be pretty much impossible to prepare at the last minute for the final, which you would experience as a waking shriekmare from which you would be unable to awaken. So my advice was to keep up. Writing the papers and the take-home final would be your opportunities to practice and show command of the ideas and methods of the course in writing. But you would also have many more informal opportunities to engage the books and try out and refine your interpretive skills in person at every class meeting.

I explained that this would be primarily a discussion class. I wouldn't lecture much after today. Mostly, I would frame analytical problems for us to work out together. How does the opening scene of this novel set up the ideas it will explore and the ways it will explore them? What's the effect of this word choice, that image, these repetitions? We would get stuck, get ourselves unstuck, get stuck again, go around, keep trying to perceive the relationship between how a text is put together and what meanings it makes available to us. (Don't be thrown by the word *text*, which is just a way of saying in only four letters *the novel or story or poem or whatever it is that we're analyzing, which means that we're noticing its form and trying to fit that to its content to make arguments about meaning*.) My role would include framing our analytical tasks, putting tools in our shared tool kit and demonstrating their use, and modeling an attitude that balances purpose and openness. Attending to the nuts and bolts of my own technique means asking "if . . . then" questions to help knit together interpretive threads (*If we accept Charlotte's point about* X, *then what do we do with Liz's point about* Y?), using the more inviting *and* rather than the forbidding *but* when we stress-test an argument (*I hear several voices saying* X *about Chapter 4, and now we need to figure out how that applies to Chapter 5, which on the face of it doesn't seem to support that reading*), and otherwise making sure we get all the juice out of what everyone has to say.

The interpretation of literature is not sorcery, I told them, though it can feel that way, or like bullshit, to many people who have sat in English classes and wondered—admiringly, resentfully, suspiciously—how those who seem more confident about interpretation come up with the things they say. But there's nothing mysterious about analyzing literature. Think of it as an exercise in pattern recognition. You notice things—word choices, imagery, details of setting, references to other works and to events and ideas outside the text, the narrator's point of view, the sequence in which the story unfolds, echoes and variations, and so on—and you try to discern some ordering logic that emerges from those patterns. You would similarly look for patterns if you were trying to figure out a family, a neighborhood, or the choices and accidents and larger forces that all flowed together to leave you sitting in a cubicle or a jail cell. I think of interpretation as a creative act in which we go into the text to gather the materials to *make* something: a persuasive argument about what meanings we find there. I'm agnostic about what particular meanings the students might want to argue for; I just want them to do it well. We would be practicing a craft somewhere between art and science, like cabinetmaking or cultivating a vegetable patch.

That craft is basic equipment for living for any citizen, any worker, any thinking person.* We swim in a sea of language, and very little of it means only or exactly what it says: "Thou shalt not kill"; "We hold these truths to be self-evident, that all men are created equal"; "Mistakes were made"; "We think of our company as a family"; "All lives matter." To function in the world, we need to understand how meaning moves on the surface of the words and in the sometimes murky depths beneath that surface, and we must attend to form—to *how* something is said—to get at the fullness of *what* it says. You can reduce the essence of this course to three words: *form expresses meaning*. If you come out of here able to see how this fundamental principle of meaning-making operates in all sorts of texts, and with the ability to make sound interpretive arguments based on it, then you'll have put our time to good use.

* I got the resonant phrase "literature as equipment for living" from Michael Denning, one of my graduate school mentors, who got it from Kenneth Burke, "Literature as Equipment for Living," in *Philosophy of the Literary Form: Studies in Symbolic Action*, 3rd. ed. (Berkeley: University of California Press, 1973), 293–304. I don't mean exactly the same thing by the phrase that Burke or Denning did, but I got the basic idea from them and modified it for my purposes—which is what I hope my students are doing with what I teach in my classes.

This is not an esoteric skill reserved for the privileged few who can afford to indulge themselves in enhancing their enjoyment of made-up stories. Reducing education to vocational training is a mistake, and to dismiss "liberal arts degrees" as impractical because there's no job called "English" or "history" is to misunderstand how education shapes a life—and also to misunderstand the liberal arts, which include science and math. But college does cost a lot, and you do need to make a living when you get out. Apart from the degree as a credential and the way that college embeds you in social and professional networks and perhaps even does you some good as a human being, what you actually learn how to do there has become essential to competing in the postindustrial job market. Whatever your major, a college degree indicates that you are good at learning, an ever-more-important metaskill as careers increasingly feature many different jobs rather than long-term stable ones. And the degree indicates that you can assimilate and organize complicated bodies of information, analyze that information to create outcomes that have value to others, and convey that analysis with purpose and clarity. Such analysis can of course lead to making and doing things, but performing the analysis is itself an act of making and doing. Whether you honed these fundamental skills in the study of foreign policy or Jacobean revenge tragedies or the solar system is usually secondary, less important than in what company you did the honing and how you went about working at it. What matters most is that you pursued training in the craft of mastering complexity, which you can apply in fields from advertising to zoo management.

So, no, "because it makes your life more, like, beautiful, man" may not be a good enough reason all on its own to study literature—though, in fact, such study can significantly increase your capacity to process beauty and truth. This strikes me as a better reason: literature offers not only a bottomless repository of ideas—inspiring, awful, useful, funny, hateful, perplexing, terrifying, thrilling, generative, ever-multiplying ideas about how to live and what's out there in the world and other such essential matters—but also endless opportunities to refine your analytical chops in an encounter with some of the most complex artifacts our species is capable of producing.

●   ●   ●   ●   ●

The scene we were getting ready to enact every Tuesday and Thursday for the next fifteen weeks might feel timeless to me, but it's not. My now-retired colleague Dayton Haskin, who's at work on a history of the study of literature in American universities, tells me that give-and-take discussions of literature in English began happening in only a few college classrooms in the late nineteenth century. They were early exceptions to a prevailing model in which professors lectured and called on students to recite back what they had heard in lectures and read and memorized *about* literature rather than directly reading the works themselves. The conversational model that feels natural to me caught on very gradually over the course of the next century, driven by broader changes in how we think about schooling, knowledge, and authority. The now-widespread institution of a class in which undergraduates talk about literature didn't begin to become normal until after the 1960s. What we do in the classroom has a history that connects it to the world beyond.[†]

I could feel the forces at play in our own historical moment pressing in on our classroom, leaving their imprint on our little commonwealth. To get to Lit Core, the students had to survive a college admissions process that has mutated into an all-consuming campaign resembling an arms race or running for Congress. On the other end, after they left Lit Core and made it (or not) through the rest of college, they would have to navigate a job market where the entry level was short on actual jobs—in the sense of what the word meant when I graduated college in 1986—and long on unpaid internships, contingent and insecure labor, and the assumption of parental assistance.

One way I can feel myself getting older is that I am gentler and less forbidding with my students than I used to be. My attitude has shifted over the years from "We all die alone" toward "One for all and all for one," in part because my own kids are now the age of my students, whose inner lives paradoxically seem a little less opaque to me now than they did when

---

† The working title of Dayton Haskin's book-in-progress is *The Birth of the English Major*. For more on the history of teaching in the college English classroom, see Jonathan Zimmerman, *The Amateur Hour: A History of College Teaching in America* (Baltimore: Johns Hopkins University Press, 2020); and Rachel Sagner Buurma and Laura Heffernan, *The Teaching Archive: A New History for Literary Study* (Chicago: University of Chicago Press, 2021).

I was closer to them in age. I also feel more sympathy than I used to for my students because they're doing their best to make their way in a world that feels more alien to me as it becomes more different from the world in which I grew up. Like a parody of an Italian American man of advanced middle years, I increasingly find myself defaulting to "Hey, they're basically good kids." And they *are* basically good kids—typically more diligent and dutiful than I was at their age and, despite being on average a lot richer than I was, less carefree and optimistic.

The students in Lit Core, all but one of them freshmen, belonged to a club that the eighteen-year-old me would not have been invited to join. As a college applicant, I had uneven grades, displayed little sign of enterprise or accomplishment, needed financial aid, and had no legal extracurriculars to speak of. Yet I was still admitted to a number of well-respected schools that could provide me with a fine education, name-brand prestige and connections, and a sufficient push toward a calling and a viable middle-class life. Transported to the present, that eighteen-year-old me would get slaughtered in the ramped-up competition for spots in the entering classes of selective colleges and universities, maybe even the not-so-selective ones.

The teenagers sitting in front of me tended to conform to the all-arounder template, much favored by admissions officers, that I think of as the astronaut type. They had for the most part aced adolescence: earned top grades across the board, as well as honors and AP credits; piled up credentials via arts, sports, and clubs; started a soup kitchen or raised money to fight cancer; and in a hundred other ways demonstrated achievement and potential—including moving heaven and earth to achieve high scores on standardized tests that, like their high-school GPA, don't tell us all that much about them that we couldn't have guessed from their zip code and parents' incomes. Their presence in my classroom was typically the culmination of a decade-long campaign to hack and claw through a grueling, perverse, and unfair admissions process that wastes much of the effort and resources that both applicants and admissions officers put into it. The system's broken enough that something resembling arranged marriage would be much more efficient and probably produce outcomes that are just as good or better.

And, at least from my perspective as a former undergraduate of the 1980s, the titanic additional quantities of time, capital, strategic maneuver, and worry expended by families to get students into today's college classroom don't produce a better result. The quality of what happens in the classroom may be a little better than before in some general ways (students in my classes today are probably more uniformly professional about school than my fellow students were back then, and fewer of them are high all the time) and a little worse in some English-specific ones (fewer people in the room read a lot of books), but on balance it's probably a wash.

The increasingly forbidding pathways to and from the classroom are part of a deep shift in the social lay of the land. In this country we're moving from a familiar and somewhat fluid tripartite class structure—working, middle, upper—toward a more rigid and binary one: haves and have-nots. Over my lifetime, higher education has increasingly emerged as one of the biggest dividers between the two groups. The cost of college, which includes the cost of doing what it takes to get in, has soared as the middle class has continued to hollow out and as greater numbers of international students willing to pay full freight have come to American campuses. That cost is increasingly out of reach for the have-nots and those who feel themselves sliding in that direction. Most people with whom I went to college in the 1980s expected to rise up past their parents' economic high-water mark as a matter of course. A lot of my students these days, including well-to-do ones, don't expect to ever get anywhere near what their parents have. My students may be more consistently professional about school than my college cohort was, but they are also a lot more anxious.

As the middle class shrinks and it gets harder for young people getting started in adult life to wriggle up through the tightening passage into the magic circle of the haves, and as college becomes yet one more aspect of American life that gets marked up with red and blue crayon and reduced to bogus partisan simplicity, English and other disciplines in the humanities have come under increasing pressure to justify their existence. That's part of the reason for too many people taking seriously the idea that your major leads directly to a career in that same field, even though this idea willfully misunderstands education, work, and the relationship between them in a nearly infinite number of ways. And the facts don't actually support the notion that English and the rest of the humanities are somehow less practical or valuable than other disciplines. While business majors, engineers, or dental hygienists might make more in the immediate period after graduation, English majors' lifetime earnings are similar to those of their peers who major in other subjects, STEM and business included.[‡] The big difference in outcomes remains between college and no college; among college graduates, outcomes among the various majors don't vary anywhere near as much as conventional wisdom assumes they do. That all underscores the silliness of arguing that "there's no job called English," especially when you consider that the number-one thing that the English majors I know do after graduating is go to law school. It's at least anecdotally interesting that the governor (Charlie Baker) of the state in which I was teaching and the students were taking Lit Core was an English major, as were his two immediate predecessors (Deval Patrick and Mitt Romney); and of the three before them, one majored in American Studies (Jane Swift) and another in classics (Bill Weld). So that's one job right there you can get with a major in the humanities.

But the numbers of majors and tenure-line faculty in the humanities have indeed declined at many schools. That decline has caused both genuine sorrow and overwrought handwringing—though there's a silver lining, as I see it, since in my experience the shrinkage in English majors has come off the bottom. The quality has gone up as the quantity has gone down, and the majors who remain tend to have a clear idea of what they're doing and why they're doing it, which makes for better English majors. Still, the decline has encouraged talk of a crisis of the humanities and questions in particular about the role of literature in the college curriculum. Why should students pay through the nose to spend three weeks on *The House of Mirth*? Why continue to require the study of literature at all when they could be using that valuable time to learn how to mine lithium?

None of the talk about crisis—in the discipline of English, the humanities, college, education, our polarized culture—will be going away anytime soon, but at some point, you have to shove that all off to the side and get

---

‡ See David Deming's cogent summary in the *New York Times*, "In the Salary Race, Engineers Sprint but English Majors Endure," Sept. 20, 2019, https://www.nytimes.com/2019/09/20/business/liberal-arts-stem-salaries.html. For a deeper dive, see the 2024 *Report on English Majors' Career Preparation and Outcomes*, by the Modern Language Association's Association of Departments of English: https://www.maps.mla.org/Resources/Reports-and-Other-Resources/Report-on-English-Majors-Career-Preparation-and-Outcomes.

down to business. I arrive at that point pretty much when I wake up in the morning, since I'd rather try to do good work than worry about the conditions in which that work is done. (I realize that it's easier for me to say this because I have a reasonably secure tenured position, but if I didn't, then I'd be trying to do good work at a different kind of job. I happen to be a professor, but I don't *have* to be one.) If you're a musician, you play with and for whoever shows up, and something similar goes for being a teacher. Yes, it's true that if you are, say, a blues musician in Chicago, it makes a difference whether the people showing up are migrants from Mississippi or tourists from Belgium, but either way, at some point you still have to play a shuffle right and bend some notes. As long as students walk into the classroom at least somewhat ready to learn and at least minimally capable of doing the work, which has so far always been the case in my experience, I'll try to meet them where they are and get something worthwhile done. And, yes, it's too bad that a concatenation of forces operating far beyond the classroom—plus some self-inflicted wounds, like some literary scholars' tendency to value obscure critique over explaining things clearly— have helped to make English a less popular major than it used to be and have encouraged some people to question the value of studying literature and learning to write well, though the skills and knowledge to be practiced and acquired in English classes are just as essential as ever. But as a guy who's partial to the fights, steel guitar, Norse sagas, mill towns, and the works of Magic Slim and Charles Portis, I'm used to my enthusiasms being regarded as marginal, so the current situation of English as a discipline strikes me as unfortunate but par for the course in the world we've got. As a gentle woodland creature whose powers are still weak on this planet (though soon I will be invincible, natch), it looks like my only reasonable option is to live with the way things are and do my best to manufacture small amounts of less-unfortunateness in my immediate vicinity.

School is school, forever and always, but it's not as self-contained as it might appear to be when you're in the classroom. The wider world impinges in all sorts of ways. Besides all the talk of crisis in education and the usual big-ticket items—rising seas, the widening distance between haves and have-nots and the holes it's tearing in the social fabric, the hateful buffoons who ooze through those holes into positions of power that allow them to screw up the world even more completely—in order to teach, I also had to shove aside a suite of more personal sources of concern typical of middle age. These included whatever my teenage daughters were doing at the time to cause me to worry about them, the incurable scarring of the lungs that was killing my father, how my mother would weather his passing and go on without him, how my brothers and I would help her do that. I also had a newish book out and had upcoming talks and readings and other book-related events to prepare for, as well as magazine deadlines to make, stories in development, all the business of a writing life to put away in a separate compartment while I taught.

.   .   .   .   .

Two course policies detailed on the syllabus I handed out on the first day of class required further explanation. One had to do with technology: put away laptops, phones, tablets, e-readers, and all other such devices during class meetings, and always bring a hard copy of the reading. The other policy had to do with engagement: good classroom citizenship means being present and prepared to get the most out of each session and take responsibility for your share of the work we're doing. It means having something useful to say and speaking up, a responsibility to your colleagues and yourself, as well as essential to getting a good grade. As a general rule, you should be actively participating at every class meeting.

Students do the work in this class, I explained, and they do it better if we're not dragging along silent or distracted partners. Because screens connected to the internet get in the way of people paying attention to each other, they directly interfere with what's special and valuable about what happens in the classroom. Humans paying attention to books and one another may seem rudimentary, but it's a vanishingly rare and precious experience in an age in which, without ever leaving home or putting on clothes, students can do the reading, study scholarship about the writers and their eras, post opinions, and even watch lectures about literature. Most of those lectures available online are terrible, so far, but if you dig, you might find substantive ones, and in time there may be more. Most of the people in the room, once they got out of college, would never again gather regularly with other people to think deeply about something they have all read, uninterrupted for seventy-five whole minutes by text messages, emails, instant messages, buzzes, beeps, dings, klaxons, flashing lights, tempting links, breaking news alerts, GIFs of naked mole rats dancing, or AI-generated video of George Soros and Satan clinking champagne flutes.

I don't buy for a second the specious let-the-market-decide argument that you just have to give in to the tech giants and live with the rule of cellphones everywhere and that teachers are therefore obliged to make class so interesting that everybody will choose to pay attention to it and not to their cellphones. It's a simple fact of classroom life that everyone who chooses to be visibly engaged in something other than what we're doing together—whether they're looking at their phone or sticking their hands down their pants—makes it harder for everyone else to choose to be engaged, and the phone is expressly designed to make it extremely difficult for most people to choose anything else. I will change this policy when it's clear that we've gotten so used to what's happening on a screen that it doesn't trigger our 150,000-year-old savannah-bred impulse to pay attention to any stimulus that indicates a change in our environment, and at this rate that should probably happen sometime within the next 150,000 years or so, but not anytime soon. Right now, while I recognize that devices connected to the internet certainly have their uses in the classroom, those uses do not begin to make up for those devices' tendency to distract attention and kill community.

A community of inquiry takes shape in a classroom as together we grapple with one problem after another, one book after another. Especially in a class organized around discussion, it's the level of the floor, not the ceiling, that most dictates this community's collective efficacy in getting the job done. Even if you get lucky and have two or three great English students in a class, they can't carry a weak group, and the gap between the standouts and the rest may well breed resentment. The capability and willingness of the typical student in the room sets the tone, and I have never had much to complain about there, since the students I've taught tend to be competent and willing. At Boston College, especially, the prevailing norm has so far been that students take the work seriously, want to do it well, and find ways to be interested in it. Some of my colleagues wish that their students were more ironic, rebellious, bookish, and otherwise similar to how those colleagues remember themselves to have been back in some sadly elapsed golden age of radical critique, but I don't take students' earnestness or their work ethic for granted, and I don't ever lose sight of the fact that the way they are makes my job much more satisfying.

They're also pretty good writers and thinkers, by the way. Academics complain and regularly publish jeremiads about what terrible writers and closed-minded sheep their students are, but that doesn't square with my experience. It's true that students often have bad habits to unlearn, and too often they get stuck emulating lousy models of what a smart person sounds like: blowtorching everything in your path with withering critique, taking offense at everything, cranking up the gasbag register to start papers with sentences like "Throughout all time, society has struggled with the problem of the misfit . . .," and the like (a list that, by the way, describes to a tee those screeds about what bad writers and thinkers students are these days). But college students can write, and they can think—when they don't get in their own way and when they're not led astray by teachers who provide poor examples. Many professors regard teaching graduate students as more intellectually substantive because those students are more like them, but I find that undergrads are often more rewarding to teach because they have fewer bad habits to unlearn. All I ask is that students do the work, keep an open mind, listen to others, and say what they mean rather than try to sound smart. Most of them can do that.

To be a contributing member of a community of inquiry, and not an impediment to it, you need to ante up your share of useful thinking— which means that you need to not only prepare well and listen but also speak up. Four decades in college classrooms have taught me that if you don't talk in class during the first two weeks, you're probably going to remain entirely silent for the rest of the semester. This brief period at the beginning of the semester in which students either do or don't become a person who talks in class is an unforgiving fact of academic life.

The stakes are higher than just grades, of course. The classroom affords you opportunities to practice exploring and building complex ideas with other people, a skill that matters beyond the academy—in the workplace and friendship and family life, for instance. You can't develop competence in human exchange, a crucial talent that my friends in the business world complain is increasingly hard to find among even the most brilliant young colleagues, by posting strong opinions in electronic anonymity.

Think about that, I told the students in Lit Core, when you're sitting in class and suddenly realize that you have something to say that would answer or pose a relevant question, identify a problem, sharpen a point, or otherwise be of use. This realization probably causes your heart to thud and your ears to burn and your skin to go hot and cold. When I was a student, I would feel all that, plus one drop of sweat trickling down one side of my rib cage (but never two drops on both sides at once). Some large percentage of students think of themselves as abnormally shy, but there's nothing abnormal about it. Even people who speak easily elsewhere can be anxious about talking in front of others in class.

If that anxiousness makes you hesitate too long, the moment will pass, and you'll end up swallowing the thing you had to say, which will spoil inside you like bad meat. Each time that happens, it becomes less likely that next time you'll manage to put your hand up and speak your piece. After about two weeks, you'll stop taking seriously the possibility of ever saying anything in that class. A kind of verbal writer's block sets in. In addition to the usual worry about public speaking, you now also worry that if you suddenly say something after eight weeks, it can't possibly sound smart enough to justify the long silence that preceded it.

But if you speak up early in the semester, and especially if you volunteer to talk at a time of your choosing, you become a person who has spoken in class. Such a person, now a committed member of the community, no longer regards it as public speaking; the anxiety swiftly diminishes, and you settle down to doing your share of the work at hand.

This is why I require students to speak up, preferably at every class meeting, particularly during the first couple of weeks, and make it a significant part of their grade for the course. You may be inclined to think that I can get away with this only because I teach the kind of highly motivated, expensively prepared, rule-following, grade-oriented students who tend to dominate the population at selective residential universities. Yes, this kind of student tends to respond particularly well to being required to speak up, but I've also established an everybody-contributes expectation with all kinds of groups at all levels, from public-school fourth graders to stateless émigrés in a care facility for senior citizens, and so far it has worked on all of them. If you make clear what's expected and why, and that there's value in the enterprise, most people will accept that good citizenship means speaking up. This policy makes me the worst kind of zealot—a convert. As a college student, and really from middle school through grad school, I mostly sat there quietly, trying not to be a bother to anyone and hoping to write papers good enough to make up for my silence in class. I didn't realize that I was guilty of intellectual bad citizenship, forcing others to do my part of the job while carrying around my spoiled-meat-stuffed carcass for the whole semester.

Making students talk goes against my strong instinct to let people do what they want, but I've come to understand that, at least in a discussion-based class, inert silence kills intellectual community. In this nose-to-screen age we may not give face-to-face community the attention it deserves, but it's essential to learning, among other meaningful enterprises. So force yourself to do it a few times at the beginning of the semester, I told the students, and then you won't have to force yourself anymore because it will come much more easily.

I do understand, I added, that we're all different in how we participate in a classroom conversation, or any conversation. Some people like to go first; some like to wait and react to what others say; some like to ask questions, and some like to answer them; sometimes you'll have a complete point to make, and sometimes you'll just want to throw something out there, even though you really don't know what to do with it. All that variety is good, as is the variety in points of view about any given text we discuss. Styles, as they say in the boxing world, make fights. I'll leave it to you to find your own way to make a meaningful contribution, which will be a lot more effective than remaining silent and thereby forcing me to decide that it's time for you to talk. They were looking even more nervous now.

·   ·   ·   ·   ·

So, I said, today we're all going to become people who have spoken in class, and you'll do that by speaking very briefly about a subject on which you are the world's leading authority: yourself. Please get ready to tell us your name, where you're from, and one thing about your relationship to literature. Telling us where you're from helps me remember names, which I do in a medieval sort of way—like Jennifer of Akron or Bob of Sarasota. Those of you from New Jersey or Long Island, please do not just say "New

Jersey" or "Long Island." We need the name of a city or town. As for something about your relationship to literature, it can be a book you love, a poem that had a strong effect on you, anything will do. The main point is to say anything at all, so don't overthink this part, and don't feel obliged to come up with your absolute favorite or with something that you feel will sound intellectually respectable. It doesn't have to be *Hamlet*. If you feared *Goodnight, Moon* or still secretly groove on Erin Hunter's warrior-cat books, that will do nicely. Also, we're not going to start at one end of the room and go around in order, since we're not going to do that during discussions. It's better if you start getting used to deciding that it's time for you to speak and putting up your hand. Who'd like to start us off?

Hands went up. They always do. Some people prefer to just get this kind of thing over with, and another significant percentage can't abide even the thought of a lull in which the professor stands there and waits for somebody to respond. I think there can be great value in thoughtful pauses, which help counter our tendency to skew classroom discussion in favor of those who can come up with swift articulate responses and penalize those who need to ruminate a bit more. But many students find such pauses awkward, and these days awkwardness increasingly equals unbearable horror, especially for young people. So off we went. Wilson from Oyster Bay, Long Island; Marguerite from Carmel Valley, California; Luke from Laurel, Montana; Nina from Montville, New Jersey; Arthur from Winchester, Massachusetts; Susannah from Gorham, Maine; Tyler from West Chester, Pennsylvania; Jenny from Millis, Massachusetts; Dalha from Portland, Oregon; Paul from Ridgefield, Connecticut. One unlined, open face after another, and I had to attach each one first to a name and eventually to a character, a mind, a life.

Marguerite and Arthur both talked about the Harry Potter books, which usually make a strong showing when I do this first-day ritual. Paul talked about another YA series, Michael Grant's dystopian Gone books ("No adults. No rules. No escape."), which he would stay up reading until 3 a.m. in the summer before he started high school. He also mentioned his all-time favorite, the dragon-intensive Eragon fantasies. Young adult fantasy, science fiction, and dystopian series are probably the most common responses. They're often the last books that adolescents choose to read for fun, the last books in which they utterly immerse themselves, before the dominion of the pocket-size rectangular overlord and the ramping up of homework in high school bring that phase of life to an end. That's the point at which they typically switch over to reading books almost exclusively for school, while games and social media and other such electronic pursuits increasingly replace leisure reading.

More hands, more names to learn. Arun from Bengaluru (Bangalore), India; Ryan from Ladue, Missouri; Charlotte from Providence, Rhode Island; Dan from Fall River, Massachusetts; Stella from Seoul, Korea; Dave from Long Valley, New Jersey, and David from Palo Alto, California; Liz from New Haven, Connecticut, and Elizabeth from Bedford, New Hampshire. Somebody mentioned *The Kite Runner*, one of those international middlebrow bestsellers, like *The Life of Pi* or *Three Cups of Tea*, that come up regularly during these exercises. Somebody mentioned *The Brothers Karamazov*, one of the classics assigned in AP English classes that also tend to make an appearance, well-ridden warhorses like *A Tale of Two Cities, Frankenstein, The Great Gatsby, Heart of Darkness*. Dan emailed me recently to tell me that he can't remember which of two books he named on that first day, but he is sure it was either Warren Buffett's *The Intelligent Investor* or Og Mandino's *The Greatest Salesman in the World*, "which contrary to the title has little to do with business and almost everything to do with self-help and spirituality. Have courage, persistence, integrity, be kind, trust in God—the type of practical wisdom that makes a big difference." Either one of these two nonfiction books about business and self-improvement would have made him an outlier, which, I would soon come to realize, was his preferred relationship to the group. Stella, another outlier, talked about Min Jin Lee's novel *Pachinko*, which tells the multigenerational story of a Korean family in Japan in the twentieth century. "It was the first book that I really critically analyzed by myself, without relying on existing literary opinion, as it was newly published when I examined it," she said. She sounded like a potential English major.

More hands, more names. Alice from Crystal Lake, Illinois; Bill from Bernardsville, New Jersey; Eva from Rocky River, Ohio; Jonah from Shoreham, Long Island; Kathi from Greenwich, Connecticut; Eli from Cold Spring Harbor, Long Island; Matteo from Milan, Italy; Colleen from Yonkers, New York. And more, thirty-four in all, including Allie, the TA, from Norman, Oklahoma, who chose to go with a childhood favorite,

Lemony Snicket's *A Series of Unfortunate Events* books, rather than a more intimidating selection from the Russian literature in which she specialized.

When everyone had taken their turn, I took mine. I'm Carlo of Chicago, I said, and from there I told one of two stories I often tell during these first-day exchanges. I can't remember which one I told to this group, so I'll give you both—one about language and one about history.

The first goes like this: Like a lot of people here I read a lot of fantasy growing up, and I still do. In high school, when I didn't feel like doing my homework, which was often, I read pulp fiction from the 1930s, which you could buy used in paperback collections for pennies: Robert E. Howard's stories about Conan the Barbarian; Edgar Rice Burroughs's stories about John Carter of Mars; stories by H. P. Lovecraft, C. L. Moore, Clark Ashton Smith. I thought I was just wasting time. But I vividly remember a moment when I was taking my SATs and I sat back and gave silent thanks to those pulp writers because they had taught me some word that had just showed up on the verbal test: *incantation* or *stygian* or *clove*, as in "The witch doctor's shrieking incantation was just reaching its climax when the tigerishly thewed swordsman leaped from the stygian obscurity of the temple's shadows and clove him to the breastbone with a crunching blow of his notched and gore-slick blade." It just goes to show that you never know when something you read will turn out to be good for you, even if you read it precisely to avoid doing what was supposed to be good for you.

The second story goes like this: One set of books that had a significant effect on me was James T. Farrell's Studs Lonigan trilogy. These are three realist novels, published in the 1930s, which take place in the neighborhood in which I grew up, South Shore. When I read them in my teens, around 1980, I found them flat and toneless, but I recognized some things that still held true in my own time, half a century after they were written, like the apparently eternal fact of packs of guys hanging out on Seventy-First Street and messing with people. The thing is, almost everybody in the Studs Lonigan books is white, and Lonigan's family moves to South Shore in part to get away from black people, while the South Shore in which I grew up was almost entirely black. Until I read Farrell, I vaguely assumed it had always been that way, and I remember thinking as I read

Farrell that I should find out more about the history of my neighborhood, which helped lead to a sustained interest and academic specialty in city life, especially the ways in which we can tease out history from novels, poems, essays, movies, music, painting, photography, design, landscape, you name it. The most recent book I wrote was all about South Shore and its transformations, and I can trace that book's origins back to, among other things, my reaction to stumbling across a confusing piece of my neighborhood's past in the Studs Lonigan trilogy when I was just a couple of years younger than you are now.

.   .   .   .   .

We had time for a quick exercise before our seventy-five minutes were up. I wrote "Call me Ishmael" on the board and said, Let's start getting into the habit of thinking about the relationship between form and meaning. Here's a three-word sentence that many people are familiar with, the famous opening of Herman Melville's *Moby-Dick*, still widely regarded as The Great American Novel. It doesn't matter if you've read the book or not—and if you have, put aside for a moment the rest of it. Let's just concentrate on these three words at the very beginning of a long book and think about the relationship between *what* is being said, which is what the term *content* refers to, and *how* it's being said, which is what the term *form* refers to. Dave raised his hand with the serene confidence of somebody who likes to talk in class and is always game to put an interpretive harpoon in a big fish like *Moby-Dick* and said, "This may be kind of obvious, but he's not saying 'My name is Ishmael'; he's saying that we should call him Ishmael, which is not the same thing." We gnawed on that bone for a while. "Call me Ishmael" has the feel of something some heavily tattooed guy in a waterfront bar would say before bending your ear. Maybe it's an alias, maybe it's a clue, but in any case, he's telling us to pay attention to how he presents himself in this book, not just to the story he's going to tell. Our narrator's warning us to keep an eye on him, that who he is and how he tells the story may be as important as the story he tells.

Phrasing his introduction to emphasize his choice of the name *Ishmael* also invites us to find out more about that name. Somebody pointed out that Ishmael is a character in the Bible. Okay, that gives us moves to make, including a research agenda. We'd want to find out who Ishmael is in the Bible, what his story is, what kinds of meanings get attached to him, and then ask why this guy who's about to tell us a really long fish story would invite us to be thinking about the biblical Ishmael. How is it going to matter to our reading of this book that in the Bible, an angel tells Ishmael's mother, Hagar—who is enslaved by Abraham and his wife, Sarah, and wanders in the wilderness while she's pregnant with Ishmael—that her unborn son will be a wild donkey of a man, that his hand will be against everyone and everyone's hand against him, and that he will be the father of nations? And there's no mention of the biblical Ishmael spending any time at sea; rather, he wanders a desert so waterless that he must be saved by a miraculously appearing well, a photonegative parallel to the Ishmael in the novel being saved by a floating coffin when he's adrift on the ocean. One handy literary-critical word for the relationship between the books is *intertextuality*, which is the practice of reading two texts together as if they were parts of one larger text. The novel's narrator is saying, "I'm inviting you to read my story along with the story of Ishmael in the Bible, which will help you understand what my story means." Whatever we do with the fact that the name of our narrator is Ishmael, it's going to be filtered through the fact that he starts by telling us to call him Ishmael rather than just saying his name is Ishmael.

We felt pretty good about all this. In addition to wanting to read books in Lit Core that they find entertaining, many students regard the one required literature class as an opportunity to amass cultural capital, and talking about biblical intertextuality in *Moby-Dick* on the very first day felt intellectually respectable enough to satisfy that ambition.

Just time for one more. I put another three-word sentence on the board: "Build the wall." Our current president at the time had repeated it frequently on the campaign trail, as had chanting crowds at his rallies. On the content front, the sentence is telling someone to build a wall. Simple enough. What about form? Does it even *have* form? Well, what about *the* instead of *a*, and what does it do to *not* add "at the border with Mexico" when you are in fact referring to a wall at the border with Mexico? There were some uneasy looks around the room. Are we talking politics in English class? How about getting back to *Moby-Dick* and, you know, Shakespeare and stuff like that? But a couple of hands went up. Calling it "the wall" implies that you know what the speaker is talking about, somebody said. It's saying that you know and I know what's going on. Somebody else said that calling it "the wall" implies even more than that. There's an extra-imperative ring to it, especially when the phrase is modified to the common variant "Build *that* wall"—it's like saying "You know what wall I'm talking about, and you know why it has to be built, and let's just man up and get it done."

As it became clear that people could speak on this subject and not be struck by lightning, that after all it was a conversation about the interpretation of language and not a test of whether you belonged on Team Blue or Team Red, the discussion broadened. The often-repeated notion that Mexico was somehow going to pay for the wall came up, and then we got into the larger implications of the three-word sentence, which came in two flavors: one, narrower, was about the importance of controlling national borders; the other, broader, was about all the disappointments and frustrations piled onto the figure of the immigrant who crosses the Mexican border illegally. After a while, with just a minute or two of class left, I suggested that we step back and consider just how much resonance we had managed to get out of the three words, and how *the* amplified that resonance. What concatenation of form, content, and context allowed those three words to say not just "We have a national responsibility to build that wall on the border with Mexico that we're already talking about, a project already under way that just needs to be completed, one that real Americans support" but also "I feel that life in America has proven disappointing in so many ways, that my expectations of the promise of this country have not been realized to my satisfaction, that the rights and privileges that I believe accrue naturally to me have been constrained and rolled back, and let's agree for the purposes of this conversation that those who cross the border and those who fail to control them are somehow to blame"? That's a lot of work for three one-syllable words.

·   ·   ·   ·   ·

1:15: quitting time. You have a short story by Stuart Dybek and three brief chapters from the textbook on interpreting literature to read for Thursday, I reminded them. Come prepared to speak up, which means that when you read Dybek's story, you should be trying to notice form and trying to connect it to whatever you think the story's about. You have the one-page handout on literary form you got today to give you some ideas of what to look for. Also, read the syllabus with care. It's a contract, and you should know what you're getting into, and plan ahead. See you Thursday.

We were under way. This group of students looked promising—willing and capable, with no obvious red flags so far when it came to classroom chemistry. I was confident that we could get into a groove and have ourselves a good semester just similar enough to past successful semesters to feel like a job well done and just different enough from them to keep it interesting. School is school, forever and always. But there was yet one more potent extracurricular force just coming into view on the horizon, still far from the classroom but inexorably closing in. On January 11, the first confirmed death attributed to a novel coronavirus that had recently appeared in Wuhan was announced. Official news of the first case outside China had come on the thirteenth, the day before our first class meeting.

3 Citizens

You can see a class in any number of ways: a bunch of people from all over, students and their teacher, a group of aspirants trying to secure the credits and grades dispensed by a gatekeeper, paying customers and a paid employee, and so on. It's also, most importantly, a community of inquiry. The main thing we have in common is that inquiry, which in the case of my Lit Core course was defined by two intentions: to discern how meaning flows through literature, which speaks more to the skill-acquisition side of the mission of the humanities, and to understand the depth and reach of the enduring theme of the misfit, which speaks more to the examine-models-of-how-to-live side of that mission. For the community to cohere and function, people in the room—students and teacher alike—had to see themselves as members of it. We didn't have to become zealots, and it was understood by all that the commitment is always partial rather than total. We all had ideas about the limits of interpretation, and we all had other things to care about: families, lives, interests, other classes. But we had to be willing to care about the intentions that defined the community and its inquiry, which obliged us to overcome any initial skepticism to ante up. That meant acknowledging and acting on a responsibility to the group and, in return, feeling entitled to make a claim on the group's responsibility to its individual members.

In other words, we had to become citizens. There are all kinds of ways to be a citizen, and it's part of a teacher's craft to make sure that the range of individuals and types in the room can all find their way to citizenship. Eli and Stella both found their way to citizenship, though by very different routes and in very different styles; and, as contributors to our classroom discussions, they did it in front of everyone else, which had the effect of demonstrating to those others that achieving citizenship was doable and worth doing—for all kinds of students, all kinds of people.

.   .   .   .   .

Eli and Wilson often had their hands up first in our early discussions of Stuart Dybek's stories, establishing themselves as our most willing trail-blazers. Wilson didn't come on as someone who thought of himself as an English major; rather, his manner said that he wanted to do well in this class, was willing to overcome his doubts to find this stuff interesting, and had challenged himself to take the lead in volunteering to talk. Eli, in contrast, seemed moved to speak up when others were hesitating, at least in part, because the prospect of a lull in the conversation clearly made him nervous. He often sat up front and to my left, but he was one of the few who didn't return to the same seat from one class meeting to the next. A ragged-edgy presence in contrast to Wilson's studied self-confidence, Eli blurted out his ideas in bursts when he talked, and he was unquiet when at rest, radiating an awkward dynamism. He could seem impatient with others' contributions or oblivious to them; indeed, when I interviewed him as a junior, he admitted that he often had no use for what classmates said: "Sometimes you go through like five or six people that say essentially nothing, and it's like this is kind of a waste. And they all say the same general idea, like, 'I thought Jackson was right. This book *is* sad. He's correct.'"

He spoke up in class because he hated long silences, because he thought the books were interesting and he had something to say, and because it was required of him and he wanted to get a good grade; but there was something fundamentally oppositional about his presence in the classroom. "I feel like there's a level of complete bullshit that's kind of necessary in English classes," he said to me with the heartless honesty of the young. "Like, there's no time you go in there and you fully know what's going on every day. I've never had a class like that. I don't think anyone's had a class like that. And sometimes you just need the participation and you just say some point, whether you think it out or you just go 'That's a thought; I'm going to say it.'" Picturing him in Lit Core, seated in a row of his freshman peers but somehow refusing to get in line, puts me in mind of a domesticated dingo I used to encounter sometimes when I was out for a run during summer visits to Cape Cod. I'd see it up ahead in the distance, sniffing around in the front yard of the house where its owner lived, and even from a block away the dingo's outline and manner of moving would trip my atavistic alert system: *That may look like a regular dog, but it's a wild animal.*

Eli was not a get-with-the-program type looking to find a way to fit in. He gave me angles and destabilized the game almost by instinct. By "gave me angles" I mean that, as effective boxers do when they present themselves to an opponent, he didn't come straight at a question or a task in a way I could predict. If I was asking an open-ended question like "Let's start by noticing any aspects of form," then there wasn't much in the way of expectation to upend. But after an open-ended start, I will increasingly shape a discussion toward a clear goal—one that arises from what the students say or one that I have in my notes as an objective for the day or, often, one that I have in my notes that the students also bring up on their own, which creates a convenient opening for me to seize on it. The more focused the discussion became—"Okay, let's try to figure out what kinds of meaning we can find in what we've noticed, this pattern of repetitions of trees, the moon, apples, wafers, and blood"—the more I had to be ready for Eli to come back at me with something unexpected. If we had been talking about X but the last five comments in the discussion had been about Y, he might go back to X or jump to Z. Abrupt forward or backward leaps and sideways bounds were built into his thought process, and I had to work to stay with him. I didn't want to shut him down, but I also had an obligation to orchestrate a conversation that clearly displayed the momentum of logical purpose. Most students, including Eli, relied on me to make each class meeting and the semester as a whole feel as if it was moving from clearly defined start to clearly defined finish.

By "destabilized the game" I mean that Eli had the advanced game-player's knack for doing something other than plugging along turn after turn, making incremental advances and retreats. In some games, including most sports, plugging along will do fine. In basketball, for instance, you try to do a good job, attend to fundamentals, minimize your team's errors (turnovers, choosing to take bad shots, allowing easy shots by your opponents), let the successes pile up incrementally (made shots on offense, stops on defense), and at the end, if all goes well, you've got more points than the other team. But many board games and card games don't work that way, especially when there are three or more players and not just two teams. To break out of the pack and finish as something other than an also-ran in the middle of that pack, you have to stop plugging along and destabilize the game by taking a chance, making a bold and risky play, throwing a spanner into the works in the hope that the ensuing chaos leaves you atop the pile. The equivalent in boxing is "making the fight," opening yourself to greater danger in order to force the action and land blows and make something happen, which a fighter will feel extra pressure to do when he realizes that just doing a solid job isn't going to be enough because he's getting outjabbed and outpointed as the rounds go by. Consider how Donald Trump handled the challenge of breaking out of the crowded Republican primary field and lining up an unlikely shot at the presidency in 2016. Trump received far too much credit for being crazy like a fox when he was pretty obviously just flailing around and winging it, but he was an idiot-savant six-pole-diagram kung fu master when it came to instinctively giving them angles and destabilizing the game—the only two things he was ever any good at.

My invoking Trump as a parallel might lead you to believe that I saw Eli as a problem. I did not. I liked having him in class; in fact, he went on to take a second class with me, and I liked having him in that class, too. It's worth underscoring that a square peg like Eli can be a valuable asset, especially in a big class, the size of which tends to make most students extra-nervous about saying something that might be received as weird by others. Square pegs help prevent falling into a rhythm in which everybody tries to outdo everybody else in saying exactly what they think I want to hear. When Eli spoke up, it was clear to all that he hadn't devoted even a second's thought to trying to imagine what I or his fellow students might want to hear. He just had something to say, more often a thought just sparking into existence than a fully formed one, and he said it without considering whether it fit neatly into the flow. It probably wouldn't work too well to have thirty-three students like that in the classroom (though I'm up for at least a taste of what that would be like), but it was good to have a few of them for at least two reasons. First, Eli's tendency to come at us out of left field offered a constant reminder to all that we weren't looking for *the* meaning of the text, that, instead, we were turning observations of the text into interpretive arguments that led to always-multiple possibilities for finding and making *meanings* in it. Second, he made me work harder to incorporate what he had to say into a conversation that felt like it was heading somewhere purposeful. Having Eli in class and on his angle-giving, game-destabilizing game made me a better teacher by making teaching that class a more challenging workout for me and preventing me from getting too cozy and set in my ways.

And Eli, who told me he'd scored a perfect thirty-six on his ACT reading test, was indeed on his game at the start of the semester. He was doing the reading and coming to class prepared—"not just pulling it entirely out of my ass like an ape," as he put it when I interviewed him. I also soon realized that even a brief silent pause would make him so uncomfortable that he'd have to put his hand up. "I've always had a thing like if no one speaks in class, I feel like I need to just say something at that point," he told me. "It just feels so awkward to sit there staring, especially for, like, thirty seconds—like, 'What's happening, guys?'" It's useful to a teacher to know that there are students in the room who can't abide even a brief silence; their hands will go up if you are patient and wait them out. Eli's discomfort with silence was especially useful because it was paired with preparation—"Beyond doing the reading, I'll jot down a note or two, something like, 'Jon Snow, big sword, means something'"—and a militant refusal to give a damn about what anybody thought of him. He told me, "I feel like I just don't have any social anxiety anymore," and that's a rare trait indeed in a college freshman, especially these days. Therein lay a story.

Because he had a speech impediment and had received a lot of speech therapy as a child, Eli was assigned to a Special Education English class in ninth grade. He said, "I hated that class with a burning passion because there were like two girls in it, everyone was either on the football team or just didn't care at all, we didn't do anything except for make fun of people and get up to shenanigans, and I was, like, singled out as the good kid because I didn't actively interrupt the class." Judging from his tone when he said this, it may well be that being identified as the good kid burned him the most. "I hated it there," he went on. "Out of spite, basically, I moved up to honors English the next year, and then I had an experience there, had a really good teacher who got me involved in a bunch of clubs and afterschool activities, and we really bonded. So I took another honors English class, AP lang, AP lit—I just ended up liking English."

Eli told me that he had never really conquered his speech impediment, though it came as news to me that he had one, since I had never noticed it in class. "They simply gave up, or I gave up, I guess," he said. "It was like, 'I don't want to do this anymore, Mom. We're spending a lot of money and a lot of time on a thing I hate going to,' and so we just stopped." I suggested that perhaps he had declared victory, and Eli said, "I definitely did. Basically I was very shy to talk for a long time, I had so much social anxiety; then I was like, in high school, 'What if I just make myself do it?' And so I joined improv and debate. Both of those are, like, hold a gun to your head, you must speak for five minutes right now." Improv and debate cured him of the fear of public speaking by eliminating the fear of saying something stupid. "At least personally, unless someone is consistently saying the dumbest thing I can think of, like I don't understand the point at all, I will not remember unless it's a good point," he told me. "And I feel like people are the same way, generally. You say something dumb and it's like"—assuming a matter-of-fact teacher's voice—"'Okay, next person.'"

His intent to major in English did not sit well with his parents. "I got into here as a computer science major," he said, "which I'm totally ditching for an English major the second I can get my dad on board, since he's paying." His father was the main force pushing Eli and his older sister, who ended up in finance, to make moves that he believed would lead to affluence and success in life. Eli's father's story of pulling himself up by his bootstraps from poverty dominated the family narrative, and he had rigidly conventional ideas about how his children could prosper. He gave Eli a list of twenty-three colleges and universities to apply to—"basically all the Ivies, even though I had no chance of getting into any of them except maybe Cornell, and then he, like, literally copy-and-pasted the USA Today top fifty schools and picked from the lower twenty-five"—and stayed on him to pick a major that he saw as leading to a good job. "It's like a 'I don't want to pay 70K a year for you to work at Starbucks' kind of resistance," Eli said. "Mainly from my dad, but my mom would make jabs like, 'Oh, you should pay attention to how they make the coffee here. You're going to do that for the rest of your life.'" Eli's father sent around in the family group chat a link to an article showing the starting salaries of different majors. "And he was, like, Caitlyn's at number five with finance; Eli's at number forty-three out of forty-three with English." When I asked if his father was aware that English majors make just about the same as everybody else when you compare midcareer outcomes rather than starting salaries, he said, "I think he's going to be dead by then, so he's not too concerned about that time." But *you* are not going to be dead by then, I pointed out to him, and Eli said, "I really hope not, no."

A detente had taken shape between son and father when I talked with Eli in the fall of his junior year. He had declared a major in English and was doubling down on creative writing and theater, "but I'm still being forced to take a minor in computer science, and I literally don't know what's happening." When I pointed out to Eli that one of the things that had changed since I went to college was that few students now expected to do better than their parents, he said, "I am fully expecting not to do better than my father, but I think he hopes I do better than him. We kind of have this game where we pretend I'm going to be a lawyer, but we both know it's not true. That was how I pitched it originally, like, 'Ah, if I go to English I can become a law student,' and he was like, 'Okay.' And then he slowly realized 'This kid's totally lying to me.'"

The momentum of Eli's strong start in Lit Core didn't last. He stopped putting up his hand regularly when we moved from Dybek's stories to Wharton's *The House of Mirth*, and he never reengaged at his original level. He missed some classes, and on other days, he was physically present but hadn't done the reading; so we heard from him less and less. He wrote an insightful, if disorganized, first paper about one of Dybek's stories—he finally wrote himself into a clear statement of his main point about two-thirds of the way through it—but he failed to turn in the second and third papers when they were due. Looking back on Lit Core in the fall of his junior year, he said that his drop-off began with his dislike of Edith Wharton, which opened the door for his native disorganization to assert itself.

When I asked Eli about his level of skepticism about interpretation, he said it was set by the text, not the conversation about it in class. "I feel like it depends purely on the book whether I'm in the 'This is bullshit' camp or the 'This is very interesting' camp. In high school, I remember, we read *Tale of Two Cities*, which I fucking—I *hated* that book, *despised* it, and I basically said nothing about it because I didn't have anything to say." He initially responded to *The House of Mirth* in a similar way. "It's usually like if the book doesn't get to the point, if it's a lot of artful language that doesn't go anywhere." I observed that, based on his examples, it seemed that his bullshit reaction was triggered by nineteenth-century diction, which many Lit Core students found difficult to navigate. He allowed that by the time we got to the end of our discussions of *The House of Mirth*, he had developed some respect for the novel, "but at the beginning, I was like, 'This is so slow,' and it was like she's cutting the pages of the novel she's reading and I'm supposed to think she's like making her own narrative by cutting the pages and I was like, 'You're doing too much. I don't care.'"

In Eli's view, entropy is always on the prowl and ready to strike at his semester, as it did when he allowed his distaste for Wharton to discourage him from keeping up on the reading and being regularly prepared for class. "I am awful at time management," he told me. "I'm a last-minute or I'll-do-it-when-I-want-to kind of person. Currently, I'm desperately behind in two classes, and I'm literally a month ahead in another class." At semester's end, he staged a last-minute frenzy of paper-writing that just barely saved him from tanking in Lit Core. Junot Díaz, Joan Didion, and Hunter Thompson spoke to him more than Wharton had, but by then he had fallen far behind and it was almost too late. "I was BS'ing everything, and then the arc was like, Okay, if I don't read this and write this, I will actually fail out of college," he said. "And so, literally, I was just chugging coffee for two days straight and just feverishly typing." The results were . . . caffeinated. There were plenty of lively ideas caroming about, but his execution was even more all over the place than usual. Still, he turned in both missing papers and his take-home final at the very last possible moment and passed the course, even if his final grade did not do justice to the quality of his thinking when he was at his best. I didn't hold his fade against him, of course. These things happen to students, especially when they're new to college, and a teacher shouldn't take it personally. And he still deserved respect for being one of the intrepid ones who went first in class discussion in the crucial early days of the semester, when we needed to establish a community norm of participating in class and of being willing to say things that might sound weird to others.

It wasn't until I started interviewing for this book that I learned that in those early days of Lit Core, when Eli and Wilson were setting the standard for willingness to contribute to class discussion, I was witnessing a reunion of sorts. "We grew up together," Eli told me. He and Wilson "were very close friends when we were, like, six through twelve. But then, he's, like, a professional hockey player, and so he traveled the country; he moved to Minnesota [Michigan, actually] at some point to play hockey there. He was going to go to Harvard, and then at the last minute it was BC," and meanwhile Eli was deciding between Wake Forest and BC, "so it was just chance that we both ended up here." They weren't pals anymore, but a remnant of the earlier bond remained. "We say hi to each other. It's funny because I don't really watch sports, and people around me are like, 'How do you know all these hockey guys that come up to you randomly at the dining hall and say hi?' I don't, like, go to parties with him or anything, but he came to my house for Christmas multiple times—even now, even last year, to make gingerbread houses like we always had."

· · · · ·

While Eli was breaking to the front of the pack at the beginning of the semester, Stella was hanging back, observing, getting a feel for the lay of the land and the people around her. Looking back when we talked in the fall of 2021, she told me, "The first few weeks you just gauge the student atmosphere, you gauge the professor's receptiveness to students responding—because sometimes professors want to dominate the conversation in the classroom, which is understandable because it's their classroom. And so I think those first few weeks, I'm just testing the waters, seeing how students react, seeing how students don't react. I've always been very vocal in classroom discussions, but there's, of course, always that level of hesitancy that I think anyone has going into any classroom."

The Lit Core classroom was particularly forbidding for her. It was a big class, especially for one in which everyone was expected to participate in discussions, and it was also a required course full of students intending to major in business, STEM, and other disciplines that weren't English. So it wasn't going to have the intimate feel of an elective seminar full of people who have had classes with each other before and know each other well. "It's understandable because we're in a Lit Core, and some of the students don't want to be there because English is not their strong suit," she said. "You could sense the dread for sure a little bit on the part of some students," a dread traceable in large part to my policy of expecting everyone to speak up in discussions. "Other students were very comfortable, but I think a lot of students felt tense, and you can feel that tension."

As a result, Stella said, "I was very intimidated for sure. Everyone around me was—well, the majority was white and I came from a very international background, and so I'm used to seeing a lot of diverse faces, I'm used to seeing faces like mine and hearing very interesting names." Stella's Korean, from Seoul (her Korean name is Minjin), but she laid out for me a cosmopolitan background: born in Thailand, lived in India until the first grade, then Malaysia, then in Korea for four years, then back to Malaysia, with a six-month stay in Canada as well. "I don't identify with Korea, really," she said. "I identify more with Malaysia as my home." She described her international school in Malaysia as a small, tight-knit, very diverse community, in stark contrast to her highly competitive school in Korea, where leading students' names were prominently posted on honor-roll boards. Being a freshman at BC was in a sense more like her Korean high school: more homogenous than Malaysia and with an atmosphere still supercharged by the aftereffects of all the ambition and competitiveness that had powered the typical freshman's yearslong campaign for college admission.

"I was intimidated by that," she said, "and, as well, by the fact that it was an English class. While I am confident in my English abilities because I am a native speaker, I think it's kind of that aspect of double consciousness where I am my own demon just because I've read a lot of Asian American narratives about always being conscious and aware of your race and skin color, which honestly, I shouldn't have been bothered by. So by the time that passed, I was like, I really should not care about this. I should participate because, if I don't participate, it's probably not going to reflect that greatly on my grade. And I also want to share my thoughts. And also, there weren't enough girls speaking up. There were a lot of guys dominating the conversation and I was like, I need to change that." Conventional wisdom holds that men speak more freely in class and in general—men talk even when they don't know what they're talking about, and women stay silent even when they do—but that hasn't been my experience in my classes, where the majority of students and the majority of regular contributors are usually women. This Lit Core was an exception. There were, indeed, a lot of guys speaking up frequently: not just the trailblazers Eli and Wilson but also a number of others—Dan, Dave, Paul, Tyler, Jonah, Luke, Bill—who all seemed remarkably at ease analyzing literature in a room full of strangers.

In talking to students about their experience in class, I was struck by how much they got out of listening to their peers. Eli was in the minority who expressed impatience with others; the majority credited other students with seeing things in the texts that they hadn't seen and relied on them for most of their insight into the books we read. Stella, who sat midway back to my right, was one of these. She listened to others with great care, not just at the beginning of the semester when she wasn't talking yet but also when after a couple of weeks she decided that she'd hung back long enough and it was time to speak up more regularly. When I observed that she seemed to come to class with full-blown interpretations already mapped out, she corrected me: "Not necessarily. I'd make annotations in advance, just like writing 'naturalism' in the margin or something like that, but I mainly made my observations based on what other people have said—because when other people say something, or whenever you said something, I would then get a new insight. I try to listen most of the time because everything that's being said in the classroom is material for me to work with." She was committed to the principle that she had something to learn from everyone in the room, "especially because we had a lot of people from different majors."

Some students, like Wilson, liked to go early in the conversation and toss an observation or two onto the pile while it was forming, but Stella, a counterpuncher, would wait until we were well into the discussion and then put the pieces together in ways that often felt like fully realized interpretive arguments. "I see what people are saying about Lily trying to take control of her story," she might say, her voice low and firm, warming to her subject as she went on. "And the language describing her as an attacker and a predator on page 17 supports that. That reading makes sense. But I'm thinking about all the scientific-sounding naturalist language we've talked about that describes her as a passive victim of larger forces, like on 236 when she's compared to something swept along on a current, or on 296 when it says she's like a sea-anemone torn from a rock. And that language is also used to talk about other characters, like look at page 270"—a passage we hadn't discussed yet—"where how people are doing in high society is described as rising above the horizon and being eclipsed, like they were planets and moons and they get pulled by gravity and their light gets blocked. So maybe one way to put that together is you could say that the theme of naturalism gets stronger as the novel goes along, like we're seeing deeper layers of how the characters' lives are determined by forces they can't do anything about. It seems like being a predator or an attacker, being active and taking control, could be just an illusion Lily has about herself that she comes to realize isn't a true picture of how passive she really is." Sometimes I would catch other students nodding along as Stella spoke, or shaking their heads like guitar freaks absorbing a monster solo, as they flipped between the pages she cited, trying to keep up with her. When she was done, everybody would kind of sit back and visibly say to themselves, *Okay, that's pretty much settled, and I'm definitely not talking next after her. Let's move on to some other topic.* I would take such opportunities to remind the class to take notes on what other students said, not just on what I said. It doesn't get more insightful just because I repeat it, I would tell them. Your peers have things to say that you will want to remember—when it's time for the final and beyond.

Stella, who had been so intimidated by others at first, was aware that her willingness and ability to go long might intimidate or bother other students. She said, "I could feel that they were at times unwilling to speak up, and so I guess sometimes my mentality was 'I'm going to dominate the floor again.'" She added, "I find my, well, my classroom personality very annoying because I think I'm a bit of a try-hard, but I've learned to just get over that." Wait, I said, you find your *own* classroom personality annoying? "I really do," she said. "I would not want to talk to me." Why? "It's just 'Wow, she's such a try-hard.' It's just like 'It's *that* student, speaking again.'" But that doesn't actually stop you from talking, does it? "It doesn't," she said, steely serene.

One thing that helped Stella overcome any hesitation about being perceived as overbearing or a try-hard was the larger principle of classroom
citizenship that she tries to keep in mind. "Just being willing to learn
in general is an attitude that I try to have. Because if you fight against
something—this is what I took away from, like, being very burnt out in
high school—if you try to fight something, then it's very hard to learn in
general. And so even with the core, the fact that we had to take a lot of
natural science courses, math courses, and I am not a sciencey or mathe-
matics student, but I tried to learn to love the material just so that I can
help myself. I think that's an attitude, especially, that comes very naturally
in English, and so I felt confident in the class after I started talking. I realized talking wasn't that scary in your class; after I learned that, I just felt
very comfortable."

Stella came to college already having absorbed one of the most important lessons any school can teach: learning how to be interested in things—
learning to ask *What can I get out of this?*—is, in fact, an advanced skill
essential to doing well in school and in life. It takes practice to develop
your facility for fitting yourself to the contours of a discipline, a style, a
genre, a scene, an angle of inquiry—and then taking full ownership of the
knowledge and skills you gain from that process, fitting them in turn to
your own purposes. So-called disruptors hog the praise in our culture
these days, and my fellow professors tend to think of students who question everything as especially brilliant, but getting with the program is not
a default setting. It takes work and skill to do it in an intellectually meaningful way that's original and not rote, and Stella already knew that.

It would be a mistake to see Stella as a natural-born round peg, but I
can understand why you might make such a mistake, since I did, based on
the first impression I formed of her as a student in my Lit Core class. I saw
a high achiever who set rigorous expectations for herself, worked hard to
meet them, and showed a stellar capacity to get with the program in the
most inspired sense: she saw what mattered about the ideas and methods
of the course and found ways to make them her own. But in my conversations with her after the semester ended—email exchanges that began
when she asked for recommendations about books to read when she was
in quarantine on her return to Korea for the summer, our interviews in the
fall of 2021, and continuing follow-ups and catchups and check-ins in the

years since—it became clear to me that she understands herself to be in many ways a misfit, a square peg who's constantly rounding and smoothing herself to fit into round holes. Identifying as a cosmopolitan rather than a Korean was one way in which this showed up; another was identifying with the diversity and community of her school in Malaysia rather than with the regimentation of her school in Korea. She also read her own square-peggery into the episode of burnout during her high-school years to which she referred during our interview.

It happened during her senior year, right after she was rejected by her dream school, the University of Chicago, to which she had applied Early Decision because she saw it as both a high-prestige school that would advance her career prospects and a paradise of eccentric square-peg types. "In high school, I would say, I was very driven, very ambitious, and I burned and crashed very hard. I refused to go to school. I refused to go to college, even. I really put my foot down and was just angry at the world for no reason. We have something called a teenager moment in Korea, and I think I had that moment then." As she looks back on it, she says, "I was caught in between self-blame and my teachers telling me that I was lazy and that I wasn't pulling enough weight in my work. I couldn't even go out and party and club just because I hated myself so much because I was like, 'You have to work,' but I refused to work. And so it was just this whole internal dilemma, and I had a lot of internal demons."

Stella also saw her family situation as square-peggish for a Korean. When I asked if there was a story her family tells itself about itself, she said, "My parents went through a very messy, terrible divorce, and my mom and I came out on the very bruised and bloodied side of the battle. A lot of people assume a lot of things about a single mom and her daughter, especially in Korean culture, because there is this expectation of a heteronormative nuclear family. And so there isn't really a story between us, but I think it's just that my mom is everything to me and vice versa, and we don't see ourselves or our situation as being sad whatsoever. It's the two of us, and we're very comfortable with that." As a result, she says, "I actually grew up in a very liberal family in a way. My dad is very conservative, very Korean, but he kind of gave up on my studies because as a kid I really didn't study. My mom, she was very much like, 'If you got a C, if you tried your best, it's fine.'" She credits her mother with instilling a love of books in her when she was a child. "She would always carry a book in her bag," ready to pull it out for Stella to read whenever they were waiting at a doctor's office or restaurant. And Stella's mother read fairy tales in English to her daughter, even though she herself wasn't completely fluent in the language. Stella traces her passion for English language and literature to that influence.

Her mother, Stella said, further urged her to depart from the straight and narrow by seeing hard work as something other than just a path to prosperity. "A lot of people, they say they work hard because they want to achieve the future or lifestyle that their parents never had," she said. "I don't think that's the case for me. My mom always stressed the idea of a happy life, and she said, 'Whatever you want, go for it, pursue it and sustain yourself. Just be happy.' And so I never felt tied down in any way, and I still don't feel tied down, even though I am working and even though I am financially limited." In the fall of 2021, when I first interviewed her, Stella had taken a leave of absence from BC to work full-time in Korea to support herself and her mother, who was unemployed. "I just simply believe in setting my own course and learning from the mistakes of my parents," she said. "I just want to be my own person."

.   .   .   .   .

At first glance, you see mostly the differences between Eli and Stella. Loose cannon versus good soldier. Mercurial leaps and dips versus steady progress. White guy from Long Island versus cosmopolitan Asian woman from Korea, Malaysia, Thailand, India, Canada, the world. Literary guy struggling against a father who believes that there's a direct correlation between college major and lifetime earnings versus literary girl encouraged in her love of books from day one by her mother. Eli chafed at *The House of Mirth*'s nineteenth-century diction while Stella drank it down like fine wine. Stella systematically incorporated her classmates' comments into her own thinking, while Eli looked for inspiration to come fizzing and bubbling up from within. Eli went up and then way down and then partially up again, starting out strong and fading and then staging a frantic last-second rally, while Stella went up and up and up, starting out diffident and watchful and not quite sure of herself (in addition to her early reticence, she did not get an A on the first paper) before coming into her own as one of the strongest students in the class (she rewrote the first paper, got an A on it to replace the original B-plus, and received nothing but As after that).

But despite any number of apparent differences in classroom persona and style, Stella and Eli had a lot in common. They were in the small minority of students in the room who regarded English as their best subject. They were two of the three out of thirty-three who would go on to declare an English major. They both spoke up in class: Eli right away but then less and less as the semester went on, Stella not right away but with increasing frequency and authority once she got acclimatized. Other students who told me things like "I was intimidated by how smart and confident everybody else seemed to be" had the two of them, among others, in mind. Both even shared an apparent trajectory toward law school: Stella said she was set on it; Eli was engaged in a complex dance of assumptions with his father, though such dances sometimes result in your doing exactly the thing you thought you were only pretending to plan to do.

And, though they came to their shared status from different directions and in wildly different ways, they both anted up and became citizens— which was, from my point of view as the person charged with making the class work, the most important thing about them.

4 Noticing

Having gotten the preliminaries out of the way on Tuesday, we had our first real day of class on Thursday. On this day, we started handling the stuff itself—a work of literature—with analytical intent, which meant trying to figure out relationships between how the story is told and what it's about. *Form expresses meaning* was our mantra: notice the *how* and connect it to the *what*; or sometimes we'd start with the *what* by identifying a theme or a mood or some other aspect of aboutness and then consider the meaning-shaping effects of *how* it's delivered. We didn't ever have to come to earth-shattering conclusions, especially not on this day. If everybody got to handle the material with this sense of purpose and hear everybody else do it, and we could practice moving from noticing form to making arguments about meaning, that would be plenty for our first real class meeting.

The assignment was to read Stuart Dybek's "The Palatski Man," the first story in *Childhood and Other Neighborhoods*, his debut collection, published in 1980. In the next few class sessions, in addition to discussing more stories from *Childhood and Other Neighborhoods*, we would also work through some chapters of a textbook on the interpretation of literature—chapters on topics like plot, character, setting, motif, symbols, and so on—but we'd move quickly through those, pulling out tools and terms for describing what we see to put in our shared kit. Terms like *third-person omniscient narration* (the narrator is not confined to the point of view of any one character and can range freely among them or independently of any of them) or *in medias res* (starting the story in the middle of the action with no preliminaries) provide useful shorthand, and they also helped us think of ourselves as craftspeople. Authentic craft language, as opposed to obscurantist jargon, has that salutary effect. "Give-and-go off the pick-and-roll" conveys a lot more technical information and a sharper sense of self and intent than "You stand here and I'll go around you, then you go over there, and I'll pass you the ball and move toward the basket, and you pass it back to me." But such tool-kit stocking would always be secondary action in the service of the main event, which was analyzing Dybek's stories.

I started class promptly at noon, and we would end right at 1:15. Squeezing everything we could out of every minute allotted to us was a norm I wanted to be sure to establish. A typical course at BC features roughly two thousand minutes of class time in a semester. That seems like a lot if you think of it as one very long lecture, but it seems like not very much if all thirty-five people in the room are trying to get better at the craft of interpretation, increase their fund of knowledge, and augment their capacity for finding and making meaning (and joy) by having a thirty-five-way conversation about a half-dozen formidable works of literature. I try not to waste my time or the students', and I am always aware of how much I'm being paid and how much they're paying—or somebody's paying for them—to be in the room. College can't be reduced to just class time, of course, but I found it useful if we all bore in mind that if, at the time, a year at this school cost about $80,000, including room and board and expenses, and each student had a little over ten thousand minutes of class time per semester, it came out to about $4 per minute. You know how a roomful of students will start rustling their papers and collecting their stuff when there are just a few minutes left in a class? All I have to say when that happens, once I've introduced the dollars-per-minute idea to a class, is "Hey, people, we've got fourteen dollars of class time left," and they settle back in to get the juice out of the tail end of our high-priced time together.

First thing, beginning as students arrived in the minutes before noon, I made a point of going through names again, matching to faces, asking when I wasn't sure. I would do that at every class meeting for the first couple of weeks. While I'm learning names, I am inevitably going to make mistakes, but I try to make extra-sure to avoid those that will embarrass students or make them feel that I'm lumping them into an unindividuated category. If there are two Asian women in a class, for instance, or three goths, or four bros with flow, calling one by another's name will make that whole group self-conscious and less likely to participate. Another good reason to use a bit of class time on learning names: I'm reinforcing the message that I'm going to know who's present and contributing. I also asked Allie, the TA, to learn everybody's name as fast as she could, so that she could make an ostentatious habit of standing off to the side with a notebook at the beginning of class and marking down who was present and who was not, perhaps audibly muttering to herself things like "So Nina is *here* . . . and Cora is *not* here." She would also help me keep track of who contributed to discussions, which was a great luxury for me. I monitor all that in my head as I teach, just as a matter of course, but having Allie keep her own independent eye on participation provided an extra safeguard against students slipping through the cracks.

I talked for a few minutes to set up our discussion. We were starting with "The Palatski Man," an urban fable that traces a girl's path toward womanhood via her encounters with an enigmatic neighborhood character who sells candy apples and *palatski*—a treat made from two crisp wafers stuck together with honey—from a horse-drawn cart. Along the way, the story tells us something about her relationships with her brother, parents, and community and also about what's gained and lost as she matures. In thinking about the fit between form and meaning, I reminded them, we don't have to start with full-blown interpretive ideas. We can just notice things about how the story is told: word choices, images, repetitions, anything that looks like a pattern or a break in a pattern, even if we have no inkling of what to do with it. If we first make a pile of these observations, we can then start looking for the organizing logics they reveal.

They had brought with them a couple of one-page handouts I'd distributed on the first day of class that offered some help in preparing for discussions. The handouts were antidotes to paralysis. One sheet provided a list of different aspects of literary form, some general guidance about the kinds of things you might look for in setting, imagery, figurative language, symbolism, diction, repetitions, allusions, narration, structure, and so on. The other offered a simple template to help prep for discussions of Dybek's short stories. First, try to identify the beginning, middle, and end of the story. How do you break it into these parts, and what's your reasoning for saying that the beginning ends here or the ending begins there? Second, pay some attention to the character system. Who's the protagonist? What's the function of the secondary characters in relation to that protagonist? I find *character system* useful as an analytical term because it obliges you to think about whatever principle organizes the characters into a coherent network, in the way that gravity helps organize planets into a pattern of orbits around a star. Third, what is the arc of the narrative? Who or what changes as the story moves from beginning to middle to end? What's the nature of the change? This is all basic stuff that gives students some concrete things to look for and do as they read the story and prepare for class, and it also tends to reinforce the foundational principle that seeing form leads directly to making interpretive arguments about meaning. Why do you think the beginning of the story ends here and not there? If you think the story's ultimately about Mary, the girl who grows up, what work does this supporting character or that one do to help us know more about her?

I also reiterated some fundamental expectations for any interpretive work. Meaning is always plural and has to be argued for. There's no singular meaning hidden in the text by the author, nor do I think I know what the answers are. As I see it, if lawyers should always know exactly what answer they want to hear from a witness on the stand, humanities professors should never know exactly what they want to hear from a student in class. If I really do know what I want to hear, I should either just say it myself or ask a better question. So I'm not hiding answers behind my back and making you guess at them. The author created the text, but interpretation is also a creative act, in some ways an aggressive act, in which we— each of us, and also all of us together—go into that text and *make* something: an analytical reading. We'll be piecing together arguments: claims about meaning supported by evidence. We'll test the strength of these connections we're making as we go. If they feel strong, let's push and see what additional meanings we can stack on them. If they feel weak—if we find ourselves tossing out too many brilliant-sounding but unsupported claims or doing violence to the text to get it to mean what we want it to mean, both of which bring on that uh-oh feeling of stepping precariously out on shaky footing over a substanceless void that we've all felt from time to time during English classes—then we'll look for more evidence or change what we're asserting to match the evidence we do have.

Finally, I reminded them that everyone's expected to pull their weight. On Tuesday, we each said something about ourself and became A Person Who Has Talked in Class; today, our objective is for everyone to contribute to the discussion of the text. So find your way into the discussion today, even if it's just to notice something or ask a question about something you find puzzling. We are, I told them with a touch of mock here-we-go drama, about to arrive at The Pause, which happens when I finish my introductory comments and ask the first real question of the day. When The Pause arrives, students tend to look down at their books, as if to say "Hmm, this would be a good time to reread a key passage or two and review my notes in the margins of the text while waiting for somebody else to go first." Instead, you should prepare in advance for The Pause. You know it's coming every day, and you'll know what to expect from what I said about this class at the end of the last class. So be ready to treat The Pause as your cue to take action.

.   .   .   .   .

Time to get to it. Of all the possible ways this story could begin, it begins this way: "He reappeared in spring, some Sunday morning, perhaps Easter, when the twigs of the catalpa trees budded and lawns smelled of mud and breaking seeds," and so on into an anecdote about Mary's older brother, John, forcefully intervening to run off a jerk named Leon Sisca, who told Mary she was a dumb girl and lashed her bare legs with blessed Palm Sunday palms. Then we meet the Palatski Man, who will return every Sunday until the fall, when school resumes and "the green catalpa leaves fall like withered fans into the birdbaths, turning the water brown." What's being set up in these opening paragraphs? What's so significant that the story wants to get it said right away? If you think of a text as having a finite amount of energy and only one chance to introduce itself to us, this text uses its energy and its one chance to make a first impression in particular ways. Let's just start by noticing some of them. So, what did you see?

The Pause wasn't going to last long this time. I'd lowered the bar to participation almost to the floor by letting students know that simply pointing something out would do and that there was no particular right answer that others could revile them for missing, and I'd also raised the stakes by making participation a clearly expected norm and essential to getting a good grade. A full house, carrots over sticks. These were, for the most part, good kids, all-around achievers, astronaut types. For years they'd been hitting the marks set by teachers, coaches, parents, guidance counselors, and anxiety-stoking profiteers at the College Board and Stanley Kaplan and *U.S. News and World Report*. And, even if many of those present were at least a little skeptical about the whole business of interpreting literature, I had just set a pretty easy mark.

I was ready to wait for a response, resisting any fugitive urge to keep talking to fill a potential silence, but my patience was not tested this time. Hands went up. Wilson, Eli, Marguerite, Liz, Dave, Luke, Dan, Tyler—all looked to be potential regular participators. Somebody noticed that the catalpa trees are blooming at the beginning of the opening passage, withering at the end of it. Somebody pointed out the number of Polish names and words, and also Hispanic names; we had a sense of who lives in the neighborhood and that it might be changing. Several people noticed all the Catholic imagery and vocabulary: palms, mass, crosses, the Virgin, Jesus, Easter, and such. Somebody noticed that the second sentence, in which Mary makes her entrance, moves from the second person to the third person: "Or Palm Sunday, bending palms to be cut into crosses and pinned on your Sunday dress and the year-old palms removed by her brother, John . . ." What might that be about? We couldn't say yet, but we added it to the pile.

The main thing was that we were in business, getting into the swing of a conversation and getting used to that feeling. Early classes are a little like practicing with a recently formed band; regardless of what you play, it's important to share the feeling of flowing together into a groove. I didn't have a sense of characters yet, and it's not always true that people who jump right in on the first day will continue to play prominent roles in the class, but I was picking up some initial impressions. Marguerite seemed genuinely curious about what we were going to find at the bottom of this story. Dave exuded relaxed confidence, Eli nervous tension. Colleen and Susannah and a couple of others had turtled up, refusing to meet my eye and careful not to move a hand in any way that could be construed as raising it, but they seemed more intimidated than uninterested, and intimidated is much easier to fix. Both Liz and Wilson visibly said to themselves, "What the hell, I'll give it a shot" before deciding to raise a hand.

Wilson had been the very first student I called on to speak at the beginning of our discussion, when we got to The Pause, establishing himself as a pioneer willing to go ahead onto unknown possibly perilous ground and show others that it was okay to speak up. He was especially effective in this role because he didn't seem to think of himself as some kind of literary ace; rather, his in-class persona was that of a regular guy who wasn't sure about this interpretation business but just happened to think this story was cool and wanted to do a good job and get a good grade. Phil, a hockey teammate of Wilson's (Phil later made the Olympic team and was drafted by an NHL team), had walked in with him and sat next to him. Phil had not raised his hand and wore a pained look that suggested he was not convinced that we were doing anything that was going to lead anywhere he wanted to go. Ryan, who sat near Wilson and Phil, had a skeptical look similar to Phil's, but he put up his hand and added something to the pile. It looked as if it unsettled him to do it, but he forced himself to make the effort, and that counted for something.

I was content to let the class pile up the observations for a while. There was plenty to notice; different people would see different details in the story; and different people work at different speeds. Also, I wanted to give them all some time to perceive that their peers were not saying anything otherworldly, a revelation that would help them talk themselves into taking the risk of saying something. But, in addition to establishing the principle that simply noticing things is useful, I was also trying to model the process of building an argument—which may start with noticing details but presses on to connect those details to what the story's about, which is the heart of the process of making assertions about form and meaning. So after fifteen minutes or so, I did a reset. Okay, we've been noticing and cataloguing some of the many choices the story makes about how to introduce us to its world and its characters. These are ways in which the story sets up what it's going to pay off later on. Let's move to the next step, which is to start thinking about what it *does* with all this rich setup. Can you make out a problem or conflict or process that the story needs to work out? Who or what changes, and how? Let's start with the question of where you mark the break between the beginning and middle of the story, and why you put the break there.

There was another little pause, but, again, hands went up. The beginning ends when the Palatski Man has been introduced, because he's going to be the cause of change in Mary's life. The beginning ends when John has been set up as the exemplary neighborhood kid, because when Mary eventually eclipses him, she's going to outgrow the neighborhood. The beginning ends much farther into story, at the first break of white space in the text, only after we hear the story-within-the-story about a supporting character named Raymond Cruz, who goes beyond the neighborhood into the wider world and disappears. Some of the students in the room started to relax now that we were moving from structure to theme. These were students who tended to regard identifying and analyzing theme as the real work of engaging literature, and they might dismiss noticing details of form as mere magpie list-making. Thinking about theme often comes more naturally to students who did well in high-school English classes, where theme, plot, and character are often the main subjects of discussion. *Is Ahab justified in seeking revenge on the whale? What does the green light at the end of Gatsby's dock represent?* I have profound respect for high-school English teachers and maybe even more respect for elementary and middle-school teachers (visiting my kids' third- and fourth-grade classes always made me feel as if the college classes I was teaching were an epilogue to the educational main event), but I do find myself gently urging students who have grown used to being rewarded for theme-spotting to expand their analytical repertoires. Over the next few weeks I wanted them to come around to seeing how, in the process of assembling an interpretive reading, just noticing a lot of passive verbs in the first paragraph or a structure that breaks a text into little fragments (both of which would turn out to be keys to Joan Didion's "Slouching Towards Bethlehem") can be just as important as spotting a Great Theme—and often more useful in making arguments.

Still, we do need to consider theme—or, as I like to think of it, about-ness. So what does the arc of "The Palatski Man" suggest that the story's *about*? We started with the change, and therefore the aboutness, that's easiest to see: Mary grows up over the course of the story. At first she's a little girl hiding behind her older brother's protection, but in time, she becomes the bolder and more experimental of the two. She's the one who proposes that they follow the Palatski Man out of the neighborhood and into the urban wasteland where he gathers with other scruffy itinerants, known as ragmen. She's the one who in the story's climactic scene takes the first sweet bite of the red candy apples the Palatski Man offers them, and she's the one who tastes the shocking bitterness of the giant *palatski* that he breaks up and distributes like a eucharist among his strange congregation. John tells her not to be afraid, but he's the one who mistakes the bright red fluid in which the candy apples are dipped for blood, and he refuses to taste the giant *palatski* because he fears that it might be poisoned. The surprise of its bitterness is a secret that Mary keeps to herself. At the end of the story, having made it back home to what she used to think of as the safety of the familiar, she rises from bed to look down from her window at the Palatski Man standing below with his horse under the streetlight in a whirlwind of blown leaves, the moon reflected in his dark glasses, holding out one last *palatski* to her. In the story's final sentence, "She ran from the window to the mirror and looked at herself in the dark, feeling her teeth growing and hair pushing through her skin in the tender parts of her body that had been bare and her breasts swelling like apples from her flat chest and her blood burning, and then in a lapse of wind, when the leaves fell back to earth, she heard his gold bell jangle again as if silver and knew that it was time to go."

Talk of swelling breasts inspires a little bashfulness in freshmen, but not much. I was in a room full of people who were still technically adolescents, and this story was singing their song. We talked for a while about Mary's maturation, the destination to which the story is heading. What else can we connect to it? My job here was to play contagiously crunchy rhythm guitar so that they could take turns trying out lead licks. I wanted to let them wrestle with a topic, even let them flounder a little, but also give just enough shape to the conversation by gathering up what had been said and using it to perform periodic little nudging resets, often by way of *if . . . then* statements. If Nina and Arthur are right that apples and blood suggest maturation, then what else in the story might point to the consequences of that maturation? If we're pretty confident that Mary's maturation is the thematic throughline of the story, then what does that do to our reading of setting?

The latter question got us going on the contrast between the neighborhood and the world beyond. The neighborhood feels knowable, solid, with its churches and schools and parents and orderly ideas about how when a girl enters middle school, she graduates from dresses to skirts, and "green ribbons for her dark hair, and shoes without buckles, like slippers for a ballerina." The world beyond, the indeterminate ground between the neighborhood and downtown, is a wild, ungridded place of slag heaps and cinder roads and a strange scarecrow-haunted wheat field in the center of the city. It's full of mystery and danger and short on familiar guideposts, and it's where Mary encounters surprising sweetness and bitterness and takes the upper hand in her relationship with John. How does the physical world imagined by the story express meaning? The comments started opening out into a conversation about the process of growing up, how ventures into the literal and figurative wider world—like, you know, say, *going to college*— revise your understanding of yourself, others, your home ground.

And so another reset: Can we expand our reading of the story by trying to connect the transformation we've been talking about to other things we mentioned at the beginning of class, like all the religious imagery we found it so easy to spot when we were just noticing things? The story expends a good deal of its energy on that imagery, so we should be able to find a way to connect it to our developing sense of aboutness. So far, nobody had been cashiered or hospitalized for saying the wrong thing, so students were starting to decide that it might be okay to relax and, as they say in the fight world, let their hands go. Somebody suggested that Mary's relationship to Catholicism might be changing, and I encouraged them to dig around in that idea. They started to consider how she's moving from innocence to knowledge, not only in personal experience but also in her faith. If the *palatski*'s like communion, then she's finding out that there's bitter strangeness in that ritual, not just the sweet familiar reassurance she used to expect. Somebody pointed out that near the end of the story, Mary tries to say her nightly prayer but falls asleep instead, waking out of a half-dream to have her final glimpse of the Palatski Man. Is she falling away from her religion, or at least from an innocent version of it?

Having tested out various ways to connect form to theme, we could now try putting the pieces together. Again, we didn't need to arrive at some kind of all-encompassing analytical climax, but it would be useful to at least consider how we might merge previously freestanding arguments into parts of one mega-argument. The last three words of the story are "time to go." Yes, the story was originally published in a magazine of science fiction and fantasy, but we don't necessarily think that Mary's going to get dressed, go downstairs, and go somewhere with the Palatski Man, do we? What if going to the mirror is as far as she'll get? So in what possibly less-literal sense is it time to go? We tried out some ideas. Time to grow up, time to depart from the familiar and safe, time to understand herself and her family and her faith and her being and place in the world in new ways. Time to leave the Old Neighborhood, in other words, even if she continues to live in it—a bittersweetly adult sort of transformation.

We knocked around the possibility that she's done with the neighborhood and also the contrasting possibility that her experiences have infused this most familiar of places with fresh mystery and possibility that renew her relationship to it. We didn't need to decide which reading we favored. A work of fiction is not a policy statement. It can have it both ways and end on a tension, an unresolved chord. However we read the transformation of Mary's sense of her neighborhood, it spoke to college freshmen. They had just been home for Christmas, felt the fresh oddness of a once-cozy fit as they slept in their old beds in their old rooms, with familiar stuffies and trophies and posters of bands or anime characters or athletes they used to adore. They'd said to themselves *Maybe I should get rid of some of this meaningful but embarrassing stuff and make room for other things-to-be-named-later that will be more in keeping with who I think I'm going to become.* Or maybe they'd just said to themselves *In not too long I'm going to be done with living here. Time to go.*

Time for another reset. If we haven't heard from you yet, I said, you've got just enough class time left to find your way into the conversation. And let's remind ourselves that we aren't trying to come up with one single argument that takes everything into account. We want to leave room for other approaches, loose ends, other ways of seeing. So is anybody sitting on something they noticed that we haven't touched on yet, something that might fit or that doesn't seem to fit with what we've been talking about?

We got a few more people into the game that way. As far as I could tell, almost everybody had spoken up, but I'd compare notes later with Allie to see if anybody hadn't.

Only about $20 worth of class time left. Like fitting licks into the groove of a song, over time I've gotten better at bringing a class session to what feels like a rounded conclusion after 50, 75, or 145 minutes, the standard lengths of classes that meet three times, twice, or once per week. Wrapping up, I reminded everybody of what we'd been doing: noticing form, connecting to theme, seeing patterns and gathering up loose ends and using them to adjust and connect the arguments we've been trying out. I also noted that we seemed to have decided that we didn't know what to do with the odd movement from second to third person we noticed at the beginning of the story, and that was okay. We were not trying to explain away every last bit of mystery in this richly strange tale. I saved the last minute to set up what was going to happen next time we met. As you can see on the syllabus, you'll read a couple more Dybek stories and a couple of chapters from the textbook. We'll start with "Sauerkraut Soup," and among other things we'll try to figure out the effect of the author's structural choice to tell the story out of chronological order. I will do minimal preamble next time, so The Pause will arrive just a couple of minutes into class. Be ready for it. Have a good weekend.

Stuart Dybek once said in an interview, "Reading is a tremendously creative act; it's not a passive act. It's like dancing is to music. . . . You bring your experience, you bring your own imagination."* The text provides the music, and the reader performs the dance—a creative act in its own right, guided by and drawing on the music but not programmed by it. Rather, the dancer *makes* something, using the equipment provided by the music and her or his own imagination, experience, and training. There are many ways for any given dancer to respond to the music, and the dance might even go against the grain of the groove, though it can't be so out of step with the music that it does violence to it, thereby severing the connection between dance and music. The vast majority of dancers will go with the grain, and there's deep craft pleasure in picking up the groove and getting

---

* The interview can be found on YouTube: https://www.youtube.com/watch?v=6ROFYDSipRc (see esp. 37:09–37:46).

inside it, responding to it. That's what we'd been doing today in class, and that's the main skill we'd be working on this semester.

·   ·   ·   ·   ·

The crucial work of establishing habits, expectations, and a sense of community at the beginning of the semester deserves plenty of attention and shouldn't be rushed. Among other things, it's worth devoting some effort to building community because everyone does better work in a classroom where participating in class discussion no longer feels like public speaking and becomes more like having a purposeful conversation with colleagues you know and trust. When I'm tempted to become impatient at this stage, I sometimes remind myself of Adam Gopnik's magazine profile of Kirk Varnedoe, a prominent art historian who also coached a peewee football team called the Giant Metrozoids. After the first practice, in which Varnedoe has the kids run around and scrimmage but doesn't teach them any plays, Gopnik realizes how much Varnedoe has accomplished. "He had taught them how to stand and how to kneel—not just how to do these things but that there was a right way to do these things. He had taught them that playing is a form of learning—that a scrimmage was a step somewhere on the way toward a goal. And he had taught them that they were the Giant Metrozoids. It was actually a lot for one hour."[†]

It was essential that I make clear that I was going to wait for answers after asking a question. Better a few early awkward silences at the outset than fifteen weeks with a class full of people who don't believe I'll wait as long as necessary for an answer. At this point in my classroom career as teacher and student, I've built up stamina to the point that I could go at least a minute or two, smiling faintly while looking around and waiting them out, and most people can't stand to go anywhere near that long. It's useful to remember that a discussion of literature is not talk radio or TV news: silence in a classroom is not dead air, and it shouldn't automatically unnerve you. I appreciate a nice stretch of cogitative classroom silence, and I think there should be at least one of them in a good class discussion. People don't all operate at the same speed, and the typical class discussion

---

† Adam Gopnik, "Last of the Metrozoids," *New Yorker*, May 10, 2004, 85.

tends to over-favor those who think fast and can articulate those thoughts right away. Many people, including some of those with the most insight to offer, need a little more time to cook and digest a thought.

Mainly, I needed to establish from the beginning, by asking genuine questions and visibly expecting responses to them and not supplying those answers myself, that the students would do the work of the class. I would be coming less than halfway to them, and they would have to come more than halfway to meet me at the place where learning happens. They needed to see and accept that I would be framing the problems and they would be doing the problems (and, in time, also helping to frame them), that there were many possibilities for finding and making meaning in any work we read, that class discussion was not just a game of hide-and-seek that would be more efficiently played if I simply came out and told them the answer. By taking seriously the different observations and ideas that came up in response to the problems I laid out for us, I could establish that there wasn't *an* answer, that there were just stronger and weaker arguments for a near-infinite number of interpretations.

In these first few classes, I was also setting tone, mood, and other intangible but essential conditions for learning—a strategy that often entails trying to convey two opposite messages at the same time. For instance, *You're all doing your best to earn good grades as individuals, and you're each responsible for your own effort and accomplishments, but we're also a community of inquiry, which means we also have responsibilities to each other.* I had reinforced the individualistic part of this message on the first day when we went over the syllabus—the papers, the final exam, grading—but it didn't need much reinforcement. College students already think of themselves as highly motivated lone operators who are out to maximize return on investment. But I had to build up the face-to-face, flesh-and-blood community-of-inquiry part, working against the grain of our tendency these days to consent to everyone getting sorted into the magnificent isolation of a highly curated, individualized electronic niche. That's a principal reason why I try to create a warm and encouraging tone in the classroom, why I make a visible point of learning and using names, and why it's worth insisting that students use each other's names when referring to what others say—not "what she said," but "what Jenny said." It's also why I make a show of melding individual contributions into a greater whole. Reduced to a kind of Mad Lib, the template for that melding might look like this: if we take what [NAME 1] says about [FORM] and what [NAME 2] says about [FORM] and try to put them together with what [NAME 3] and [NAME 4] say about [THEME], then we arrive at [INTERPRE-TIVE CONCLUSION], which leads to [NEW QUESTION]. I'm trying to make clear to students that there's a larger conversation going on that they can get in on, to their own benefit as well as the greater good. They can use class discussions to workshop ideas, practice moves, test out and refine their chops—all of which will help them do what they need to do on papers and the final. And students are modeling that same process for each other, as well as giving each other lots of ideas about how to interpret each text. I can put analytical tools in our shared kit, but other students do the greater part of demonstrating what can be done with them.

Another contradiction: *Any honest attempt to engage the texts in ways that might lead to finding meaning in them is welcome, even if you're fumbling around in the dark, but there are a lot of us in the room and talking just to hear yourself talk isn't okay.* Sometimes this means encouraging a student who's reluctant to say what's on her mind to go ahead and spit it out. Say she despises a particular character. That's an analytically inert response on the face of it, but is there something about the way the character is presented, the way he fits into the character system, the words used to describe him, and other moves made by the text that produced that response in her? I'm willing to dwell on it a bit and let her try to work it out—and to encourage us all to try to help work it out—if it looks like there's something for us in there, some insight into how the text functions as a machine for producing readers' responses. She's modeling something very useful for the group if she can find the analytical payload in her own visceral reaction: from *I just hate that guy* to *The narrator uses words that evoke disease, waste products, and reptiles to shape a reader's response to this character.* Sometimes, though, I have to gently redirect or even shut down a conversational thread that's not getting anywhere. We'll try to do something with the fact that you hate this character, or that this scene reminds you of a Shakespeare play you read in high school, but at a certain point, we can't wait around forever for these feelings to turn into something useful, and we'll move on. We also don't want to wait around for very long at all if all you're doing is trying to sound brilliant or well-read. That's a judgment call I have to make, but in making that call I'm also modeling another lesson for everyone: we're willing to be patient in locating the analytical purpose in what's being said and building it into our conversation about this text and into our developing repertoire of interpretive moves; but, like a wilderness rescue team with multiple lost parties to save, if we can't find that purpose after a reasonable amount of searching, we will cut our losses and search elsewhere.

That brings me to perhaps the broadest, most all-encompassing contradictory condition I was tacitly establishing at the beginning of the semester: *we're going to step back from the rush-rush-rush and click-click-click of everyday life to take our time in exploring these endlessly deep and beautiful works of art with a care you'll probably never lavish on literature again in your life, but we have a job to do and limited time in which to do it, every second of which is costing you (or someone) a lot of money and also carries significant opportunity costs for all of us.* If you have visited Rome or Disney World or whatever place counts for you as a glorious destination, you will recognize this conundrum: we're finally here, and we're going to do everything we can to take all possible pleasure in being in this special place, but we're constantly aware that we made sacrifices to be here and have to go home soon.

I wanted them to appreciate that what we did in this class was actually much like what we do in other phases in life. Talking about form and meaning in "The Palatski Man" is not that different from talking with friends or family about form and meaning in a beguiling song or a disturbing movie or a relative's eccentric behavior or the State of the Union address. But I also wanted them to recognize that what happened in Stokes 209 South for seventy-five minutes on Tuesdays and Thursdays was special and pursued at great cost of money and time and other resources, so we should feel an obligation to proceed with purpose and get somewhere.

·   ·   ·   ·   ·

When I'm deciding whether to teach a book, I don't devote much thought to whether it's considered a Great Book, as long as it's a good book and it teaches well. Dybek's *Childhood and Other Neighborhoods* qualifies on both counts, and I like to start the semester with it in Lit Core for at least three reasons. First, short stories lend themselves well to the kind of close reading we were practicing in these first few weeks of the class. Each story is only a few pages long, which makes it easier to notice resonant details that lead to recognizing patterns, and I assign just a couple per class meeting. Even with the addition of a chapter or two from the textbook on interpreting literature we were working through at the beginning of the semester, that's a light reading load for a college course. It would get heavier when we got to the novels.

Second, Dybek wrote some of the stories in this collection when he was about the same age as the students in the class, and they're often about young people trying to make their way in life. Those young people typically feel like misfits both coming and going as they navigate between where they come from and where they might like to get to. In Dybek's stories, they're almost always coming from a neighborhood much like the one in which he grew up—Pilsen, on Chicago's Southwest Side—and often looking out on a wider world of art and literature and education and experience that changes not only the characters but also their understanding and appreciation of where they come from. College students can often identify with that broader situation, even if they didn't grow up in a Polish-Mexican inner-city melting pot/lasagna of a neighborhood like Dybek's.

Third, these stories fairly beg for interpretation, which encourages even skeptics to take the analytical plunge. In "The Cat Woman," order breaks down in a neighborhood when an old lady stops drowning its excess kittens. In "Sauerkraut Soup," a young man with high-cultural ambitions and a horror of following his father into factory work suddenly can't keep any food down, which leads to a near-psychedelic freakout on the grass median of Western Boulevard, which leads to salvation in a bowl of soup at an otherwise generic diner with padded stools on Forty-Seventh Street. In "Visions of Budhardin," the story the students (and their professor) find most puzzling of all, a former neighborhood pariah seated inside a mechanical elephant makes a return visit in latter years to the place where he grew up, where he recalls the early sexual adventures that caused him to be rejected by the community as a monster. Still inside the elephant, which has sort of turned into his actual body while also remaining a machine he operates from within, he runs amok, assaulting a nun and setting fire to the parish church. An angry mob seizes him and rolls him down to the river, where he escapes on a garbage scow with a renegade altar boy.

Reading "Visions of Budhardin" tends to cause students to have a near-psychedelic freakout of their own. Even two and three years later, a lot of them remembered it with the vividness of an exotic drug experience. "That was a crazy story," Marguerite recalled. "Crazytown. That one just blew my mind. I was like, 'What is happening here?'" Paul said, "That was like the weirdest thing I've ever read. I remember I was in the lounge doing my work and I got to that one; he was with some other guy and with the girl, and I was just like, 'What am I reading?' Wow." The weirdness of the story also inspires interpretive impulses. Dave said of Budhardin in his elephant suit, "I mean, it's an absurd image to the point where it has to mean something, even if it doesn't mean something. The absurdity of it *not* meaning something has significance." The story can't just be about a guy in an elephant suit, can it?

Some were put off by the story's demand to be interpreted. Eva, who liked math because there's a correct answer, said, "I knew it was meaningful, but I couldn't figure it out, so it just frustrated me." It appealed to others for precisely that reason. "The elephant story really stuck with me," Luke told me. "I think about that one a lot, actually. I really liked the symbolism in it, and it was just really out there." Tyler said, "Budhardin's elephant was my favorite. I wrote a paper about that. It was so good. I love that story. I just thought that there was so much double meaning and imagery in it. I had so much fun writing that paper because I was just discovering new things as I went. I can write a whole 'nother paragraph about, you know, the duality of his elephant suit representing like the emptiness and—oh my god, I had a field day with that story." Nina told me that sometimes in the class she was "shocked as to how we got to an interpretation" of a text, and she cited "Visions of Budhardin" as an example. "That one was odd, in my opinion. I was very confused by that one. I had no interpretation, and I think I was just shocked that people were having—like, being able to closely read it."

Wilson was thrown by the story, as well, but still he thought he ought to give the elephant a chance and tried to prevail on his hockey teammate Phil to do the same. "Phil was the only guy I really talked to in the class," Wilson told me later. "And I remember he was like, 'Dude, what *is* this?' I was like

'We got to trust it.' You know, I was like 'We have to trust the material. Like, obviously, the professor knows what he's doing and we just got to, like, go with the flow. And even if we don't like it, we just got to read it, you know.'"

By the time we got to "Visions of Budhardin," we'd had a few classes together to get into our rhythm, and I had seen enough to be confident that this group would be ready to stretch a little. I expected that they wouldn't quail in the face of the story's weirdness. If designing and teaching a syllabus is like bringing along a young boxer, I felt that we were ready to mix it up with a tall, shifty southpaw.

The textbook chapter they had read for this class meeting was about setting and symbol, so when I went over the chapter at the beginning of class I emphasized how it could help set up our discussion of the story. The setting of the story is Dybek's usual Pilsen-like neighborhood, and the very first lines begin to situate us in historical era and cultural context: "The elephant was there, waiting, in the overgrown lot where once long ago there had been a Victory garden, and after that a billboard, but now nothing but the rusting hulks of abandoned cars." If the story has the abstract feel of a parable or a Zen koan, as we go on, we'll see that it's also concretely grounded in the precisely described landscape of a certain kind of church-haunted Chicago neighborhood that used to be filled with Catholics from Eastern Europe and in the decades after World War Two filled with Catholics from Mexico and points south. As for symbols, well, there's that elephant, for one.

For a change of pace, and to counteract any temptation anybody might have been feeling to decide it's safer to sit out this discussion because this story's just too weird, I broke them up into groups of four to pick over the opening of the story for a few minutes and generate items for us to discuss when we reconvened as a group. I'm no virtuoso of small-group teaching techniques, which I use sparingly, but I do know that this kind of thing works best when everyone has a clear sense of the job to do, how to do it, and what it will lead to. So I asked each group to go over the first couple of pages of the story and make a list of formal choices, elements of theme, and crazy-ass-seeming inexplicable stuff, then decide which items on their list they would most like the whole class to talk about when we reconvened. Everybody in the group had to contribute to the list, and each group had to pick one member to report to the rest of us. They would need to have two or three favored items from their list ready to go, in case another group beat them to their top choice. The students hiked their chairs around to form eight clusters scattered around the room, there was a pregnant moment during which everybody wondered who was going to say something to get their group started, and then eight people separately said to themselves, "Fine, looks like it will be me," and went first, and then others responded, and the room rapidly filled with a rising hubbub of voices. I walked around, mostly eavesdropping, jumping into a group's conversation now and then to make sure that a silent partner did not stay silent.

They got into pulling apart and examining the opening of the story, which begins with the rich and successful adult Budhardin sitting on a stool inside the elephant, operating it with levers and pulleys. A pack of kids gather, and instantly they're throwing garbage and dogshit at the elephant, carving initials into its hide, trying to set its tail on fire. Lumbering about with impossible agility, weeping real tears from his elephant-suit eyes, and gushing silver dollars and rings from his vacuum-cleaner-hose trunk, Budhardin embarks on a tour of his old neighborhood that will raise painful memories and open old wounds. One discussion group seized on the image of his smoldering tail as a slow-burning wick that's eventually going to lead to an explosion; another on the hose, five-gallon ice cream drums, and other everyday materials used to build the elephant; another on the way that Dybek's diction conveys the immediate and unthinking quality of the children's violence; another on the mix of ethnicities represented by the names mentioned in the opening pages: Budhardin, Crystal, Sanchez, Shwartz, Ghazili.

Once we had shuffled our chairs back around to reconvene, and the individual groups had reported on what they talked about, we started to feel our way toward aboutness. We got into a discussion of the meanings associated with elephants: they have long memories (an elephant never forgets), they're imposing (the elephant in the room), they're smart and sensitive and tinged with sadness (circuses and war). That they're also associated with the Republican Party didn't strike anyone as relevant, allowing us to have a brief sidebar on the importance of listening to your bullshit alarm when you're tempted to make a connection that has no support in the text. Attuning yourself to that alarm is a skill for living made ever more important these days by the nonstop cyclopean gusher of nonsense, lies, and non sequiturs coming at us from the electronic realm—the extra-vulnerable blind side in almost every citizen's cultural pass-blocking scheme.

Okay, if the figure of Budhardin in his elephant suit evokes the associations we've been talking about (those that don't set off the bullshit alarm), what else in the story does this figure resonate with? We talked about this for a while, and I took an opportunity to contribute a slightly extended riff of my own—which I will do sometimes, mostly to model some aspect of the process of interpretation. This time that aspect was bringing personal experience to bear on responding to a text. I told them that I was just coming off a stretch of several years in which I'd been going back frequently to the neighborhood where I grew up, to work on a book—and that experience helped the elephant suit make sense to me. For all its magical-realist strangeness, the story also feels strangely familiar, because going back to the neighborhood in which you grew up can indeed make you feel elephantine: big with memories and emotion; protected but also made ponderous and sensitive by unwieldy layers of sentiment and experience; at once freakishly alien and also nostalgic for half-forgotten but instantly recognizable shapes marching trunk-to-tail out of the past.

Talking about elephants led us to a discussion of sympathy in the story. Budhardin is like the creature in Mary Shelley's *Frankenstein* in that he's a feelingful free thinker who's instinctively loathed and shunned by those around him—in Budhardin's case, for precocious sexual experimentation with both female and male peers, and then, after the community turned on him, for his campaign of payback against Christ that features using pornography to get altar boys to sell him their souls. But, like Shelley's creature, who may be the most thoughtful and passionate character in her book but also murders a significant proportion of the other named characters, including a child, Budhardin also does things that are impossible to defend. When the wizened Sister Eulalia tries to stop him from destroying the church, their struggle appears to turn into a sexual assault: "He fingered her with his trunk, pulling away what was left of the habit." And that's actually his *second* attempted rape in the story. Also, at the story's end, his final escape with the "angelic" altar boy Billy Crystal on a garbage scow down the river—to Europe or maybe the Yucatan, "depending on the current"—amounts to transporting a minor across state lines for what could conceivably be lewd purposes.

How does the story, the narration of which shifts back and forth between going inside Budhardin's head to recover his traumatic memories and standing back at a distance to observe the elephant's violent progress, cultivate your sympathy for this character at least some of the time? And, if it does so, what happens to that sympathy when he does awful things? We chewed on that one for a while. The preponderant feeling was that elephants are enormously sympathetic figures, and the story exploits that quality in testing what Budhardin can do without completely scuttling the reader's identification with him. And yet the image of a guy in an elephant suit, as opposed to an actual elephant, seems to acknowledge that any identification or sympathy he elicits from us has limits. The queasiness we feel as we approach those limits—the language of the story sometimes describes him as if he were a real elephant, but it always comes back to reminding us that he's just wearing an elephant disguise—may be part of the engine that makes the story go, part of what it's about.

Even if we had all the time in the world, I assured them, we'd never come up with a reading of this story that takes every last detail into account. It's not like the answer is five or man's inhumanity to man. So, since you've got a paper to write next week, let's lower our sights and instead just practice formulating partial arguments that we think might work. Think of each argument we propose as doing nothing more than taking a bite out of the aboutness of the story by making a claim that con- nects form to meaning—*a* meaning or *some* meaning, not *the* meaning— and considering what textual evidence you'd use to back up that claim.

We spent the last fifteen minutes of class on that. Some of the topics that students proposed and refined began by zeroing in on an aspect of form. For instance, if you start with the elephant, you might get to *The story uses the figure of the elephant to show the effects of memory and community in shaping Budhardin's identity.* Other topics started with a theme and addressed multiple aspects of form associated with it. For instance, you find it interesting that almost everybody in the neighborhood, from juve- nile delinquents to nuns, seems to agree that Budhardin has to be isolated, shamed, and silenced, often violently. Okay, how does the story convey that shared feeling? You might end up with something like *The story uses images of churches, cars, and fire to show that the neighborhood regards Budhardin's sexuality as a problem it has to solve or control in order to protect itself.* The ideas came out of our conversation, and that was fine. We were practicing putting together elements of argument into a claim that would stand up because we could find textual evidence in the story to support it, and in doing that, we were free to draw on each other's observations and insights—which students could also do in their papers. Yes, having everybody come up with an entirely original reading of a text would be lovely, but our main concern in this exercise was laying pipe that wouldn't leak, and it didn't matter where the water came from. Just as musicians cop licks from other musicians on the way to sounding like themselves, being part of a community opens a way for students into the process of interpretation because it's easier to contribute just a piece of an argument or to put together pieces contributed by others than it is to come up with all the pieces and put them together all by yourself.

Walking up the stairs back to my office after class, I felt that the session had gone pretty well, that we had risen to the challenge of the story. We'd sparred with the tricky southpaw beanpole and not gotten our ass handed to us—had, rather, put in some good work. We weren't trying to reduce the story to a comprehensive interpretation or explain away every last bit of strangeness in it; we were just trying to make analytical headway and execute sound interpretive moves in the whirlwind of its weirdness.

On to the different set of problems offered by the next sparring partner. There was one more reason to start the semester with Stuart Dybek's stories: the whiplash effect that would be produced by the violent contrast between his warm, lyrical inner-city magical realism and the cool mandarin exactitude of Edith Wharton's realist prose when we moved on to the next book, *The House of Mirth.* Another whiplash would happen when we moved from Wharton to Junot Díaz's maximalist, profane, quotation mark–less, unglossaried Spanish- and Spanglish- and Elvish-suffused prose in *The Brief Wondrous Life of Oscar Wao.* There's value in learning to deal with different kinds and styles of writing, making a way through all kinds of landscapes of language, and there's nothing more challenging for most young readers than reckoning with writing that hews to outmoded conventions. Wharton is fairly modern—certainly not as opaque to them as Chaucer or Shakespeare—but her style's just archaic enough to throw them. After they wrote their first paper, about the Dybek story of their choice, we'd take on Wharton.

5 Icebergs

Students sitting in rows in class will put up the usual affective barriers to shield their emotions from peers around them—the facial control and behavioral self-policing we all deploy to get through the day without giving others too many naked glimpses into our inner life. But they often don't think of extending coverage to the front, where the professor's looking back at them. In part, this is because they don't really see the impossibly old and strange professor as fully human in the same way as they see their classmates as human, and in part, it's because it doesn't occur to them that the professor really sees them and might even take an interest in an individual student's inner life. So sometimes it seems as if I'm standing in front of rows of washers and dryers, watching intimate underthings go around and around through the clear window in each: this student's having a terrible week, these two are in love and had a fight, this one's a million miles away, this one's scared, this one's experiencing a surge of joy, and so on. I'm not registering these perceptions on purpose, nor am I devoting primary attention to them. Rather, they run as a sort of chyron at the bottom of the screen while I attend to the primary business of managing the class.

But I have learned that these casual impressions of inner life gathered sub rosa and in passing can be wildly misleading; in fact, they're probably wrong more often than they're right. Without the extensive one-on-one conversations I had with Dan and Tyler, I never would have guessed from their classroom personas that there was a vision of an idyllic Tahitian beach at the center of Dan's tumultuous being or a surging mass of tightly contained emotional upheaval at the center of Tyler's outwardly sunny one. Caught up in the calculations and improvisations of teaching, my main concern was to consider and engage those outward personas, which form just the tip of the iceberg of selfhood. That meant, in practice, making sure that we got the substantive juice out of Dan's contrarian stands and tangents without letting them derail the discussion and remembering to push now and then to get more than just an acceptably correct go-along-to-get-along answer out of Tyler. A teacher could easily fall into thinking of Dan as difficult and Tyler as easy, and that would be a mistake in both cases, especially if it led to shutting down Dan too much and not extending Tyler enough. You can't always get to know all of your students well enough to avoid such mistakes, but it's good to remember that they have inner lives that you're probably not going to be able to map accurately by extrapolating from surface appearances.

.   .   .   .   .

Other students remarked that Dan seemed oddly at home while talking with me in front of the rest of the class. When during my interview with Alice the discussion turned to the subject of speaking in class, for instance, she remarked on Dan's air of seeming to talk one-on-one with the professor while everybody else looked on, and Phil wryly noted in an email at the end of the semester that he would miss my chats with Dan. They were reacting to Dan's manner as much as to the frequency and content of what he said in class. I don't mean to imply that he seemed perfectly at ease. I could see that he felt everyone's attention on him when he spoke, that it made him nervous, and that he was especially conscious of how his Massachusetts regular-guy accent set him a little apart from the others. He sat front and center, and his bearing and dress were as a rule more formal than is the norm at BC: he'd wear a collared shirt or a sweater, sometimes jacket and tie or a suit on a day when he had a presentation to give in one of his business courses. But when he spoke, he'd lean back in his seat and shift a little to one side as if settling in for a good talk with me. He would often take a while to loop around to his main point, and he was the only student who would regularly take issue with what I said. I might, for instance, be summing up a stretch of discussion preliminary to moving on to the next thing—"So we've been talking about how Lily Bart finds herself faced with a set of possibilities that she finds unacceptable, whether it's marrying Percy Gryce or Rosedale, or living with limited money as Selden's wife or lover, or living with even less money on her own in the style of Gerty Farish . . ."—and he'd put up his hand to question the completeness of the list of possibilities I'd just made, or wonder whether some of them were not as unacceptable as I was making them out to be, or cast doubt in some other way on what I'd just said. He did it respectfully, always, and with an air of enthusiasm for the subject at hand, but he wasn't shy about doing it, and he didn't seem to think that it was a big deal to come back at the professor with contrary views. Rather, he seemed to feel himself honor-bound to do it.

The part of me that wants to keep things moving from one logical step to the next in the classroom might be a little annoyed that he had waited to reopen a topic until I was putting it behind us; until I had, in fact, just reached the comma before introducing the next thing to talk about. But mostly I was pleased by his willingness to come back at me, in the way that the scenery-chewing replicant Roy Batty is pleased—"That's the spirit!"— when the cornered human gumshoe Deckard smashes him in the face with a length of rusty pipe during their showdown at the end of *Blade Runner*.

Other students didn't know exactly what to make of Dan. Was he arrogant and entitled? Overeager to rack up class participation credit? More familiar with literary matters than they were, even though he was clearly a Future Businessman of America type and, confusingly, had a working-class accent? Even when they resented his willingness to engage me, or found it presumptuous, they were also intimidated by it, and it won their respect. I wondered about him myself. He did not seem to think of himself as a special talent who enjoyed unique parity with his professors; instead, I got the impression that he was not fully socialized, or refused to be fully socialized, into what most of his peers regarded as the normal way to act in class at an exclusive and expensive university. Yet he also struck me as a natural citizen of school, operating at a high level of assumed belonging that dispensed with the usual undergraduate diffidence and eagerness to be in accord with professor and classmates.

I had a feeling from the beginning of the semester that Dan reminded me of somebody, and at first I couldn't identify who that was. Then, in a conversation during office hours at some point early in the semester, he and I got onto a tangent about the everyday uses of narrative, and he mentioned that he'd had a lot of practice at making up stories to tell his younger brothers that featured their stuffed animals. That's when I realized that he reminded me of Didi, my older daughter's number-one teddy bear from way back: small body, big head, open face with small even features, a manner combining gentleness and fierceness. That is, he reminded me of Didi if Didi was a Latino who had been reading *Fortune* and *Forbes* since the third grade and had attended a voc-tech high school in Fall River, Massachusetts. But unlike Didi, a sweet lisping naif who thinks he's terribly fearsome and wise, Dan's teddy-bear outer form didn't prepare you for the do-or-die work ethic, philosophical gameness, self-improver's penchant for introspective stewing, and roiling striver's ambition within.

Dan told me that he was one of the few kids in his hometown social circle to go to college, and he was just about the only one among his academic peers who went on to a fancy private university. Most of his fellow top-ten-in-the-class graduates from his high school—which made a big deal of ranking its top graduates, like Stella's Korean high school—went on to public universities in the UMass system or the local community college. His long-standing love of architecture had led him to a vocational high school so that he could study drafting, a move that he came to regard as a mistake, though he still covered himself with glory there: he was student government president, founded a finance club and a debate team, and ended up ranked sixth in his class. He believed that if shop and academics grades had been fairly weighted, he would have been ranked second, behind only a friend of his who was a certified genius and rightly deserved to be first. He relitigated the injustice in detail during our first interview in the fall of 2021, noting that he'd "had several meetings with the superintendent about it."

Dan's father, a great exponent of reading and the life of the mind, stressed practicality above all else in what Dan read, studied, and did with his time. The father of one of Stuart Dybek's neighborhood-guy characters sounds just like Dan's father when he says, "Don't you see that one well-designed bridge is worth more than everything Shakespeare ever wrote?" But even a well-designed bridge was too frivolous for Dan, who by the time he came to college had set aside his passion for architecture as overly arty-dreamy and was committed to concentrating in finance in the undergraduate School of Management and going on to work as an asset manager at a hedge fund. This goal raised the stakes on everything he did from the moment he arrived. He walked me through his freshman mind-set as an anxious stream of consciousness: "Okay, I think I have some sort of natural interest in and calling for investing, a natural affinity. Maybe I'm dead wrong, but I think I do. And one day I hope to be, like, sort of like a Buffet type where I have a big influence on commerce not only through the companies that I manage and run or invest in but also maybe in positions like Treasury or central banking, things like that. So I enjoy it, and I think I can make the world better through it, more so than I could make the world better through any other branch. So in Lit Core, well, I thought 'I'm going to give this effort because I got to get a good grade because if I don't get a good grade, I won't get a good job afterwards. And if I don't get a good job afterwards . . .'"

Unsurprisingly, Dan nearly burned himself out in his freshman year. "Mentally, the transition to college wasn't a good one, and I think that's because I was trying too hard for my grades," he told me. "I had a bad perspective on life then. I worked like an absolute maniac, over-studying, studying unintelligently, just mismanaging life." He hadn't yet learned, he explained, to balance schoolwork with human contact, to find at least a little time to do what pleased him or just chill out, to figure out what the big-ticket items are on a syllabus and use them as a guide to proportioning his own efforts. He suffered from debilitating stomach troubles as he went around in a desperate and solitary state, constantly extended to the breaking point, as if buffeted day and night by a set of G-forces only he could feel. His weekend visits home to Fall River felt like desperately needed reprieves from the crushing doom of college.

There was a curious moment in class that I didn't understand until I began interviewing Dan in his junior year. We were discussing a chapter in *The Brief Wondrous Life of Oscar Wao* in which Oscar's sister, Lola, runs away from home and lives with her boyfriend and his father in a scrofulous dive on the Jersey Shore, a decision she rapidly comes to regret. Oppressed by the stink of cat piss and flat Schlitz and the palpable hostility in the atmosphere of the house, she worries that son and father "would bury the hatchet by gangbanging me." In the middle of a discussion about how the temporary switch to Lola as narrator affected the novel's developing portrayal of how families enforce social and cultural norms, Dan raised his hand and said, "These guys are degenerates. There's no value in what they do. They're just degenerates." As usual, he was coming at me from an angle I hadn't expected, since we hadn't gone anywhere near the subject of assessing the boyfriend and his father as models of moral virtue, so I asked him to say more, but he'd said his piece on the subject, and we didn't do much with it before returning to the throughline of our discussion.

Only later did I come to understand that *degenerate* had a specific meaning to Dan—as does being at the beach, and Lola's boyfriend and his father *live* at the beach. That specific meaning derives from Dan's understanding of the conflict aroused within him by his powerful drive toward achievement. He told me, "I've always had this struggle between, like, just being like an 'All right, all right, all right'"—he delivered Matthew McConaughey's laid-back mantra with the unconvincing stoner drag of a guy who's never been stoned—"type of thing and not putting much effort into anything, just going about my day, trying to have as much fun as possible and just enjoying life, versus taking life seriously." When I asked what having fun would consist of, he said, "Oh, hanging out with your friends and, um, doing stuff that would probably be perceived as degenerate stuff." Degenerate in what sense? "Like just clowning around, mostly. You know, it's like girls, cars—not weed for me. I never smoked weed in my life so far. Probably will, at some point, definitely will, just because I want to see what it's like for scientific purposes," and he laughed a little. And drinking? "I have drank, but never to get drunk. I've had different alcoholic beverages in my life, but I've never tried to get drunk." So he wasn't just dismissing Lola's boyfriend and his father as losers; he was also observing that they were living a downscale version of the idler's dream. Scuffling on the Jersey Shore wasn't Tahiti—Dan used the image of a Tahitian beach more than once when he wanted to describe to me the opposite of his driven existence—but it wasn't eighteen hours a day of manic studying, either.

Keep all that in mind when I tell you that Dan loved Hunter Thompson's *Fear and Loathing in Las Vegas*, by far his favorite book of the semester in

Lit Core. "Gonzo journalism was the best thing I got out of your class," he told me. "Changed my perspective, enjoyed it, didn't realize it was there. For an example, I like architecture. That's my art. So, you know Zaha Hadid? Her architecture looks like its own class or style. And when you've never seen one of her buildings before, you didn't even know that was a thing. Well, that's what gonzo journalism was to me. It's like, 'Wow, there's this entire art form out there that I didn't even know about.'" When I asked Dan to explain his love of a writer who on the face of it couldn't be more different from him, he said, "He paints the picture of himself as a beast— not even a beast, but he doesn't care, he is a free spirit. That's how he paints himself. But under the surface is a highly intelligent individual who's extremely, like, aware of what's going on, and I think his free-spirited nature was really just a little bit of moral courage." Dan admired Thompson for getting off the utilitarian treadmill and making his own way—turning degenerate behavior into his calling, making the Tahitian beach of the mind his home—and *still* succeeding: "Hunter Thompson was a real smart guy. He could have maybe tried to become like a *New York Times* real reputed journalist, and he just wasn't—he didn't like it, so he didn't do it. And so he had courage."

For Dan, who paid a great deal of attention to conventional markers of prestige like grade-point averages and rankings, it was like Thompson partied all the time in high school and didn't study, didn't join any clubs, didn't bother trying to rank high in his class, and still got into Williams on the strength of a terrific essay about why he chose to live like such a degenerate. Compare that to Dan's view of the experience of his friend, the certified genius who ranked first in his high-school class and devoted his whole young life to achieving and went on to UMass Amherst, not Stanford or Yale. Dan nodded and granted the point when I argued that college rankings don't mean anything, that it's mostly up to you, that you can get a great education at UMass Amherst or throw away four years at Yale. "I know there's nothing wrong with it," he said, "but I think he would have conducted his life differently in high school had he known he was going to end up at UMass Amherst."

For a fundamentally gentle guy who yearned to be on a beach in Tahiti doing nothing much, Dan could be pitilessly tough on himself and others. He pushed himself to the point of illness and repeatedly described his own errors and choices as "stupid"; during an interview, he asked me to tell him what was wrong with him so that he could work to improve his weaknesses. (I told him, because he insisted that I answer the question, that he was a little too hard on himself and perhaps overfocused on judging everything he did by a single standard of utility.) When I asked him my routine question about how his family perceived itself, he said, "Hard workers, decently educated, decently intelligent, and screwed over by society." His stepfather had been a truck driver; his mother had stayed home to raise five sons; his father had attended Boston College, starting out at the night school and working his way into the School of Management, but had chronic health problems that subsequently prevented him from working. Dan explained that they were "lower middle-class pillars of the community" who "played by the rules of the game, did what society told them was right—bought the house, had the kids, got the nine-to-five, bought into college, didn't commit crimes. Then they see that the mavericks, liars, cheaters, nonconformists beat the hell out of them in the game, and they feel as though they bought into a scam. Their perception and, in my opinion, real-world reality is that school and politicians failed them. The game gave unfair advantages to those with inherited wealth, those willing to cheat, and those who were just plain savvier." Then came the pitiless part: "At the end of the day, the schools and politicians and society owe you nothing. You owe yourself common sense." So he regarded any response to feeling screwed over that featured grievance or self-pity as "a little crock of you-know-what. It's a cop-out. It's an excuse."

He could be even tougher on his peers—though only in conversation with me, not with them. "I'll tell you what," he said. "This is a good quote for your book. I do not mean this to be in any way disrespectful. The entire education I've received at Boston College so far—the professors and staff here are what makes the school great. But the kids here are, for lack of a better word, shit." Taken aback, not least because I think the undergraduates are the single best thing about the school, I asked him to explain what he meant. "This, like, arrogant prep-school atmosphere here that I don't very much enjoy. People are too guarded and too fake. But the faculty are incredibly kind people and very intelligent people, very helpful people. The staff are very nice, too. The Office of Disability Services has been incredible to me; the Office of Financial Aid, same thing. The offices here are run well, and all the teachers are great. I haven't paid a lot to come here, relatively speaking, but, and this is the quote, the entire education I received here so far at BC, I think, except this one-on-one element, I could have gotten for a dollar-fifty in late charges at the public library." That last part was a quotation from the movie *Good Will Hunting*, the crowning line of a scene in which a regular-guy genius with a heavy-duty working-class Massachusetts accent ("a duollah-fifty in late chahges") humiliates in public a snooty graduate student who bears zero resemblance to any actual graduate student who has ever lived.

Dan had more to say about college being too expensive, at least partially replaceable with online browsing, and such, the standard Peter Thiel–flavored critique of higher education as an overvalued bubble that you'll hear these days, but it seemed pro forma, less heartfelt than his criticism of his fellow students. He did not mean, however, that he thought all of them were no good. He told me that he valued what his classmates had to say about literature and that many of them were better at analyzing it than he was. I think he said such terrible things about them because he'd suffered the pangs of outsiderhood at BC, because the harsh judgment sounded bold and uncompromising to his own ears, and because it pained him to see his frivolous peers failing to appreciate and max out on the value of the privilege that had brought them to BC.

Dan was a straight arrow *and* a misfit. His commitment to not getting with the program was part of what he had to contribute to the class. He wanted to do well, and he was always respectful of me and the work we did, but he was different from other students, most of whom were very good at getting with the program, and that enabled him to come at our discussions from fresh angles and say surprising things. Giving the other guy angles is one of the highest forms of technical sophistication in boxing, and he did it almost instinctively. So I appreciated having him in the class, and I felt for him, even when he seemed blinkered in his attitudes or unfair to others. He was tortured by his own commitment to perfectibility, his reflective nature, the imperative to extract value out of life. Being himself ate him up.

Early in the semester, he gave me an essay he had written entitled "Musings in Café Europa." In the essay he's sitting in an old café in Fall River on a winter afternoon. It's 3:00, and the sun is already sinking; the small room is bright and cheery, customers speaking muted Portuguese in the cozy warmth. "Step through the door and be teleported to a cosmopolitan world free from the stresses of everyday life," he writes. It's the Tahitian beach again, this time in suitably wintry New England form. But the mention of Wall Street in the overheard conversation of other customers snaps him out of his idyllic state. "It's now 4:00 and I need to get back to reality. I have an essay to finish writing. I have been thinking a lot about it, hoping to produce something worth reading, something that accurately expresses my interest in the craft of literary analysis." As usual, he feels himself to be under surveillance in the panopticon fashioned by his parents and his own self-discipline. "If my parents, especially my dad, knew I was writing this, they would wonder what is wrong with me. 'Be practical and finish writing the paper that is due on Tuesday,' they would likely say. 'After all, you have got to learn Microsoft Excel, read about securities regulation and the Uniform Commercial Code. Sooner or later you are going to have to pay for rent. Sooner or later you will have medical bills to pay. Children to educate. Get back to work.'"

He makes a last stand against these voices: "I don't need to become a securities lawyer or portfolio manager to provide for myself and my family, I would respond. 'Be practical,' they'd say. Since when have million-page statutes and infinitely complex financial markets been practical? Coffee shops, kindness and compassion are practical. At the end of the day, the person waking up at 4:00 a.m. to make pastries has as big of an influence as a United States senator." But in the end, he gives in to the inevitable. "I wish society would slow down and think. I wish I had more time to think. As for now, I will (reluctantly) go back to reality. Over and out."

.   .   .   .   .

Tyler arrived in Stokes South 209 each Tuesday and Thursday just before noon with headphones on, taking advantage of the fifteen-minute break between his previous class and Lit Core to get a dose of the music he used as an intellectual palate cleanser, mood adjuster, and accompaniment to the routine of getting through the day. He might be listening to pop of one sort or another, or opera, or Broadway; often, in his freshman year, he was listening to *Newsies*, a musical in which he had performed as a high school senior the previous year. A music minor and an economics major planning to go into the supply-chain logistics business, Tyler had played piano and sung since he was four years old. On YouTube you can find him singing and performing finger-snappin' choreography in an unspeakably whole-some a cappella group at BC and, in older videos, putting across "My Way" and "Hallelujah" with precociously louche showbiz affect in high-school talent shows.

Tyler exemplified the all-arounder astronaut-type profile of many students who gain admission to BC: checking boxes in all academic subjects, athletics, the arts, community engagement, leadership, you name it. He's from an affluent suburb of Philadelphia and attended a prep school for boys, where he racked up the full suite of academic and extracurricular achievements widely regarded as the key to getting into exclusive colleges. "I was a committed student, and I was very involved," he told me when we talked in the fall of his junior year. In high school, his schedule was packed end-to-end from before breakfast until whenever practice or rehearsal ended, just leaving time for dinner and homework and a few hours of rest before he had to get up and do it again. "Minimal sleep, lots of going, going, going," he said. "There was a lot of pressure at a school like that because you're expected to play at least two sports, I was in theater, I did the newspaper, as many cookie jars as I could get my hand in. I tried my best to do it because I knew it would pay off in college applications. That's what the culture was like, and a lot of kids were the same way. Everyone always had it in the back of their mind like, 'Oh, if I don't do this, how is that going to look on my resume or my application?'"

Tyler's in-class persona brimmed with sunny openness. Typically sitting erect, head up, following the discussion and contributing steadily without taking a lead role, he positively radiated interest and engagement. *This is compelling*, his manner said, *and I'm looking forward to where it goes next*. I will confess that, as a student, I probably never looked like that in class. I was often deeply into the subject matter—after all, I did end up pursuing academics as a career—but when I'm not the teacher, even when I'm listening intently, I tend to look like I'm a million miles away, detached, bored, possibly irritated, shifting between slouching back in my seat and leaning forward with eyes downcast as if vastly wearied by what I'm hear-ing and contemplating a catnap with my head on my desk. So I was impressed by the overt consistency of Tyler's engagement. Just the thought of the sheer energy he put into sustaining it wore me out a little bit.

"I feel like I'm pretty intellectually curious," he told me, "so I don't really push things to the side. I don't, I don't really have much skepticism towards—oh, I don't know what I'm trying to say. . . ." I observed that he sounded like a remarkably well-adjusted person. He answered, "Well, I guess I'm more optimistic than the average person, I would say. In an academic perspective, it helps me out because I'm open to new ideas." I asked if that also applied to what other students had to say in class. "I think yeah," he said. "A lot of kids brought more introspection than I previously thought, because we went over dozens of different ways in which, you know, Stuart Dybek's words could twist a story into a different sort of theme. There were a lot of things that were brought up in class that I had never been exposed to before. It was interesting to me, and I took an overall positive experience from it."

An overall positive experience seems to sum up Tyler's attitude in general. But while positive thinking may come to him naturally, he also has to work at it. When I asked whether he finds it easy to speak up in class, he said, "Honestly, I found I've become more anxious in college. I think high school was easier." In high school, there were no more than twenty kids in a class, they all knew each other, and they didn't feel much drive to compete with each other. "It's more cutthroat at BC than I would have ever imagined in terms of like kids trying to get the best grades and fend for themselves. So I've come to find I'm less comfortable speaking, and if I'm unsure of what I'm saying, I will feel physical discomfort, just because like, Oh, what if I get it wrong? What if someone else says something smarter than me? Like, am I really as prepared as I think I am? So it's definitely been a little bit harder in college, but I'm getting better at it." He said that he was able to participate in Lit Core because it rapidly came to seem "a familiar environment," but he clammed up in larger classes "just because there's much more apprehension."

So he had to manage a certain amount of distress coming from his classes, and then there was the bigger picture. When I asked him my standard question about family—if there was a story his family tells about itself, a shared understanding of who they are and what they're about— Tyler answered, "I could have, I would have, said yes as a junior in high school, but a lot has changed over the past three or four years" as the result of a difficult divorce. His father, an exacting entrepreneur with a knack for moving product—"he's straight sales, he can literally sell you anything"— who has also often moved himself from one company to the next, was the breadwinner; his mother left a job as hairdresser at a high-end salon to raise Tyler; and a much older brother had recently moved from law enforcement to the private security business. "It's hard for me to put an identity on my family because I pretty much have like two families at this point," Tyler said. "The whole divorce has really made things bitter, and I kind of had to serve as the middleman between my mom and my dad, which is something I would have never thought I had to do." He took on this responsibility with his usual pluck and willingness—"it's just kind of how the hand was dealt, and I just got to be strong for both of them because I have sworn to myself I'll never pick a side"—but it plainly wore on him: "I want to be there for both of them, so, yeah, things are pretty tumultuous."

When I asked if everyone in his family was as anomalously upbeat and healthy-minded as he is, Tyler said, "Um, it's probably just me. Honestly, my dad is less so over the whole situation. My mom is in a much better mental headspace. My dad is not, and my brother has just been away, rais-ing his kid and moving and working, and he has his own life." When I suggested that perhaps this was, in fact, the story to be told about his fam-ily these days, Tyler said, "I think I'm still trying to find my role in this whole situation, because when I go home, my dad lives forty minutes from my mom now, so I've got to be like, 'Okay, if I'm home from Friday to Sunday, am I going to spend twenty-two hours with my mom and twenty-six with my dad? Or like, what? Are they going to be mad at me that I don't spend more time with one or the other? Can they coexist whatso-ever?' It's just a constant struggle."

When I asked to what extent the divorce defeated his determination to look for the positive and optimistic side of everything, his commitment to asking what good can be drawn from any situation, Tyler said, "I think that's how I've always been and that's who I still am, but the whole parent situation has made me a little less jubilant because I've seen the ugly side of a relationship, especially of two people that I'm so close with. So it's kind of hardened me up a little bit, but I'm still always trying to see the good in people." I pointed out that this would be a particularly useful attitude for someone to bring to a literature class, in which each successive book comes at you like a new person, a new opportunity to learn how to read a different way, to be trained in a different way of seeing and understanding. Tyler said, "Right, yeah," though for once he seemed a little faraway, preoccupied with the difficulties we had just been discussing. But in another moment, he visibly mastered himself, calling on his reserves not only of optimism but of discipline to compartmentalize his troubles and maintain his positive outlook, and soon we were talking animatedly again about our shared interests in running and music and about an especially fascinating class he was taking in machine learning and data analysis.

I had a responsibility to avoid the trap of Tyler's easiness. Because he was always accentuating the positive, moving himself back to his enthusiastically cooperative default start point, and otherwise exercising considerable discipline in pursuit of cheerful equanimity, the path of least resistance for me as a teacher was to be satisfied when he raised his hand and contributed something constructive to a discussion. He was never a problem, after all, in the way that Dan could be when he was taking his time about talking his way around to a possible non sequitur and I was figuring from second to second whether it would be better to let him get there on his own or to jump in and try to rush him along to the denouement. Tyler was the opposite of a problem, in fact: he worked hard to make everything always okay. But the kind of acceptably correct and on-point classroom comment in which Tyler specialized, the kind that checks the box of participation and doesn't interrupt the flow, may be the tip of a more complicated iceberg.

Sometimes you have to interrupt the flow yourself a little and come back at the seemingly easy students to try to find out what else is down there underneath the perfectly fine response. Good point about all that fire imagery in "Visions of Budhardin," Tyler. What do you make of the way that it tends to appear when the community's trying to control Budhardin's desires or punish him for them? Is there something going on there, thematically, in the picture of the misalignment between the community's sense of order and Budhardin's inner life that might have helped set off your pattern-recognition sensors?

.   .   .   .   .

We live in an age of anxiety. I don't mean that ours is a uniquely anxious-making era. It's common these days to believe that, though it's hard to prove; and if you go back in history, you will find that people were always claiming they lived in the worst of times—or the best, which is just as hard to prove. I mean, yes, there's plenty of bad stuff happening these days, some of it apparently unprecedented and of existentially grave import, but I am reliably informed that the twelfth century BC was no picnic, the four-teenth century AD was also rough, and things looked pretty bleak for a lot of people around Christmastime in 1941. There's more global warming these days than in the past, but no current world war; more Covid, but less bubonic plague; less functional democracy in America, but also less slavery. . . . It's always an open question as to whether any given present can really be seen as the worst of times.

So I mean that it's an age of anxiety in the sense that anxiety is the hot trending influencer in maladies these days, especially for young people. They're being diagnosed and treated for all kinds of anxiety—social, generalized, phobias, obsessive-compulsive disorder, you name it—in astonishing numbers, and they're hyperaware of their own anxiousness and its proximate causes. They're anxious about being anxious and about the stress that makes them that way. They're also more comfortable than ever talking about it. Even a few years ago, I would not have gotten emails of the kind I regularly get now that say things like "Hi, Professor. My panic attacks are especially bad this week, so I don't think I'll be up to participating much in class. Just wanted to let you know! I hope that's okay! See you tomorrow!" Their hyperawareness of stress and its wide range of effects often dominates their thinking when they talk about themselves as students. Almost every student I interviewed, even those who described themselves as naturally relaxed or optimistic, had something to say about stress, even though I didn't make a point of bringing it up. Each had a more or less conscious set of techniques for managing stress and anxiety, a kind of personal domestic mental health policy, and most reported that they had gotten better at such self-management over the course of their college careers.

I see no more than enigmatic glimpses of students' inner workings from the front of the room, but I try to remember that each of them has an inner life, no two are alike, and the principal action of each student's semester may well be happening on that terrain. When I look at rows of similarly unlined faces looking back at me, it can be easy to forget that college students these days think of calming the waters within as a big part of the business and craft of being a student and that there's a fingerprint-like individuality to the way each person in the room goes about it. It can also be easy to forget that they're lonely, typically more isolated than college students of previous eras, and less equipped to span the technology-enhanced void to make meaningful contact with others.

I can't sit down with every student for hours, as I did with Dan and Tyler and their Lit Core classmates when I interviewed them, but there are some things I can do to help me get at least a slightly less enigmatic glimpse of students' inner lives. One is to mix in the occasional creative assignment in critical classes like Lit Core, opportunities for students to show their command of the ideas and materials of the course by trying out moves they couldn't make in a traditional analytical paper. For instance, I might try an assignment that asks the student to envision a debate between two characters from different books on the syllabus about an idea or problem with which both characters had to reckon, and sometimes a paper like that can offer a fresh glimpse of what's on a student's mind. Another way to get a look at the rest of the iceberg, which I tried out when I taught entirely online during the pandemic but which could also suit in-person classes, is to give students a questionnaire at the beginning of the semester that mimics some of the questions I asked when I interviewed my Spring 2020 Lit Core students face-to-face. The questionnaire features questions like "What story does your family tell itself about itself?" and "If I was an anthropologist studying your hometown, what's one location or event you would recommend I go to in order to get a sense of the place and its culture, and what would I discover there?" I also filled out the questionnaire and sent my response back to each student when I received his or hers so that there was a fair exchange of iceberg data. After all, though it can be hard for students to believe, professors also come from somewhere and have inner lives.

6 It's Okay to Hate the Book

What kind of reader does this book want me to be? When you start with this question, you're taking a first step toward getting something meaningful out of whatever you read—or watch, or play, or however else you might consume stories these days. Even if simply enjoying what you read is your objective, *What kind of reader does this book*—or poem, movie, game, song, newspaper, newscast, painting, website, social media stream, etc.—*want me to be?* offers a more promising place to start than *Do I like this book?* or *What's wrong with this book?* and a much more promising place to start than *Do I feel outraged or validated by this book?* Being outraged has increasingly become a default response for people who think of themselves as thinking persons, but it tends to shut down the mind rather than open it and so robs it of an opportunity to work and grow stronger and come to handle things with greater competence and find more joy in the encounter with them.

What kind of reader does this book want me to be? is useful precisely because it helps you find your way to meaning even when you dislike or hate or are outraged by a book. Whether you like a book certainly matters, but you can interrogate any reaction—like, dislike, disgust, fascination, irritation, bliss, boredom, hating or loving or identifying with a character, you name it—and exploit that reaction's interpretive possibilities when you begin by thinking of the book as a machine that produces reactions in you and ask how the machine works. This is effective even if you fight the book every step of the way, reading against the grain of what it wants you to do, who it wants you to be. Actually, this approach may be even *more* effective when you naturally resist becoming the kind of reader a book wants you to be, because resisting its demands makes you acutely aware of them.

One way I think about putting together a syllabus, especially for an introductory course like Lit Core, is to make sure that as the semester goes on, students have a series of opportunities to come up with some very different answers to *What kind of reader does this book want me to be?* We may end up encountering a demographic assortment of authors—female and male, of different ethnic and racial and class backgrounds, and so on—but that's mostly a side effect of the effort to find different kinds of language, narrators, structures, and settings that expect students to be different kinds of readers.

Here's what I don't do when I design a syllabus: run an ideological test on each text to see if it sends the correct political message or needs to be trashed because it doesn't. There are, indeed, English professors who think that hammering approved content into students' minds is the point of reading literature at all and who put such considerations first. They come in a variety of ideological flavors—from, say, performing withering critique of settler-colonial imperialism to conveying the greatness of the West—but there aren't as many of them as you might be led to believe by those who are appalled by them. Ideology-first teachers, some very good at their jobs and some not so good, prove irresistibly fascinating to anyone who fears that the academy must be saved from some particular breed of misguided true believer. It's not hard to cherry-pick the words of such teachers to convince yourself that the academy has lost its way or been taken over by fools—*if*, that is, you can conveniently forget about all the ways in which it was misguided and foolish in the past, which then allows you to imagine that in higher education, as in so many other sentimentally remembered aspects of life (Crime! Music! Kids these days!), things used to be a lot better and have lately gone to hell.

But lots of people in the business, me included, don't really think that way. I mean, yes, I can certainly get behind the principle that literature's a good place to look if you're interested in questioning or defending the way things are. Why is there so much pressure, for instance, on both Lily Bart and Oscar Wao to pair up with a member of the opposite sex? The stakes are literally life and death in both of their otherwise very different cases, and that's worth thinking about. But I don't believe that this way of reading a novel is more important than, say, figuring out how reliable the narrator is. In fact, you need to ask and answer that kind of craft question in order to engage the ideas about mating or anything else in play in a novel.

That's my rough working synthesis of the two main positions in a long-running internal debate among humanists about the value of the humanities. One side sees the principal value of the humanities in teaching lessons about how to live; the other sees that principal value in the acquisition of equipment for living in the form of analytical skills, often described as "critical thinking." Though it's been going on for centuries, it's actually not a very compelling debate, since there's an obvious "both/and, not either/or" solution to the problem it purports to address—just like the contrived standoff between Tastes great! and Less filling! in old Miller Lite ads. If you're looking for lessons in how to live, you have to work on your interpretive chops so that you can get meaning out of all kinds of texts in which those lessons might be found. If you're looking for lessons in chopsmanship, then you need some kind of application to the problem of how to live to impart the necessary urgency of a meaningful answer to the So what? question. As I taught it in spring 2020, Lit Core was designed around twin objectives that replicated in miniature this symbiotic relationship between the two principles: discerning how meaning flows through language (developing analytical skills) as we explore what happens to social misfits (considering problems in how to live).*

---

* On the long-running debate about the purpose and value of the humanities, see Eric Adler, *The Battle of the Classics: How a Nineteenth-Century Debate Can Save the Humanities Today* (New York: Oxford University Press, 2020); and Paul Reitter and Chad Wellmon, *Permanent Crisis: The Humanities in a Disenchanted Age* (Chicago: University of Chicago Press, 2021). Executive summary of the practical outcome of this debate: tastes great *and* less filling.

Taking advantage of these opportunities begins with *What kind of reader does this book want me to be?*

.   .   .   .   .

This question becomes especially important when a lot of your students hate on sight a book you're teaching. Everything's easier if they like a book and are eager to read and engage with it, but dislike creates some openings I can exploit, which is why I prefer it to indifference. I tell students that genuine dislike of a book, or of something about a book, can function in the mind like a grain of sand that gets into an oyster, irritating the organism so much that it produces a pearl in response. The pearl, in this analogy, is an interpretive reading, and one way to get moving in that direction is to ask yourself what about the text inspired such a reaction in you. If you think of the text as a machine for producing that reaction, *how* does it do that? Is it language? Characters? Plot? The problems or ideas the book cares about? I've asked myself these questions often over the years, because any number of writers generally admired by people who consider themselves educated and well-read—a list that includes Henry James, D. H. Lawrence, Virginia Woolf, James Joyce, Ernest Hemingway, Ralph Ellison, Saul Bellow, James Baldwin, John Updike, Thomas Pynchon, Don DeLillo, Salman Rushdie, and pretty much every beloved Russian writer— have a negative effect on me so potent that just a few sentences of their prose (even part of a single sentence, in James's case) can cause a book to slip from my nerveless fingers. I just don't want to be the reader they want me to be.

But that's no bar to getting something out of their work. I don't have to love a book to teach it. I've taught authors I can't stand, including some on the above list (Junot Díaz, whose work figures prominently on my misfits syllabus and in the following chapters of this book, probably belongs on that list), and my own reactions helped me do it. So did the reactions of students, often very different from mine. A teacher, like an interpretive reader, can do something with strong responses, negative or positive, which offer a promise that form and meaning operate in a text in potentially interesting ways. I bear in mind in this regard something that James Schamus, whom I interviewed for a magazine profile when he was the long-reigning head of the indie movie studio Focus Features, told me about CinemaScore exit polls of movie audiences. While an A from CinemaScore was always welcome, he said, "A B or B-minus is 'eh.' I'd rather have a C-minus or D, knowing that people have strong reactions."[†]

Which brings me to Edith Wharton's *The House of Mirth*. If you teach literature and you feel for some reason like getting taken down a peg or two, tell your former students that the statute of limitations has elapsed and they're free to say what they really think about a book you made them read. Most of the books I taught in Lit Core in the spring of 2020 fared well in this exercise, but *The House of Mirth* took a beating.

"That was not my thing," Susannah said, speaking for many. "The language, the time period." The novel's set in New York's high society at the end of the nineteenth century—not *that* long ago—and its precise, elegant, lapidary prose is by no means impenetrably alien, but there's enough distance from us to trigger a response like Susannah's. Jonah, who told me that he finds it hard to sit still and read because he gets antsy very quickly, assumed an expression of vividly remembered pain as he said, with dripping irony, "That was so fun. Oh my gosh. A chapter of that would take me like an hour to get through, because I'm such a slow reader. And it's just like, What the hell *is* this? What is she *talking* about?" Matteo, who is Italian, also found it slow going. "That was the one I hated the most," he told me. "It was very complicated. I remember the English was very literary. I have to read it three times."

Among those who identified plot and character as the main off-putting traits, Charlotte articulated the response of several students when she explained that she couldn't figure out how to care about what happened in the novel. "I kind of had a hard time with it," she said. "I just couldn't pinpoint what I wanted to talk about, what parts meant the most to me." Tyler felt the same way, but he could put his finger on the source of the problem: "I had just a harder time getting through that whole book because, like, all right, is she going to get married yet? Is she going to keep pushing all these guys away?" He was referring to the main action of the novel, in

---

[†] That profile of James Schamus, "The Professor of Micropopularity," appeared in the *New York Times Magazine*, Nov. 28, 2010, 50–55.

which Lily Bart, low on capital but richly endowed with beauty and calcu-
lating acumen, tries to pick her way through a field of wealthy suitors.
Each of them offers money and position but nothing much in the way
of pleasure, excitement, intellectual stimulation, or the prospect of anything other than a life of loveless, socially irreproachable tedium possibly
brightened by the occasional extramarital affair. She can't bring herself to
stomach any of the candidates or to say to hell with their money and hook
up with the socially acceptable but modestly salaried lawyer Selden, to
whom she might actually be attracted. The stakes couldn't be higher
because Lily apparently can't function anywhere else than at the top of
society. She's a hothouse flower, and in the wrong conditions she'll wither
and die. None of that mattered to Tyler. He's an enthusiast, an achiever, a
consummate good kid, but *The House of Mirth* temporarily turned him
into a cost-benefit-motivated corner-cutter: "So, yeah, I, if I'm being honest, I don't think I read the majority of that book, but I did my typical
student thing—what we do, we try to work smarter, and I got all the
themes from online."

Dara, Eli, and Eva reported that reading *The House of Mirth* gave them
flashbacks to bad experiences of being forced to read nineteenth-century
novels in high-school English classes. Eva, with endearingly characteristic
bluntness, told me, "I hated it. It was incredibly boring to me." Dan, too:
"Boring. Simple as that." He discussed the syllabus with his father, he told
me, and "we both think that you assigned that book to us because it somehow checked a box for you in terms of curriculum"—a book by a woman,
perhaps, or an old book, a canonical classic. Seeing something move in my
face when I heard that, he added, "Is that right? Or do you like that book?
We didn't think you liked it." I told him that, on the contrary, I truly love
The House of Mirth and that to my mind, there's a solid argument for
Wharton as the great American novelist. A wordsmith of a high order who
was also sharply and originally attuned to the world around her and the
affairs of the day, she wrote terrific novels about city life and country life,
rich people and poor people, women and men; she produced at least three
stone masterpieces (*The House of Mirth, The Custom of the Country, The
Age of Innocence*); she wrote all kinds of things besides novels, including
travel pieces, ghost stories, shrewd commentaries on the design of houses
and gardens, and a little super-creepy incest-flavored erotica; and she

stayed at the top of her game for decades. Though she's respectably established in the canon, she's still an underappreciated wonder, and to my mind *The House of Mirth* is the best thing she ever wrote. "Good thing I already got my grade," said Dan.

Some students got into it. Stella savored Wharton's diction, and during our classes on the novel, she came into the fullness of her formidable powers as a participant in discussion. It was as if the slope got steeper when we reached Wharton, and others flagged, but Stella picked up the pace. Dave and Paul texted back and forth about Lily Bart's suitors as they read, having fun with it, making a running joke of following her fortunes as if she were a contestant on *The Bachelorette*. "Can't believe she's really gonna pick Percy Gryce! I'm Team Selden all the way!" That game contained the seeds of an interpretive approach, to the extent that they recognized that there was a surprising and perhaps analytically exploitable bit of overlap between the kind of reader that *The House of Mirth* asked them to be and the kind of viewer *The Bachelorette* asked them to be. Wilson, who enjoyed the novel's portrait of New York's high society because it reminded him of rich people he knew back on Long Island who angled to get into exclusive clubs, said it reminded him of *Game of Thrones*, which he was watching at the time. "The whole marriage part of it, it's very cool," he said. "I remember Robb Stark when he had to marry one of the Freys, and then he ended up marrying like the random, the no-namer, and then the Red Wedding. I was like, 'This is similar.'"

Arun said, "It was a slow process, getting used to the character of Lily and kind of understanding her motives and where the story was progressing," but he took pleasure in that process. "I think I prefer the longer forms of literature because you can spend time with them, explore the different avenues." And although on the face of it a twenty-first-century guy from Bangalore would seem an unlikely candidate for identifying with Lily Bart, the story raised a compelling cultural echo for him. "I think for me, coming from an Indian background, it wasn't as alien to me because a lot of people have arranged marriages or, like, have that pressure of getting married. So I kind of—not 'understood,' but I could, I guess, identify with where she was."

Identifying or failing to identify with Lily, sympathizing with her or wishing she'd just hurry up and die already—students' responses to the demands on them as readers exerted by *The House of Mirth* were all over the map, creating multiple pathways into the novel for us to exploit.

.   .   .   .   .

Let's dig deeper into what inspired their reactions, negative or positive, to Wharton. That means starting with language, the trait that stood out for most of them. Reading unfamiliar prose styles, especially older ones, is like running on the beach instead of pavement or track. It takes more work to get through a sentence, a paragraph, a chapter. Doing that extra work is good for you, and makes you a stronger reader, and some people come to prefer nineteenth-century or sixteenth-century prose styles in the same way that some people fall in love with the feel of running on sand, but the majority find it wearying. Now, reading Wharton isn't anywhere near as disorienting as reading, say, Shakespeare can be—when the class really does have to stop to figure out the literal meaning of what a character is saying. Twenty-first-century college freshmen do not find Wharton's crystalline prose confusing in that sense, but many bog down among the commas that proliferate in sentences like the one that clinically skewers and mounts Percy Gryce, one of Lily's most unappealing suitors, like a specimen insect: "After attaining his majority, and coming into the fortune that the late Mr. Gryce had made out of a patent device for excluding fresh air from hotels, the young man continued to live with his mother in Albany, but on Jefferson Gryce's death, when another large property passed into her son's hands, Mrs. Gryce thought that what she called his 'interests' demanded his presence in New York." There's just one comma in the sentence that similarly piths Lily's horrible aunt: "Mrs. Peniston thought the country lonely and trees damp, and cherished a vague fear of meeting a bull." But readers who see the open road of simple syntax ahead and so pass in a relieved rush over the exquisiteness of word choice that gave us "cherished"—rather than, say, "was haunted by" or "suffered from"—will miss some nuances of the portrait being painted.

When we talked about the language of the novel, we noted and went deep on some tendencies we discerned in it during our initial noticing exercises: when describing Lily's situation, the narration makes a lot of word choices that have a resonance of business, war, predation, or science.

There's constant talk of credit, speculation, interest, and capital in Wharton's account of Lily Bart's career in New York's high-society marriage market. This language acquires an ironic edge when you consider that the women of the novel may have the lioness's share of drive and ambition, but they're shut out from Wall Street, where the plodding, stertorous male characters enjoy copious access to money and power. So the female characters do their mergers, acquisitions, and other deal-making in the ballroom and boudoir. There's also hunting and military imagery: "She began to cut the pages of a novel, tranquilly studying her prey through downcast lashes while she organized a method of attack." And there's frequent recourse to the language of natural science: Lily's compared to a "waterplant in the flux of the tides," a "sea-anemone torn from the rock," "spindrift on the whirling surface of existence," a celestial body in eclipse as others rise above the horizon. She comes to perceive that "the blind motions of her mating-instinct . . . had been checked by the disintegrating influences of the life about her. All the men and women she knew were like atoms whirling away from each other in some wild centrifugal dance."

Seeking a larger pattern in the interplay of these different recurring *registers*—a useful term for a particular strain of vocabulary in a text, a specific flow of language like science talk or business talk—we made out a basic tension in the novel. Lily the entrepreneur-warrior-hunter may try to actively determine the course of her own life, but she's also portrayed as passively in the tidal grip of large impersonal forces. We didn't all agree on which of those forces might be most powerful. Money? Desire? Different social expectations and rules for women and men? But we didn't have to agree. We were just trying to understand how the text thinks and works, what kind of readers it asks us to be, the tools and opportunities it gives us to make meaning.

Seeing how Lily is at once free to choose and helplessly locked into a life course created an analytical path along which even students initially put off by the novel might find their way into it. Lily's older than they were, in her late twenties, and her marry-or-else situation might seem alien to them, especially because, these days, college freshmen are, if anything, under pressure *not* to marry too early. Yes, there's a deep default expectation that they will eventually find the right person and have a family, but right now their parents typically want them to take it slow with any

serious relationships, fearing that commitment and babies could compli-
cate undergraduate and postgraduate education, professional development, and other phases of the twenty-first-century upper-middle-class
launch sequence. But the larger questions Lily's situation raises can seem
more familiar. Do you feel like a warrior or a water plant? An entrepreneur or spindrift? It's often both at once, which can be disorienting in
ways that students recognize. In both school and personal life, they have
repeated occasion to wonder to what extent they're authentically operating as free agents and to what extent they're just going through the
motions dictated by their programming and the demands of social class
and the exclusive institutions and select groups to which they want to gain
admittance. Because our culture constantly urges them to develop interests and dreams and pursue them—that's usually the essence of the essays
they wrote to gain admission to college—acting on even the most impassioned impulse can feel like obeying orders from on high. All of that reso-
nates with the predicament of Lily Bart.

So now we're talking less about language and more about plot, character, and theme, the other big category of reasons why many students found
it hard to get into *The House of Mirth*. One question we can always ask to
close the range on any text on the Lit Core syllabus is What's the nature of
the misalignment between the misfit and the order in which she or he is
embedded? What's the problem, in other words, and what does it tell us
about the world imagined by the text? We can see as the novel goes on that
Lily's not going to figure out that problem in time. When she dies at the
end, the proximate cause is an accidental-ish overdose of sleep medica-
tion, but the deep cause can be seen as ejection from her natural habitat of
luxury and fine things, which the novel keeps showing and telling us she
must have in order to feel that she's truly living. She's boxed in by sexual
inequality in access to capital, the male gaze, mandatory marriage, and all
the rest of the forces impinging on her, but at times, it looks like the cause
of death is low thread count.

Many students balk at this. *First-world problems*, they say. *Why is she
so weak and whiny?* I understand this kind of reaction, and I have a similar one. Reading the novel, even rereading it for the tenth time, you want
to say to her, *Look, if you have to marry and they're all bozos, just pick the
richest and most agreeable or malleable bozo and settle for the security he*

can provide, and you can emulate your high-society peers by having your romantic adventures on the side. Or marry Selden, if you're actually attracted to him, and endure the not-very-unspeakable fate of being merely upper middle class rather than super-rich. Or don't marry anybody and find your way into a bohemian tale or a proto-noir or a shopgirl story or some other formula. But don't just stand there and dither until the world gets around to squashing you like a bug. But that's not really playing by the rules of the text. In this novel, it's high society or nothing for Lily, a natural-born ditherer, and she's too aware of the unjust strictures on her as a woman to allow herself to do what she has to do to assure her place in it. That should turn our attention to those strictures, rather than to questioning the verisimilitude of her melodramatic doom.

Another way to close the range on the novel was to think about a resonant recurring motif: it's full of scenes in which everybody looks at Lily, whose range of options consists mostly of deciding how to present herself to be looked at. The most striking of these is a set piece in which Lily stars in a tableaux vivants exhibition put on by society ladies at a party at a Fifth Avenue mansion. Tableaux vivants, in which people dressed and posed and employed props and sometimes elaborate settings to recreate famous paintings or other well-known images, were a widespread practice among the well-to-do in the Gilded Age. In the novel's tableaux vivants scene, Lily steals the show with a solo recreation of Joshua Reynolds's *Mrs. Lloyd*, a painting of a dark-haired woman in close-fitting white, alone in the woods, steadying herself with one hand on a stone plinth while she bends gracefully to etch her new husband's name on the bark of a tree. Reactions to Lily's performance vary, from those of her friends Selden and Gerty Farish, who think to see "the real Lily" in that moment, to that of Ned Van Alstyne, speaking for the apoplectic bankers and other alpha walruses in attendance: "Deuced bold thing to show herself in that getup; but, gad, there isn't a break in the lines anywhere, and I suppose she wanted us to know it!" In other words: *Nice rack.*

I put together a PowerPoint so that we could look at photographs of actual tableaux vivants and also the Reynolds painting of Mrs. Lloyd, which prompted a conversation about what's happening in this scene. To what extent is Lily *doing* something by striking this pose, and to what extent is she passively having something done *to* her by others? Opinions ran mixed. Every time somebody said that she's being objectified, somebody else said that she was doing what she could to shape her destiny within the conditions she was given. When somebody pointed out that the painting shows Mrs. Lloyd writing, seizing control of her own story, somebody else pointed out that she's writing her husband's name, not her own, and that acquiring a husband is exactly what's expected of Lily. This was a useful deadlock, worth lingering on for a bit. The motif can say both things at once, and be *about* saying both things at once, and that bind was not unfamiliar to us. Nobody in the class had ever posed in a tableau vivant, but they'd taken selfies and yearbook pictures, written admissions essays, been on Instagram and dating sites, gotten dressed and decided how much makeup to put on, presented themselves for inspection in all sorts of ways. Maybe the stakes of those performances didn't rise to the melodramatic life-or-death level of the novel's, but, still, they prompted similar questions about being an agent and being an object. Is arranging to be looked at, submitting to being looked at, *doing* something or having something done *to* you? The blueprinting of Lily's performance by Reynolds's painting also raised echoes. We don't fashion from scratch the selves we present to others in person and online and elsewhere. We draw on templates and models; we reenact, even when we try to be original.

And, the novel suggests, we're always caught up in this sort of performance; it's a large part of what being a self consists of. Go back to page 1 and the very first scene, in which Selden runs into Lily on a train platform. Seeing her before she sees him, he's struck by the spectacle of Lily Bart in passage between other, richer people's country houses, her emblematic condition. "Selden paused in surprise," the novel begins. "In the afternoon rush of the Grand Central Station his eyes had been refreshed by the sight of Miss Lily Bart." The spectacle of her everyday self-presentation has an effect like that of a tableau vivant, which is like that of a great work of art: "He had a confused sense that she must have cost a great deal to make, that a great many dull and ugly people must, in some mysterious way, have been sacrificed to produce her." And, like a work of art, she inspires not just appreciation but interpretation: "it was characteristic of her that she always roused speculation" (note the business-resonant word choice), "that her simplest acts seemed the result of far-reaching intention." In the novel's opening scene, Selden's already modeling the routine of thinking about form and meaning in the spectacle of Lily Bart.

·   ·   ·   ·   ·

The character of Selden opens another pathway for students to take into the novel. He stands out in its character system as the one voice telling Lily that she doesn't have to play by the rules. The other men want to marry her or, if they're already married, keep her on the side as a mistress. Most of the other women regard her as a rival or a threat or, in any case, a problem. One exception on the female side is Gerty Farish, a dowdy do-gooder Lily's age who lives alone in a modest apartment, has no husband prospects, and devotes herself to charitable settlement work. But Lily can't live like Gerty. The threadbare, it'll-do quality of that life would destroy Lily as surely as a desert habitat would destroy a tropical creature—and, in the end, she pretty much literally decides that she would rather die than live like Gerty. So Selden's offering what looks like the only way out of the trap she's in. Cultivating an air of cool detachment, he preaches what he calls "the republic of the spirit," which he defines as freedom "from everything—from money, from poverty, from ease and anxiety, from all the material accidents." He dangles this vague utopia in front of Lily early in the novel, just in time to convince her to abandon her brilliant and sure-to-succeed campaign to land Percy Gryce as a husband, thereby starting her down a long road of variously refused and scuttled marital offers to her eventual OD in a rented room.

But what kind of a possibility is Selden offering, really? He's talking freedom from material conditions to a character the novel presents to us as only able to flourish in a suitably luxurious environment, and he's talking freedom from social norms to a character who's much more constrained by them than he is. As a single man, he has access to a profession—lawyering—that allows him to make enough money to support himself and function in high society, though not enough money to support Lily in the style she would require. He's welcome in high society because he's not only presentable, discreet, suitably moneyed, well-connected, and not Jewish or anything else unacceptable, but also, crucially, he's willing to play by its rules and keep up appearances. He not only lives by but also helps enforce high society's norms, even to the extent of joining in the general shunning of Lily when he wrongly suspects her of having compromised herself with a married man. So when he urges her to imagine herself outside the boundaries of what's expected of her, he's inviting her to do something that he, as a man who values his own sense of autonomy, won't do and doesn't have to do: ignore material conditions and refuse to play by the rules.

At the end of the novel, Selden rushes to Lily's side, presumably to declare his love at last, but he's too late. Several students reported that they cried, which led to a class discussion of novels as machines for producing tears. It's all very tragic—*if* you think he represented some kind of alternative to the world that killed her rather than exemplifying it. I find myself convinced by the argument that he exemplifies it. He's the leading consumer of Lily Bart as spectacle, as the opening pages of the novel make clear, and he never offers any support to her that would oblige him to step even slightly out of line. I can see the potential value of the change of perspective he's offering Lily in his speech about the republic of the spirit—*it's a rat race, get out of it*—but in a naturalist novel that sets the bar at marry or die and posits a world with different rules for women and men, it seems selfish and irresponsible to blow up her marriage prospects and offer nothing tangible to take their place. I feel that I can see Selden coming a mile away, and as a father of daughters, I want mine to be able to spot a guy like him and be prepared to repel boarders. Put a man-bun on him and he'd fit right in at Brooklyn Boulders, where he'd be trying to meet babes by demonstrating a totally excellent slackline technique, preaching freedom from all bogus convention between surreptitious bouts of checking his text messages because he has a client who doesn't like to be kept waiting.

The thing is, students tend to like Selden. He's the only character who speaks a language of selfhood and freedom resembling the one they're used to: independence of thought, transcending convention, following your bliss. Since Lily has made it plain between them that Selden doesn't have the money to marry her, it's not exactly clear what kind of relationship he has in mind—friendship, a short- or long-term romantic liaison, maybe both. But it might well fall into the category of friends with benefits, which feels familiar to students when compared to the alien-feeling hyperawareness of formal limits and constraint that otherwise pervades the world of the novel. Lily's a virgin pushing thirty, as far as we can tell, and that seems exotic and even somehow dystopian to twenty-first-century eighteen-year-olds, even those who are also virgins.

This all created an opportunity for me to make some analytical headway by poking a little gentle fun at Selden and therefore—even more gently—at the admiration he commanded. I waited for a moment when the pro-Selden voices were dominant, then suggested that we take another look at what he's really saying, whether there's anything to his offer other than possibly some quality time with a beautiful woman for him and a death sentence for the beautiful woman. In the course of recapitulating what he's offering and making the case I just outlined for seeing it as a line of doubletalk, I delivered his republic of the spirit speech in the voice of a trustafarian giving a TED Talk, mixing in for effect some extra *dude*s and a culminative *So maybe you could come over and we could, like, get in the shower and just, you know, hang out in our own, like, republic-of-the-spirit kind of situation?* It wasn't all that funny, but it didn't need to be that funny to make them laugh. Students don't expect professors to kid around, they don't expect class to involve kidding around, and they definitely don't expect *The House of Mirth* to be funny (even though it is). So expectations were low, and it was just funny enough.

There was a certain self-consciousness, a touch of shyness, in their laughter. *Hey, are you making fun of this character, of this Great Book, of me? Is it okay to do that? Are we still being serious about analyzing the book?* But stop for a moment to consider what they had to get in order to laugh at Selden, at the book, at themselves, at me. That last part, laughing at me, is important. I had told them about my being a father of daughters, and I doubled down on playing an oversuspicious dad who doesn't like the looks of this guy. I wasn't contemptuously dismissing their reading of Selden; I was taking it seriously by coming back at them with a counterargument in the form of kidding around with the book. To get the kidding, they had to understand its plot and themes, their own response to it as a reader, and our discussions of the character system and Lily's situation and the language of the novel. They had to get that a reading is an argument, and that what was happening was argument and counterargument.

Kidding about the book is like investigating your own readerly reactions to it or like comparing it—as various students did—to *The*

Bachelorette, Game of Thrones, Bridgerton, the works of Austen and Dickens and other nineteenth-century novelists they read in AP Lit, and whatever else it reminded them of. These are all ways of handling the goods, staying active as a reader, triangulating the range on the text so that you can work in closer to it. I sometimes say "We're not just talking about our feelings here" as a way of reminding students that we're building arguments, but it's worth remembering that one way to arrive at an argument is to start by considering how the text made you feel. The text is a machine for generating those feelings, after all, and those feelings are connected to the rest of your mind.

The House of Mirth is the kind of book that most students would be unlikely to read on their own. Many of them got through it, and eventually got into it, only because it was assigned in a class for which they would be receiving credit and a grade, and they needed class discussions and my minilectures to get there. Dalha told me, "That's why I liked class, especially for the discussions in class, especially for that text. Just because sometimes I was like, What did this whole paragraph—what was it trying to say? Because the language was like, so *far,* at least to me." Even Eli, who hated the book on sight, came around to it by way of class discussions. "This is the thing," he told me. "I did not like it at first, but I thought the discussion we had about how the choices a character makes for relationships influence the idea of the narrative and the themes was very interesting at the end. And I've always had that mind-set in the back of my head since that book. But the book as a whole I did not like." If he came away from his encounter with *The House of Mirth* with a newly acquired habit of thinking about the character system as a way to figure out what a book's about, then he got something useful out of it. And there's extra value in the fact that his first reaction was negative but he pushed through it, was willing to consider what the book expected of him and why and how it produced that reaction, and didn't settle for simply disliking the book.

That's part of the value of teaching a text that students find off-putting or otherwise not instantly likable. It gives us a chance to model and practice a set of moves—identification, analogy, interrogating your own reactions to the text, putting your finger on *how* the form of the text encourages those reactions—they can employ when they find themselves put off by a book . . . or a movie, a painting, a song, a human being. Even the most broadly interested and forgiving person will react negatively to at least some books, and when it happens, it's more important than ever to ask *What kind of reader does this book want me to be?*

.   .   .   .   .

"I remember Selden got very vocal support in our class discussions. People seemed to think he was the moral choice, if only Lily could learn the error of her materialism. I still think they greatly overestimated the merits of the life she would have been able to have with him." That's part of an email from Carrie, a former student who took Lit Core with me the first time I ever taught it, in fall 2017. She had a sterling undergraduate career, during which she worked for me as a terrifyingly hypercompetent research assistant, and went on to an apex-predator law school. I fully expect her to be playing an outsize role in running the world sometime soon.

The House of Mirth, catching Carrie just a few weeks into her very first semester of college, made a big impression on her. The other book that caught her just right and became a touchstone was Sylvia Plath's *The Bell Jar*. These two dark stories of doom-haunted young women grabbed her and wouldn't let go, and she went willingly into their embrace. Interrogating your own reactions to help find your analytical way into a text is an advanced readerly skill. Some readers come to it late, though it's never too late to learn how to do it. Some, like Carrie, develop the skill earlier in their reading career—perhaps while making their way through Brian Jacques's talking-animal Redwall books or the Harry Potter series—and show up at college with this skill already in their repertoire.

The House of Mirth was so important to Carrie that she wrote about it, as well as *The Bell Jar*, in her law school application essays. In those essays she wrote, *These are works that feature the interior lives of women, particularly women who feel as though they do not neatly fit into any role society has offered them. Although that description sounds somewhat trite, these are not simple stories of girl power and standing out in a crowd. Rather, the protagonists feel displaced, anxious, and isolated. The best treatment for these feelings is the realization that they are very commonly shared. While this may be lost on the novels' heroines, who do not have the benefit of reading their own books, their readers discover it when they see their own private thoughts reflected back on the page. Perhaps these anxieties are not particular to young women. I do not know. I do know how important it was for my angsty teenage self to realize that I had decidedly not fallen through the cracks of society, and in fact had excellent company in the form of these books' authors.*

In our email exchange, Carrie speculated that perhaps the Lit Core students who liked *The House of Mirth* were those who identified with Lily Bart. That could be, but a reader doesn't have to identify with a character or even like a book to find a route into that book. Any response at all, even a negative one, can potentially be interrogated and put to analytical purposes. No response, in contrast, doesn't leave student or teacher much to work with, and it's worth remembering that a text that gave one reader a life-transforming experience may not show up at all as even the faintest of blips on another's radar. A teacher is tempted to see a class as a group entity—*This is a lively bunch*, or *My Lit Core class had a flat day*, or *College students these days are so [fill in the blank]*, and so on—and lose sight of the fact that it's also an assembly of individuals, each having her or his own individual experience of any given book. Compare Carrie to Kathi, who seemed sincere in saying that she found Lit Core consistently interesting and did the reading "most of the time" and who achieved a memorable victory of enduring value to her when she conspired with me to overcome her anxious silence and speak up in our class discussions. When I asked Kathi about her reaction to *The House of Mirth*, she said she remembered nothing at all about it. Edith Wharton? Lily Bart has to marry or die, but the choices are all bad? We spent five class sessions on it over the course of three weeks a year and a half ago? You had to figure out what kind of reader it wanted you to be? She just shook her head apologetically. Nope. Nothing. Didn't ring a bell.

7 Speaking Up

Colleen and Kathi weren't speaking up in class. They had each taken their turn to introduce themselves during the first-day icebreaking ritual, but that jump start had not led to their consistently volunteering to speak in subsequent class meetings. Neither Colleen, who usually sat halfway back and to my right, nor Kathi, who usually sat near the back and to my left, displayed the seethingly slack affect of somebody who believes she's in the wrong place and is counting the seconds until she can get the hell out of there. Rather, they usually looked engaged—paying attention, taking notes—and at times, I thought to detect on each of their faces the alert and slightly pained look of someone who has things to say and isn't saying them.

When I first started teaching, my attitude toward students who remained silent in discussion classes could be summed up with the words of Bernard Hopkins, the fistic sage of Philadelphia: "Bernard Hopkins gonna do what Bernard Hopkins gonna do." If students didn't want to talk, it was on them. They were free to choose not to speak and would have to accept the lower grade that came as a consequence. After all, I had not talked much in class when I was a student, and I had resisted professors who tried to make me talk. But, though I still regard the Hopkins credo as words to live by, I have learned the error of my ways when it comes to applying it to silent students. Silence is usually not their preferred state—and, indeed, was not my preferred state when I was one of them. I had things to say, and it bothered me that I often couldn't make myself say them.

Trying to help silent students find a way into the conversation and thus into full citizenship in the classroom turns out to be no big effort for a teacher, and the results can be life-changing for the student. It also benefits the teacher because the quietly contagious excitement of previously stymied students who have finally found a way to speak up improves classroom chemistry, and nothing makes teaching and learning easier or more joyful than good classroom chemistry. A classroom in which everyone there has anted up as a participant is a much better—more effective, more dynamic, more transformative—classroom than one in which some people are holding back from being full participants in our communal inquiry.

But thirty-three students is a lot of students if you're trying to orchestrate a purposeful conversation about a work of literature—or about anything else, for that matter. That's all the more true if almost all of them are freshmen with little or no experience of discussion in a college-level classroom. It's a roomful of rookies, even if they're game, talented, and hardworking rookies who have already had to accomplish a lot just to get in the door. (Picture a discussion with thirty-three relatives, almost all of them freshly married into your extended family, on the subject of what to do about Uncle Frank and his dogs and Glocks.) Inevitably, some students don't find their way into the conversation. Occasionally, such a silent student really does hate the professor and/or the course, thinks it's all bullshit, and deeply resents having to take it (if, like Lit Core, it's required), but that kind of utter rejection is rare—and vanishingly rare at a place like Boston College. People tend to want to do well at whatever they do, a universal quality that's especially well-developed in students who get into a selective college. They're used to doing well in school, and most of them have evolved a facility for figuring out how to engage enough with any subject to accomplish that. And Lit Core is almost never anybody's first academic encounter with literature; typically, they have had to reckon with fiction, poetry, and drama along the path from kindergarten to college.

So it's much more likely that silent students are just a little more worried than others about saying something wrong or irrelevant or incoherent or just plain stupid that will produce the long, awkward silence they fear most of all. Or maybe they find it a little harder than others to time the flow of give-and-take so that they can jump in at the right moment with a relevant comment. Or they might be hit a little harder than others by the alienating effects of impostor syndrome, homesickness, or skepticism about literary interpretation—any of which might make others' apparent ease of entry into our discussions seem especially forbidding. Whatever the reasons for silent students' silence, it's a problem that I can and should address with them—in keeping with the bedrock principle that you must go and get an education rather than wait passively for someone to hand it to you.

A couple of silent students in a class of thirty-three doesn't present a major problem for a teacher. Most of the students in Lit Core were speaking up, making an effort, anteing up and following up with bets large and small; it was shaping up to be a fairly lively class, especially considering its size. I didn't want to leave anyone behind if I could help it, but I didn't have to worry about the class as a whole. Sometimes you do have to worry about a class as a whole. If there are too many silent students, trying to orchestrate a conversation becomes a chore, and their frustrated teacher may give in to the angry temptation to see them as a united front of incurious dullards who constitute the vanguard of an entire generation of interchangeably vacuous sheep who don't read and don't like the right music and aren't as intellectually vibrant as the teacher's generation, even if the teacher's generation did more bong hits. That response tells us more about the teacher's weaknesses than the students', of course. Every once in a while, I'll have a class meeting that doesn't work: too many long unproductive silences occur; we're not getting anywhere; I end up deciding to cut my losses and just explain things in order to cover ground I'd planned for us to cover together by discussing it, surprising ourselves along the way with fresh insights. When this happens, I will feel hot little flares of anger at my students, but I have learned that this is really just a deflected form of getting mad at myself for screwing up or at fate for visiting a bad day on us. The useful response to a bad day, even if you do end up writing it off as the result of bad luck, is to double down on craft: frame the question at hand in a different way next time, set it up better, be clearer about what we're doing and why, slow down, and, above all, take the small fiasco as a reminder to put more rather than less trust in the students to do what needs doing. I'm responsible for orchestrating a good class, but, as I have to regularly remind myself throughout the semester, the key to that is making them responsible for doing—and therefore learning—something useful.

Something similar applies when the class as a whole is moving along well enough that I have the luxury of doubling back to pick up strays. I should have gotten to Kathi and Colleen much sooner in the semester than I did, but it was a big class and it took me too long to notice that they were straggling. Still, before we got any deeper into the semester, I asked Kathi and then Colleen to come to my office during office hours to meet with me one-on-one. "There is an expectation that we hear from you in class," I wrote in an email to each of them, intentionally avoiding the first person to avoid making it seem as if I was personally expecting them to talk. I wanted, rather, to strike a dispassionate and procedural note, more like *This is how this class is properly done.* Form expresses meaning, even in an email. "If you are having trouble finding your way into the conversation, let's figure out a strategy that works for you." Finding out more about them, both in these meetings and in subsequent conversations with each of them that continued well past the end of the semester, dispelled the illusion of sameness generated by the opacity of silence. Silent students may have their silence in common, but the distinctive quality of each one's silence conceals depths of individuality. They may not be talking, and they may not always be thinking about what I want them to think about, but they are thinking—which means that, if I consider myself any kind of pro at all, I should try to figure out a way to reach them.

.   .   .   .   .

I started with Kathi. As she told me later when I interviewed her, she's from Greenwich, Connecticut, and attended a small private academy abundantly endowed with capital, posh tiger moms, and expectations of moving on to a suitably exclusive college. There were no boys in her classes until the ninth grade (the tenth grade in English classes), and she didn't adjust well to the change. She had spoken up in middle school, where classes had been small and she had felt comfortable among girls she knew well, "but as the years went on and we started being mixed with our brother school, I kind of didn't know how to act around boys." She clammed up, and it didn't help that she didn't get along with her English teacher. "She just didn't like me for some reason," she said. "Maybe it's because I was a bit of a jokester, but nothing, you know, malicious. And I also have ADD, and maybe that might have distracted the class at times. She kind of set a bad tone for my English experience, especially because I had her twice. You couldn't get out of her class. I wish, in retrospect, I wish I had a better English teacher, because there were so many good ones. My sisters both had good ones." Fortunately, she said, she ended up with one of the good ones for half of her senior year. "Everyone just knew he was the best guy, like the funniest person ever, a great person. And he really cared about his students, in and out of the classroom. I remember one day he pulled me aside after class and just said, 'How are you doing?' Nothing about English, but he just genuinely cared. People could joke with him, but at the same time they respected him completely. I won't forget him." Still, a pattern of remaining silent in class, especially English class, had been set and reinforced.

As a freshman in college, she said, "I was this, like, anxious little ball, not wanting to—scared of doing, like, one wrong thing, you know, antsy, just finding my place in college." She actually had a strong crew in Lit Core—her best pal, Charlotte, and also Liz and Bill, two more members of her recently formed friend group—and they all encouraged each other. "I was so tortured. I'd be, like, 'You can say something' to Charlotte, and she's like, 'No, no, you say it,' like, 'I'm not saying that.' We were all, like, 'All right, you're going to say something this class.'" Her friends found ways to speak up, and Bill in particular became a regular contributor, but she sat there rehearsing things she could say and then not saying them. She had formed the erroneous impression that there were several upperclassmen in the room (there was just one, Luke, a sophomore), which she allowed to intimidate her, "and there were a lot of boys, specifically hockey boys." There were, I agreed, an unusual number of male students in that class who—like her friend Bill—felt comfortable talking about literature, and it couldn't have helped that one of what she called the "hockey boys" took the lead as a participatory icebreaker at the beginning of the semester. "*Wilson,* yes, I know, I *know,*" said Kathi, looking back at her terrified freshman self, as if to say *You see what I was dealing with? I get to college and there are serious-business hockey boys who are going on to the Olympics and the NHL, and on top of that they turn out to be suave literary sophisticates, too.*

When Kathi came to see me at office hours, I proposed a plan that would lower the bar to participation for her. We had a split class meeting coming up, in which I would keep half of the group in our classroom and Allie, the TA, would take the other half to another room. That cut down each group from thirty-three to sixteen or seventeen, a much more manageable and less intimidating size for discussion. At this next class meeting, we decided, she would know the opening question in advance, which would allow her to prepare an answer, she would put up her hand, and I would call on her right away. Going first would prevent her from building up a disabling head of anticipation and dread as the class meeting went on. It would also eliminate any need to worry about being preempted by someone else or timing and adjusting her comment to fit into the flow of discussion.

On the evening before our next class meeting, I sent an email to all the students reminding them to come to class prepared with a passage—a scene, a moment, a phrase, a detail, a paragraph, a riff, whatever—from chapter 2 of *The Brief Wondrous Life of Oscar Wao* and at least the beginning of a thought about why that passage matters. In class the next day, I offered a quick opener to remind us of some main thematic threads and formal traits we'd identified and begun discussing at the previous class, our first on the novel. Then half the students left with Allie. Normally, Kathi would have gone with this group, since Allie had Kathi's half of the alphabet this time, but I'd written to Kathi the night before and told her to stay with my group so that we could execute our scheme. "I will still plan to look at you right at the start," I wrote to her. "Any passage or line, and an observation connected to it, will do. The important thing is to do it."

I got down to business with my group, Kathi included. What passages had they chosen, and why? Kathi put up her hand, I called on her, and she said something on-point about a passage she'd chosen—neither she nor I recalls what it was, but let's say it was about how Lola's mother, Beli, is pushing just as hard for her actively rebellious daughter to be a regular girl as everybody seems to be pushing Beli's passively dissenting son, Oscar, to be a regular guy. When a student who doesn't normally talk says something, I want—without making an embarrassing fuss—to make extra-sure to reinforce the contribution by noting its usefulness. So I said something like, Okay, that gets us off to a good start. Kathi's pointing out how in this novel the business of enforcing norms is consistently tangled up with the business of gender in more ways than one. It's not just dictators and masculinity; now we also have a mom-and-daughter pair, which looks like a more complicated pattern starting to form. We'll start by making a pile of these observations, then we can step back and look at our pile and see what larger patterns we can make out. Who'd like to go next and add to the pile?

So Kathi had spoken in class and lived to tell about it. She had not babbled meaningless nonsense that caused a dark abyss of embarrassed silence to yawn open after she spoke; she had not been struck down by apoplexy or lightning or subjected to gales of mocking laughter from distorted faces out of a nightmare. She looked like she felt pretty good about it. In fact, she felt so good that twenty minutes later, she put her hand up again. I try to call on students in reverse order of how often they raise their hands, so when a student who rarely talks puts up her hand, I go right to her. Kathi made a second point, this one building on something someone else had just said. Even if she had prepared this second point in advance, she'd still had to find an opportune moment to slide it into the conversation, another big step for her. Restraining an urge to dart across the room to high-five her, I again underscored that she'd contributed to our collective effort, something on the order of, So Kathi's pointing us to the importance of X, which we can put together with what Dalha was saying about Y and David said about Z, and that's starting to look like a clear set of connections between form and theme that helps us see how temporarily shifting the narrator to Lola does meaningful work.

Part of my job is to show students that they're participating as full citizens in an ongoing project, our crafting of interpretive arguments about the meanings that flow through a text, and one way I can do that is to recognize and reinforce such participation when it happens. *See this thing Kathi has done! She has brought us thick pelts and succulent tubers from beyond the river, so that we may enjoy full stomachs and cozy warmth. Truly she is a contributing member of our clan! These are my words; I have spoken.*

.   .   .   .   .

Colleen was next. Like Kathi, she was a white suburbanite who had grown up outside New York City and attended an all-girls school—Catholic, in Colleen's case, and single-sex all the way through the end of high school. But the superficial resemblance ended there. Kathi, the daughter of a BC alum who worked in private equity and a mother who devoted herself to medical charity, had grown up in an exclusive town synonymous with insulated suburban privilege in a big house so full of pets that her family called it The Zoo, and she had attended a school that specialized in sending its graduates on to elite colleges. She had a sister at Dartmouth, and another would go to the University of Virginia, but Kathi had been so sure that she was going to her dad's alma mater that she had barely bothered to apply anywhere else. By contrast, Colleen, an only child, was a first-generation college student, daughter of a maintenance man and a secretary in a doctor's office at a hospital in the Bronx. She had been just about the only one of her schoolmates who left the environs of New York City and went "away" to college, a few hours north in exotic Boston, and she had applied to BC despite being assured by her school's guidance counselor that she had no chance to get in. All four of Colleen's grandparents had been immigrants from Ireland to the Bronx, and she had grown up just to the north of the Bronx in an apartment in a small housing complex in Yonkers, which may be technically a suburb of New York City but feels more like a midsize mill city—bigger than any city in New England except Boston, in fact, and with an urban mix of Irish, Italian, Latino, and black populations. Colleen had spent summers in the Bronx with a grandmother in her mother's old neighborhood around Webster Avenue and Gun Hill Road, which Colleen described to me as "kind of rough," her pale serious face coloring with a deep blush at the thought that I might erroneously understand her to be trying to claim some kind of street cred.

Colleen felt a different sort of pressure than Kathi to do well in college. Kathi, who would end up majoring in communication and minoring in sociology, mused about potential futures as various as working at a startup and designing jewelry, and while her loving and supportive parents wanted her to find a passion and work hard to succeed at it, they weren't counting on her to support them in return in their old age. Because Kathi, who looked the picture of sleek, tan good health, had had a grave medical scare in high school—a previously undetected heart condition surfaced when she went into cardiac arrest on the way to class and nearly died—she and her family had strong incentive to regard each day on earth as a gift to be treasured in any way that felt meaningful. Colleen, by contrast, knew exactly what she *had* to do with her life. She had wanted to be an elementary school teacher for as long as she could remember, and she would be majoring in elementary education and applied psychology in BC's school of education. She believed that school is where people can equip themselves to move up and make good in the world, and she wanted to help kids do that. She had applied only to colleges and universities with strong education programs—ten of them, as many as she could fit on the FAFSA form that low-income students use to apply for federal financial aid. Even with robust aid, college was a big stretch for her family, and as an only child, she was acutely aware that her working-class parents had made sacrifices for her and were counting on her to move up and prosper.

When I asked Colleen if she felt that a lot was riding on whether she spoke up and did well in Lit Core and at BC in general, she said, "Yeah, well, everything, really. It means everything to me and to my family as well." Beyond the money—"I used to spend a lot of my time worrying about finances, but I'm trying to focus more like 'There will always be worries'"—there was the expectation, the looming sense of high stakes. "My dad, he doesn't say much, he's kind of a tough guy. But I bought him a BC cap and he wears it all the time. Like, that's his way of saying, 'Oh my God, I'm so proud of her.' And then my mom, she always tells me she was never a good student, but any time I'll call her—like, the other day I was complaining about housing and she was like, 'All right, I'm on it, I'm going to check it out.' So knowing that she would do anything to help me further my college career—they're incredibly proud of me, and I'm incredibly proud to be their daughter and to be getting a college education." And, of course, speaking up wasn't just expected in my class, and it wasn't just part of how a student does well in college: it's what teachers *do*. If Colleen couldn't talk in class, how was she going to become a teacher?

Like Kathi, Colleen did the reading and respected and envied other students who seemed to be able to talk with no discomfort, but, also like Kathi, she couldn't get herself across the barrier between silence and speaking. She was a lifelong reader, starting from a childhood taste for fantasy that hit the usual marks: Erin Hunter's warrior cats, Percy Jackson, Harry Potter. She loved books, she knew how to get into them, she wasn't overly skeptical about interpretation, and she had things to say; but, as she described her freshman self's thought process when we talked in her junior year, "I think I just get in my head too much and I'll be practicing what I want to say, if I have an idea, but then I'm just worried that it will sound like not knowing what I'm talking about or the wrong thing." And, of course, like many others in the room, but with an extra shot of class anxiety that made the heart race and the sweat flow even faster, she worried that everyone else had gone to high-powered high schools where they learned exactly the right thing to say and could say it effortlessly whenever they felt like it.

So I set up the same kind of plan with Colleen that I had with Kathi: I'll give you the first question in advance, you prepare something, I'll call on you first, we'll rip the Band-Aid right off. We were still discussing *The Brief Wondrous Life of Oscar Wao*, and I asked everyone to concentrate on a four-page passage late in the novel in which several of its most vivid recurring images—a mysterious golden mongoose, a sinister faceless man, repeated instances of spoken or written language reduced to unreadable blanks—all show up in proximity to each other. I called on Colleen when she raised her hand in response to my first question, which I'd shared with the class in advance. She observed that the faceless man and "paginas en blanco" were both images of something that we—the reader, the characters, the narrator—can't read or don't want to read or are afraid to read. Beautiful. I did my reinforcing due diligence by saying to the class that Colleen's getting us started by pointing out a meaningful connection between two recurring images that each can seem kind of opaque by itself, and we went on from there into a discussion of how the novel uses facelessness and blankness to think about a literal or figurative dictatorship's many efforts to stop people from knowing or believing things that could threaten its grip on power.

When I interviewed Colleen in her junior year, I asked her what had changed for her that allowed her to speak up in Lit Core. "I've thought about that a lot," she said. "It was such a turning point, just that spring semester from the beginning to the end. Fall semester, I was incredibly homesick, even though I'm only three hours away. So then spring semester, I was like, Okay, you know what? College is short. I'm going to enjoy it, and home's not going anywhere. So I was like, All right, great, I'm so happy to be back at BC, I'm gonna have a good time." That mind-set was just beginning to take solid shape when she got the email from me reminding her that she was expected to contribute in class. "I will always remember how you said, Okay, let's work on this." Already thinking like a teacher-in-training, looking to pick up craft from her own teachers, she said, "That was just a huge takeaway: really looking out for your students and seeing them as their own person. And then I had the conversation with you about participation and I was like, Okay, great, I'm going to push myself."

Colleen started raising her hand in Lit Core classes—not a lot, but consistently enough to create a new habit to replace her previous one of swallowing her ideas unsaid. When she pushed herself to do this one thing, she found it easier to push herself to talk in other classes, and other dominos also fell. "Looking back now, I think I've grown in every way, like academically, socially, even emotionally. In my own friendships sometimes I struggle with being quiet. So now I try to say, Okay, well, maybe I'll just start the conversation and then the other person will keep going. And instead of being like Oh, I have nothing to say, well, at least I'll get them talking. It's like participating at the beginning of class, so then you know that you can participate later as well."

.   .   .   .   .

When I asked Kathi what had changed for her, she said that first she'd had to overcome her negative attitude toward thinking interpretively about literature. "Being completely honest, I was like, at the beginning, Okay, this is a core requirement, kind of like, what am I doing here?" She was impressed by other students who had a lot to say, but she also resented them. "Yeah, that's never going to be me. I'm not going to find some weird meaning." She thought back to her bad experience of English classes in high school with the teacher who disliked her; now here was another teacher asking her to "read into" things. Her first reaction was to dig in and resist.

The beginning of the change happened on the first day of class, when I drew on my own experience as a student to describe the nervousness that many people feel about raising their hand in class. "I just remember you said, when you were encouraging us to participate, what happens when you have something you want to say, like you start sweating and then you start to get anxious," Kathi said. "And then I started noticing it with myself, like, I have this comment that I want to share with the class. And then I would not be able to focus on what you were saying and only thinking about what I was going to say to the class." For a few weeks she stewed about it, remaining silent but trying to be more receptive to what was happening in Lit Core. "I kind of opened myself up to it, changed my perspective, and I was like, I could get something out of this." That's what was going on inside her when she got the email from me reminding her that she was expected to speak up. "I remember you met with me and you were like Why aren't you talking? And I was like, Wow, I have this class, I have this teacher, I should open myself up to, you know, finding a deeper meaning. I told myself, I'm a freshman at BC, and this is a completely different course" from the high-school English classes she hated so much. "Obviously you're a different teacher, you're not Miss So-and-So. Let's try to change my attitude a little bit. It's a new experience."

Listening to Kathi and Colleen talk about how they'd done the hard work of pushing themselves to make a change with just the slightest of prods from me, I felt a kind of near-miss horror when I thought how easy it would have been to say to myself *This one's not talking, that one's not talking, but the class is going fine and everyone's a consenting adult and that's just how it's going to be. These two have made their choice, and they'll have to take the hit on their grade.* That's what I would have said to myself earlier in my career, before my daughters got to be of college age and before I'd caught enough glimpses inside the heads of the students sitting in front of me over the years to mend my ways. The genuine satisfaction I feel about the quiet triumphs of Colleen and Kathi in my class is tempered by the realization that I let them go far too long—unnecessary weeks in which they could have been participating and contributing—before intervening, and by the even more sobering realization that over the years I haven't made the minimal effort to reach other students in their situation. I don't have *that* many students, and the effort required of me really is minimal: ten seconds to dash off a not particularly kindly email, twenty minutes of somewhat more gentle conversation in office hours, a scrawled reminder to myself on my class notes to keep an eye out for Kathi's or Colleen's hand, a little extra reinforcing emphasis added to my response to whatever they said. Colleen and Kathi had to make a manyfold greater effort to take what felt to them like a big step, and the payoff was significant and enduring.

Silent students may all seem alike to a frustrated teacher—*What's with college kids these days?*—but each student's silence has a particular provenance and texture, a substrate of lived experience and academic history and inner life. All this backstory goes into creating a mechanical problem that we can address with some fairly straightforward mechanical solutions straight out of the behavioral psychology textbook: lower the bar to speaking in class by setting up the moment in advance; gently reinforce it when it happens; and if the problem's really bad, you can even rehearse and reinforce class participation with the student one-on-one in office hours. Becoming aware of this simple truth opens up possibilities for turning silence into speaking up and the greater engagement and fulfillment that comes with it. And that makes a class better for everyone in the room.

8 Unreliable Narrators

It feels advanced, somehow *adult*, to tangle with an unreliable narrator in a literature class. Students feel that they're in big-league literary company now, running sophisticated set plays against complex zone defenses. No need to content ourselves with pokey old plot and character and theme as they did in high school and even grade school; now we're getting down to business. The narrator's unreliability presents itself as the key to a puzzle, and the need to solve that puzzle makes the book feel like a challenge, a serious game. In the case of Junot Díaz's *The Brief Wondrous Life of Oscar Wao*, the puzzle has a lot of pieces that seem to be scattered all over the place, as in one of those murder mysteries (which *Oscar Wao* sort of is) that strew the reader's path with so many potential clues and red herrings that much of the pleasure lies in watching the detective cut through to the essence of the case. Except now we're the detectives.

In telling the tragic story of a lovelorn, heroically abject Dominican American dork from New Jersey and his extended family, the novel expends significant tranches of energy on an assortment of things that aren't always self-evidently connected. It goes deep on the history of the dictatorial Trujillo regime in the Dominican Republic and the shadow it casts over Oscar's family line and the diaspora in which they take part.

There's copious Spanish and Spanglish in the book, and no glossary. The same goes for Oscar's enthusiasm for science fiction and fantasy, anime, Dungeons and Dragons, and such, the language of which pervades the book to such a degree that the narrator describes beatings by Trujillo's goons in terms of hit points. The novel also has plenty to say about school, especially Rutgers, which Oscar attends along with his fierce sister, Lola, and her one-time boyfriend Yunior. And there are faceless men, talking mongooses, missing and blank pages, and other enigmatic recurring figures. Also, there are no quotation marks around dialogue; there are long discursive footnotes, many of them about Trujillo's monstrous excesses; and there is no end of what those inclined to convene emergency all-school assemblies would describe as hurtful and triggering speech about people's bodies and identities. Between heavy use of such offensive words and constant references to Oscar's fatness and female characters' hotness, or lack thereof, it's not a book that many teachers or students feel comfortable quoting from in class.

Yunior does most of the narrating, though he does not enter the action as a character and identify himself as the narrator until halfway through the book. It was Díaz himself, on a visit to Boston College in 2012, who showed me that concentrating on Yunior-as-narrator is the way to come at this novel in the classroom. During the Q and A after the reading, somebody asked Díaz why he chose Yunior to be the main narrator of *Oscar Wao*, which after its publication in 2007 won all sorts of prizes and rapidly worked its way into the canon of books frequently assigned in college and even high school English courses. To jump-start our discussion of Díaz's novel in Lit Core in spring semester of 2020, we watched video footage of his answer in 2012: "The book does everything to obscure the fact that its subject never speaks," Díaz said. The reader of "a book which constantly refers to people's missing voices, and missing chapters, and missing pages has to ask, Why is the biggest absence of the book the person who's most present in some ways? So the question is, Why does Oscar not speak? As a reader, in some ways that's the book's final chapter. I mean, the book actually invites you to write the final chapter." At the end, Yunior admits that he can't complete the story of Oscar's family on his own, leaving it up to a very minor and belatedly introduced character to maybe someday pick up the still-scattered pieces and put them together—

which means, Díaz said, that it's really left up the reader. Yunior "puts the pieces together that he has, and he leaves it for the next person to come along to write the book—to, like, to kind of finish it." Ticking off items on his fingers, Díaz said that among the questions that such a figurative final chapter should answer would be not only the main one—"Why does Oscar not speak, and why is Yunior telling the story?"—but also a cascade of further mysteries related to it: "Who the fuck is the man without a face and who the fuck are the talking mongooses? You know? What the fuck does all this nerd shit have to do with any of it?" This led him to his main point: "And it's okay to read the book and not write a final chapter, but the book actually yields an enormous amount of rewards if you think it through and come up with some answers for yourself. Suddenly it becomes a very different book. In fact, I can tell you, people who take a stab at answering the question Why does Oscar never speak? are given a completely different novel than anyone who's read it and doesn't ask that question. The novel becomes incredibly sinister in ways that it's not sinister right off the bat."*

It becomes even more sinister when you consider that Oscar's an aspiring writer, prolifically unpublished, and that he may well have written his own story in the form of letters and fantasy fiction—but Yunior won't let us see any of that, forcing us to rely on him instead. Díaz explained why Yunior's an ideal narrator for a novel that aspires to at once exemplify conventional masculinity and offer a "feminist-allied" critique of it. Yunior, he said, "participates in most of the practices and privileges of a kind of Central Jersey Dominican immigrant patriarchal masculinity," yet "his imaginary allows him to conceptualize alternatives." Like a soloist topping off a dense thicket of modal noodling with a nasty blues lick, he followed up that high-theory mouthful with a cogent kicker: "In other words, Yunior's a fucked-up dude who can dream of a better way but just can't get there."

He didn't add that Yunior is also his ideal narrator because, like the characters Spike Lee and Woody Allen play in their own movies, Yunior strikes an idealized version of the author's own pose. Like Díaz, Yunior tries hard to impress the reader by presenting experiential and intellectual credentials to effect a double envelopment I think of as the high-low split,

---

* You can find Díaz's remarks on YouTube: https://www.youtube.com/watch?v =FI5dtK1OfzI. The Q and A begins at 28:25.

a move also attempted by Saul Bellow and Don DeLillo: *Did I mention that I'm a regular guy from around the way? Did I also mention that I'm a literary sophisticate who grapples with Big Ideas?* (If you want to see the high-low split done more effectively—more subtly, modestly, convincingly—try Stuart Dybek or Gwendolyn Brooks.) Díaz might well have been talking about himself when he described Yunior at BC in 2012. The storm of public commentary that developed around Díaz in 2018 after multiple women accused him of forcible kissing and verbal abuse, which inspired others to speak up in his defense, was all about the extent to which he should be seen as a writer who gets credit for advancing a feminist-allied critique of patriarchal masculinity while enjoying the power over others that this conventional order conferred on him. And Díaz's response to the accusations, especially in an essay in the *New Yorker* about being raped at the age of eight, could be read as presenting himself as a fucked-up dude who can dream of a better way but just can't get there.

Taking up Díaz's invitation, I made Yunior our main focus. That's the promise of an unreliable narrator: figure out what it means that this character is telling the story—and telling it in such a shifty way that you're forced to consider what other ways to tell it may appear through the cracks and in the recesses of the narrator's version—and other pieces will fall into place.

.   .   .   .   .

There were a few students who didn't warm to *Oscar Wao*. To Stella, it felt like a literary comedown after the elegance of *The House of Mirth*. Dara said, "I'm kind of exaggerating, but it was kind of traumatizing, like with the violence and everything. I remember reading it at night, and I was like, 'Now I have to go to sleep.'" Bill just said he didn't love it, declining to specify why. But most everyone else I interviewed expressed enthusiasm for the novel, and several told me afterward that it was their favorite reading of the semester.

They found it exciting and welcoming, even when it confused them. Despite all the unfamiliar words, most found it easy to read, especially after *The House of Mirth*. And even though the book was almost as old as they were, Dalha and Matteo and others found the rhythm and texture of its language familiar, contemporary. That went for the pace, too, which, after Wharton, felt like switching channels from *Koyaanisqatsi* to *Ren and Stimpy*. As Tyler put it, "That was also a good combination of theme as well as just engaging material—like, there was always something new happening. He almost got killed multiple times. So I thought it was sort of on the surface level just super interesting and engaging." Beyond the surface level, Paul said, "I remember it was written very well, in a way that was enjoyable to read. And then, in combination with class, looking out for the themes and motifs and metaphors and all that, I really enjoyed it." Eva and Luke appreciated the fictional window the novel opened onto Dominican culture and history. As had been the case with *The House of Mirth*, Arun found resonance between Oscar's situation and his own: "Again, yeah, because he had some complications with his immigrant background, his family and stuff. I guess maybe everyone can somewhat, I guess, see themselves as Oscar in some situations. That was something that definitely helps understand the character in the book." Arun, Nina, Dave, and Susannah all singled out the mystery of the narrator as an attraction. Jonah, who finds it hard to sit still and read, conferred his highest praise on *Oscar Wao*: he bought the book after we finished reading it, having previously rented it for the course, and he said that he intended to read it again at some point.

We had three weeks to get through *Oscar Wao*, one week before spring break and two after, so we could start slowly and ease our way into it. We weren't going to get all the pieces assembled right away, obviously, and since we were reading it in measured chunks, we weren't even going to find out that Yunior's the narrator until after spring break, so we started by working with what we had in front of us: getting a sense of the style of the book and starting to consider what at least some of the pieces had to do with each other.

When we were offering first impressions of the book, just making a pile of what we noticed, Wilson raised his hand to say that he thought that the lack of quotation marks was "genius." When I asked why, he said, "Who knew that you don't need them to understand that people are talking? It just flows along with no break and you can still see what's happening." Why is that genius? "It makes it feel more like one big flow, one story, like it's all coming from one voice, even the stuff that other people are supposed to be saying. And, I mean, it makes you think, like, what *else* don't you need?" On the subject of what you might need or not need, we also considered what all the unglossaried Spanish and Spanglish and all the unexplicated references to science fiction, fantasy, anime, and gaming do to a reader who might not speak those languages. I gave them the URL of an online glossary created by an obsessive fan that does, in fact, explain what most of those possibly unfamiliar words and references mean, but the novel itself throws them at you with no such safety net.[†] Some students said they felt shut out by all the language that was initially opaque to them, others that their curiosity was piqued in ways that made them want to figure things out from context, ask friends, look things up, become more active as readers. There were a couple of native Spanish speakers in the class, and others who had studied Spanish, and they all had pretty much the same range of reactions: in some ways they were made to feel like insiders by understanding more than other readers did, but some noted that the Jersey Dominican specificity of the novel's Spanish vocabulary actually pushed them away by undermining the sense of authority they expected to enjoy as Spanish speakers.

Others zeroed in on how from the beginning we're forced to wonder why both the at-first-unnamed main narrator and Lola are so hard on Oscar. The main narrator knows Oscar and seems to be his friend, but he relates with altogether too much relish Oscar's descent into pariah status. And Lola, for her part, is so worried that her brother will be picked on and shunned that she, too, keeps reminding him that he's a fat loser as she urges him to change in self-defense. Either way, it's continually hammered home to us that Dominican boys and men just can't be unlaid nerds, which makes Oscar a classic misfit. His sensitivity and the meanness he encounters on all sides brought back memories of high school that were still fresh for the students, a familiar situation rendered by the novel as high tragedy worthy of ambitious and stylish literary treatment.

We were talking, I reminded them, about something that every book does to its reader. A book trains, creates the reader it requires by defining an identity (one technical term for this is a *subject position*) for you to inhabit while you read it. This is true of any text. If you watch a slasher

† The fan's DIY glossary can be found at http://www.annotated-oscar-wao.com.

movie, on some level you agree to take appreciative note of the well-stocked knife rack in a remote cabin visited by a group of curious and attractive young people and to await with interest the inevitable spectacle of those knives ripping through those screaming attractive young people. If you watch a romcom, you agree to anguish over whether the couple who have met cute and now claim to loathe each other will ever find a way to get back together again, even though you know they will. And when you read *Oscar Wao*, you agree to be simultaneously drawn in and kept at a distance by the avalanche of wildly various allusions, jargon, and historical references—the importance of all being underscored by a couple of dozen long footnotes in tiny print, just enough to show that we'd need hundreds more of them to get all the references. So nobody other than the narrator is *supposed* to get every last thing, which makes us wonder what we're missing and what it might mean.

We stored away for later consideration the question of why, or to what effect, the book wants us to feel and wonder that way. We also stored away for later consideration the significance of the obvious fact that while the narrator is eager to persuade us that Oscar's a defective Dominican male because he directs the energy he should be devoting to bedding girls toward learning Elvish and nerding out on E. E. Doc Smith's Lensman series, that narrator *also* knows Elvish words and is so conversant with the oeuvre of Smith that he can refer to such esoterica with a knowing off-handedness bound to leave many readers behind.

We spent some time on dictatorship and the question of what it might have to do with Oscar's story. In our discussions, we noted that much of what we learn about Trujillo has to do with his famously enormous appetite for sexual predation, an endlessly consummated desire to possess every woman in his domain who catches his eye. He's not just an all-powerful political leader; he's a monstrous totem of masculine potency, and much of what we learn about Oscar goes toward characterizing him as the opposite of that: always in love but never doing anything decisive about it, too soft and shy and serially beaten down to do more than suffer. This turned into a discussion of dictatorship as an all-purpose figure of any order that's not only enforced by overt violence but is also so pervasive in a culture that it gets into your mind and eventually obliges you to enforce it on yourself and those around you. That's how a totalitarian political system works, but it's also, at least to some extent, how social norms work—like those defining how to be a man or a woman. *Does doing this or wearing that make me gay, or maybe guarantee that I'm not?* That was a subject bound to resonate in a room full of eighteen-year-olds who were trying to figure out who the hell they were, and it also got us thinking again about the narrator. Dictators—like any political leader, only more cartoonishly—enforce and secure their rule not just by busting heads but also by controlling the stories that we tell about our history, our relationship to power, ourselves. That's one reason they so frequently imprison, torture, murder, and otherwise silence writers. All the more reason to keep an eye on this mysterious, pushy, highly motivated, prolix and yet withholding narrator.

So, okay, we had picked out some pieces of the novel and spread them out on our workbench and even tentatively put together a couple of them in a provisional way. When we got back from spring break, we'd lay out the rest of the pieces and try to solve the puzzle.

·　　·　　·　　·　　·

The first half of the semester had gone pretty well, I thought. This Lit Core class was turning out to be a good group: game, hardworking, serious enough about doing things well but with a sense of humor. There was skepticism, of course, and not everybody did the reading every time, and some of them just didn't like English or me or BC or school or whatever and weren't inclined to commit much of themselves to this required core course. But between class discussions and papers and one-on-one conversations in my office and on email, I could see that the norm in this community of inquiry, the middle of the road where most of the students hung out, was to do the work I asked them to do and care about what I asked them to care about. When I asked a question, I had confidence that they'd take a shot at considering and answering it—not just whoever spoke up in response that time but also many of those who didn't. When they asked a question, I'd do my best to answer it, if there was an answer and I knew it, or, even better, to turn it into a problem we could all constructively wrestle with. And they had shown me that they'd generally be up for wrestling with whatever came at them. That's really all I could ask for, and all I need.

At the most basic level, I have to feel that I'm getting back more energy than I'm putting into a class. No individual student has to match my expenditure—after all, what we do in class is part of my profession, a chosen craft that I've been at for decades and get paid for—but as a group they have to come back at me with more energy than I'm putting in.

I felt, crucially, that we had come to have sufficient faith in each other. I had been doing my best to show them the clear purpose in everything we did. I wanted them to always know how each move we made, each problem we set for ourselves and tried to solve, would advance us toward the twin objectives of a humanities class: developing intellectual skill (understanding how meaning flows through language) and considering how to live (examining what happens to social misfits). For their part, they had showed me and each other that I could count on them to meet me at least halfway, to make an honest effort to pick up and use the tools I handed them, to sit with problems and even flounder a little and not give up. There was never going to be one right answer in this classroom, which continued to bother some of the more computation-minded among them, but we had, I hoped, clearly established that there were more and less effective ways to come up with an answer that worked. And I had done everything I could to demonstrate that mastering those ways was a learnable craft, a basic life skill available to all, not sorcery or bullshit or some mystical something that only a select crew of literary sophisticates could do.

This group had fairly good chemistry, especially for a big discussion class, which was the result of some combination of luck and my efforts at making the classroom a place where people felt they belonged and could speak their minds, although the necessary proportion of each ingredient in the combination remains a mystery to me. Sometimes a class's chemistry just doesn't work out all that well, no matter how hard or expertly you try, and sometimes it works out just fine, no matter how sorry a job you do. In this case, good chemistry had helped forge the students into a reasonably strong group of in-class talkers. There was a sizable minority who contributed steadily and prolifically: Stella, Dan, Dave, Paul, Tyler, Marguerite, Wilson, Luke, Jonah, Nina, Arthur, Bill, and more. There were just enough loose cannons—Eli, Dan, Jonah—and plenty of troupers. Almost all of the rest qualified as anted-up regulars, contributing enough to satisfy the letter of my expectations, and several of this group—Susannah, Dara, Arun,

Jenny, Charlotte, Matteo, Dalha, David—could be counted on to have something valuable and even surprising to say, although they weren't always among the most talkative. A handful had fallen off the pace and gone silent, and it was high time for me to address those cases individually, which I had already begun to do with Kathi and Colleen. Arriving at spring break, I felt like the coach of an NFL team going into the bye week with a 6-3 record and a reasonable expectation of making the playoffs. We had our system down, a sense of how to work together to get things done and meet fresh challenges, enough confidence and trust in each other to believe that a judicious combination of plugging away at our respective jobs and taking chances when inspiration struck would produce good results.

A college semester is like a shuttle flight—mostly takeoff and landing, without much middle. You're lifting off, getting settled in with the whole journey still in front of you, and then suddenly it's time for tray tables to come up and seatbacks to return to their upright position. I could see the remainder of this semester laid out before us. We would finish Díaz after spring break, then move on to Proulx's dark but vivid *Accordion Crimes*, then turn at the end to the nonfiction of Joan Didion and at least nominal nonfiction of Hunter S. Thompson. Though Didion and Thompson wrote about the counterculture of the late 1960s and early 1970s, a period in some ways just as distant and alien for these students as Wharton's Gilded Age, the texts we read in this final unit would serve as a sort of airlock between literature and news by letting us apply the skill set we had so far honed on fiction to writing that purports to tell true stories about the actual world around us. It was particularly easy in the spring of 2020 to make the case that the kinds of interpretive skills we were working on were also basic equipment for citizens. We were three-plus years into the presidency of Donald Trump, who even his admirers would concede was the most baroque and brazen unreliable narrator to ever hold an office that specializes in them, and the 2020 presidential campaign was in full swing. Part of the something very adult about learning to reckon with an unreliable narrator is that you feel you're learning something useful about how to reckon with people in general, about how to live. These are skills we use in every phase of our lives as we decode and evaluate the stories we're told, not just by politicians, bosses, pundits, advertisers, and influencers but also by family, friends, lovers, strangers, ourselves.

9 Surprise Midterm

Over spring break I flew down to Texas and spent a couple of days tagging along on the tour bus with Midland, a country band about whom I was writing a magazine story. At a backstage meet-and-greet with fans at NRG Stadium in Houston, where Midland was headlining opening night of the rodeo, there was polite laughter all around when a woman said, "I hope we don't give you the virus" as she reluctantly broke from a photo-op clinch with Mark Wystrach, the band's almost self-parodically handsome lead singer.* Everyone could feel the pandemic coming, but it didn't seem quite real yet. Public health experts suggesting that the rodeo should be canceled were still being shouted down by those claiming that this virus was a hoax or a New York and California kind of thing, blown out of proportion by coastal elites. The magazine had just grounded all travel for reporting, but only after I had already flown to Texas, so I was able to stick around to finish what I'd come to do. The coming of Covid felt at once like an unprecedented disaster and something very ancient and familiar—a plague descending on the herd, the tribe. I had an inkling of what to

---

* The story about Midland appeared as "They're Bringing Back Cheatin' Songs," *Washington Post Magazine*, July 18, 2020, 18–25.

expect because we knew a family in Xi'an who had been locked down for months. They mostly stayed home, the daughter out of school and the parents prevented from going to work. The father was the only one who left the apartment regularly, and every time he returned home he would go through an elaborate routine of doing laundry and showering to expunge any trace of the virus.

Still, I wasn't really ready for what was coming. Even knowing what was on the way, I was like a dog at the edge of the highway who can see cars approaching and knows they are moving fast but can't truly appreciate their speed or calculate what it has to do to reach the other side safely. All I could manage was a vague sense that I would likely have to hole up for a while with my wife and daughters, which would first entail prevailing on our older daughter and her boyfriend to get out of his rented room in a shared basement apartment in Cambridge and move into our guest room for the duration of the crisis. My parents were retired, living in an apartment in Manhattan, and my father had serious lung damage that wasn't ever going to get better. Should they dig in where they were, or should my brothers and I convince them to leave the city and ride out the plague time in the house they owned outside New Hope, Pennsylvania? Should they come stay with us or with one of my brothers? How much time did my father have left, and how would we balance the prospect of him having to spend that time in isolation from kids and grandkids with the need to protect him from a respiratory virus that seemed very likely to kill him if he caught it? Then there were my brothers and their families to worry about, as well as friends, neighbors, and colleagues. And students, of course. Could we just get back to business as usual when spring break ended? School normally seems timeless and eternal, a constant of existence, an immovable object, but the coming of Covid looked to be an irresistible force. It was hard to picture the impending collision and its consequences.

After spring break, we tried to get back to business in Lit Core. We had one class meeting in which we discussed the Trujillo-haunted backstory of Oscar's mother, Beli, but we were all distracted by the spectacle of the city and the nation, the world, shutting down. We watched other schools in town close and send students home—Harvard, MIT, BU, Northeastern, Tufts, Brandeis—and wondered when BC's administrators would accept that they had to do the same. Like the people who ran the Houston rodeo, like all the other dogs at the edge of the highway, they had been trying to proceed as normally as possible and thinking that perhaps just a little adjustment here and there would do the trick. But, like everyone else, they had to give up on that. Finally, an email went out announcing that campus would close, except for some dorms that would remain open for the few students who couldn't or wouldn't go home for some reason. Classes would shut down for a grace period of a couple of weeks while faculty and staff scrambled to retool, then restart online. There was this app called Zoom, see, and . . . well, we'd figure it out, details to come.

Lit Core had one more class meeting in person to discuss what would happen next. When in my later interviews with students we talked about how they felt at this moment, they remembered vividly how unsettled, freaked out, sad, angry, and scared they had been. Several of them had also been hung over. The email announcement the previous day that the university would be closing had set off a frenzy of drinking, smoking, cranking of tunes, dancing, weeping, late-night declarations that I love you guys, and the sort of half-hearted vandalism that well-behaved kids will indulge in when they kind-of-sort-of lose control but not really. One Lit Core student woke up covered in his own vomit. "I'm not like someone who can't control himself, but it was just a whole different—a crazy time," he told me. "You'd walk through the dorm and all the tiles of the ceiling would be on the floor." The blowout left many of them looking worse for wear when they filed into class just before noon the next day and found their usual seats. They were also worried about parents, grandparents, siblings, friends, and themselves—including at least a couple of kids in the room who had significant medical conditions that put them at greater risk.

Above all, they were profoundly disoriented by the widespread feeling of being hurled off the path to life—adult life, the rest of life, the good life—just as they were finding their feet on it. Getting through the fearsomely guarded gate of college admissions had put the most obviously daunting obstacle behind them, but a lot of them had struggled in the fall semester with the usual challenges posed by freshman year. They'd found it difficult to cope with a college course load while learning to be in charge of themselves, making new friends, and fashioning a revised next-stage self that could manage all those needful things. Come spring, though, they were just starting to settle into more workable academic and domestic routines, fall in with friend groups that felt as if they might last, see possible majors and interests and scenes that could prove sustaining and even exciting—a whole range of interestingly shaped vessels into which they could imagine pouring themselves. Now that was all being yanked away, and they'd have to pour their new selves-in-progress back into old containers. It felt like a defeat to go back to hometowns they thought they'd left in their dust, family homes in which they were the dutiful or sullen children and their parents still called the shots, old bedrooms still stocked with childhood furniture and wall art and trophies and stuffies. And was the more or less painful financial stretch that many of their families were making to send them to college going to be wasted, in part or in full? It felt as if they'd boarded a very expensive and much-anticipated flight to Kathmandu, gotten seven hours out over the ocean, and then been informed by the pilot that they had to return to Newark because passengers were exhibiting mysterious flu-like symptoms.

An inbuilt affinity for disaster impels me to read a lot about earthquakes, floods, invasions, storms, plagues, climate change, and such. In those books, I've often encountered the principle that it's critically important to get schools open as soon as possible after disaster strikes because it gives kids and their parents a sense of restored order and normalcy. Accordingly, my main objective in this class meeting was to reassure everyone that school would go on, that their teachers would be looking out for them, and that we in this community we had built in section 20 of Lit Core would all find our way together to the finish line of the semester. If they continued to put in the work, they would come away from this course with the competences and knowledge and cultural capital and academic credits that they were supposed to get out of Lit Core, and I would do whatever I could to ensure that they and their families would get their money's worth. It wouldn't be exactly the same as we'd planned and expected, but we would all adjust and, as the guy says in *The Outlaw Josey Wales*, endeavor to persevere.

The university had just issued news of an emergency policy change I could pass along to allay students' academic anxieties. For this semester only, it would be easier to withdraw from classes without penalty; there was temporarily no limit on the number or type of courses a student could take pass-fail, instead of for a letter grade; and the deadline to declare the pass-fail option would be moved much deeper into the semester, all the way to the end of classes, so that a student could wait to have a pretty good idea of how things were going to come out before making that decision. I wouldn't even know what each of them had decided until it was time for me to assign grades at the end of the semester, so their decision wouldn't affect how I responded to their work.

This all made them feel better. I could see it in their faces, in their bodies. Yes, they were young adults, newly and excitingly in charge of themselves and on their way to running the world, but in this time of crisis, they were relieved to hear that grown-ups in familiar positions of authority had a plan to take care of them. There was a tenderness, a tentativeness, a quality of hurt in the students' manner that day that reminded me that they were just kids—and kids (as well as nonkids, of course) do sometimes really just need to hear that somebody they trust is going to make sure that everything's okay. I felt better because they felt better; I felt like I was doing some good.

Dan raised his hand. He said, "If all the weaker students who were going to get a lower grade anyway take the pass-fail option and drop out of the curve, then do the stronger students who keep taking the class for a grade get penalized because the curve gets skewed so it's harder to make an A?" Ah, Dan, our leading loose cannon, taking the opportunity to fire off one more smokily defiant blast. The blend of confidence and nervousness in his voice indicated that he felt that this hard thing had to be said whether anybody liked it or not. He had fallen into the posture he usually struck after making a point he knew would be controversial: sitting back in his chair and inclined a little to his right, his right hand to his face, the set of a man who has just landed an I-boldly-submit-to-you zinger, but a little over-stiff in the backbone, betraying concern that he might have overstepped and offended. His fellow students looked as if they'd each been slapped in the face by a bespoke service that customizes the force and angle of the slap to fit individual recipients' unique facial structure and psychological profile.

I took a second before responding, and I tried to keep my tone gentle and explanatory, but I wanted to be firm enough to head off his mistaken perception of a threat to his GPA before he stampeded others in the same direction. I said, Well, first, the university's saying that everybody makes their own decision about whether to take the course pass-fail, and it's not useful to think of that decision in terms of strength or weakness. There's a lot of uncertainty; we're each going home, or wherever, to a different situation, and everybody will have to decide what their own situation will allow them to do, what other academic demands and family demands and life demands they will have on them, what they feel is going to work best for them. And, second, there is no curve. There never is, in my classes, and that hasn't changed. It's never happened yet in a class of mine that everybody does A work, but, in theory, if that did happen then everybody gets an A. And if nobody does A work, then nobody gets an A. All I can tell you is that in this class, I will do my best to make it just about as possible as before to do good work and do well, though some of the mechanics will have to change. We'll figure it out, and we'll make sure nobody gets cheated by the adjustments we have to make.

.   .   .   .   .

I started receiving emails from campus entities to which I'd never paid any attention before, like something called the Center for Teaching Excellence. My default response to any email I get from any administrative office at any school at which I work has always been to delete it after a two-second skim of the subject heading and lead paragraph, but now I sifted through explanations of how to use Zoom, Canvas, Panopto, Perusall, and such to teach online. I was grateful for the expert advice, but I found it opaque, and I knew there was no way that I was going to get briskly up to speed on the newest latest, which has never been a strength of mine. If each of us has a technology threshold—a point in life at which anything else that comes along afterward will cause you to say, "That's amazing! What will they think of next?"—then mine falls somewhere around Space Invaders and ATMs, well short of the personal computer and cellphone. I'm basically an eleventh-century guy who likes email because it's just a regular old letter carried by an extremely fast horse, so I was looking for at best a workable bare-bones arrangement that would allow me to deliver the essentials of my courses without screwing up too badly or too often.

I started paying attention to those emails from the Center for Teaching Excellence, and I knocked around some ideas with colleagues at other schools and in my department, though we couldn't help each other much.

Those who had advanced technical command found it difficult to talk down to the level of those who didn't, and those who didn't had little to contribute. Mostly I talked with my wife, Tina, who was figuring out how to move her own courses online. She's no tech wiz—in fact, she radiates a natural force field that causes electronic devices to malfunction when she touches or even passes near to them—but she's naturally far more inclined than I am to find out how others are addressing a problem, adapt their most useful ideas, and otherwise execute the best-practices tango with competence and grace. So she was going to get fancier about breakout rooms and jamboards and such than I was. The sudden shift to online teaching felt like a surprise midterm exam for which Tina was prepared and I wasn't, and no amount of cramming would get me up to speed.

On YouTube I watched an online-teaching-themed update of Gloria Gaynor's "I Will Survive" by a historian at Missouri University of Science and Technology named Michael Bruening. He had a pleasing voice, the rewrite was deft ("It took all the strength I had not to lay down and die / Kept trying hard to mend the pieces of my syllabi"), and the aesthetic of the video felt like the dawning of a new order. The up-canted camera angle, the sound of his voice and acoustic guitar acquiring a lonely echo as it bounced off the hard expanse of white ceiling and bookshelved wall behind him, the previously overlooked HVAC register up high in the background becoming a slightly sinister visual character in its own right—it seemed like a taste of life on a planet we would all soon inhabit.[†]

I contemplated and even did some preliminary test samples of a shift in the rhythm of my Lit Core class in which I would record lectures or write letters that would lay out course content. The idea was that students could watch or read these on their own time (*asynchronous* was the term of art, I learned) along with doing the reading, and then we could use live (*synchronous*) class time on Zoom to have a Q and A session in which the students could ask whatever they needed to ask to clarify and deepen their grasp of what they'd gotten from me in the lectures or letters. But I soon realized that this approach, while it seemed well suited in some ways to teaching online, felt like too much of a departure from what we had been doing. If the whole point of the class had been to have a conversation in

† Watch Bruening's chef d'oeuvre at https://www.youtube.com/watch?v=CCe5PaeAeew.

which we analyzed literature together and the students did the essential work, switching to a model based on my telling them what I thought seemed like a different project entirely. And we'd be giving up on community, recasting the class as not much more than a series of parallel but essentially solitary attempts to master material I fed them. It was already that to some degree, as any class is, but it was also to a significant degree a conversation among members of a community of inquiry, and I didn't want to give up on that.

Finally, I decided to try to just keep doing online pretty much what we had been doing in person: do the reading, meet at noon for seventy-five minutes on Tuesday and Thursday, try to solve analytical problems in conversation together. It wasn't going to work anywhere near as well as before, but it was better than any alternatives I could think of. I did make a few changes, though.

I cut Annie Proulx's *Accordion Crimes* out of the syllabus, replacing it with a handful of short stories we could cover in much less time. *Accordion Crimes* is a hell of a novel, sweeping and vibrant and full of music and word-music and spectacularly dire storytelling, but we had already lost a couple of weeks to the pandemic, and it seemed foolhardy to try to squeeze the same amount of material into considerably fewer class meetings. I was sorry to see it go, but I was also a bit relieved, given the new situation. Proulx's fiction often grows from her research on strange and often terrible things that actually happened to people in the past, and *Accordion Crimes* enthusiastically visits an unrelenting litany of bad luck and affliction on its characters. There's the one who falls into a steaming geyser and manages to crawl out, parboiled half to death, only to fall into a bigger, hotter geyser; there's the one who succumbs to a galloping fatal infection after paying a turn-of-the-century charlatan to sew goat testicles into his scrotum to revive his potency; you get the idea. Reading this stuff during the initial upsurge of a deadly global pandemic might have felt a little too tonally on the nose.

I added a new kind of writing assignment, a weekly exercise that would give students a regular chance to order and articulate their thoughts about what they were reading in advance of discussing it. Usually no longer than three hundred words, written in response to a question about the reading for that week, these exercises would not be miniature papers; rather, they would be a written form of class participation, another way for students to show that they were doing the reading and thinking about it as they got ready for class. I came to like these exercises a great deal and now use them in most of my undergraduate classes. They help hold students accountable for reading and thinking in advance of class; they help them prepare for class; and, as a bonus, they have allowed me to finally do away entirely with midterms and finals, which I never liked and used sparingly anyway. This is all in keeping with basic principles of behavior modification. If you're looking to improve performance, it's better to provide lots of regular, timely, low-stakes opportunities for students to practice what we do and show that they're keeping up than to rely on infrequent, high-stakes exams that primarily function as deferred reward or punishment after the fact for a student who has or hasn't been doing the work. If a student's slipping, I want to know right away, when we can still do something about it. (And if you're thinking that ChatGPT will now make these exercises less effective, that concern has occurred to me but hasn't yet become significant enough for me to alter the policy. The more I base the writing prompt on our class discussions, the more difficult it is to outsource the job to AI.)

I also had to switch to reading and grading papers electronically, since the students had scattered far and wide and I could no longer collect printed-out papers. This was a reversal from my previous policy of insisting on receiving everything as hard copy. I much prefer to read on paper, and I can line-edit and comment on hard copy by hand much faster than I can do it on a keyboard, but that creates an enormous disadvantage for the students that I should have put more weight on before the pandemic forced me to change. I have the worst handwriting I've ever seen, a pseudocursive connected-print chicken scratch so bad that I frequently can't read it myself. I do plead mitigating historical circumstance: I attended a terrific K–12 school, the University of Chicago's Laboratory Schools, which is still to my mind the best school I've ever had anything to do with, but the teachers there included a significant number of period-appropriate Deweyite acid casualties who had little interest in enforcing The Plastic-Fantastic Establishment's handwriting norms. Whoever's to blame, the fact remains that it's often difficult to read the comments I write by hand on papers. In the past, when I returned a stack of papers, students would line up after class to ask me to read my comments to them because they couldn't make them out. This problem had only gotten worse as reading other people's handwriting became an esoteric practice for young people. So the pandemic forced me to make a switch I should have made years before—to receiving, marking, and returning papers electronically, which is how I do it all the time now in every class.

·   ·   ·   ·   ·

Snugged up like a wintering rodent in the office under the eaves of my house, I spent the shank of March revising the syllabus and retooling for online teaching, revisiting some deferred writing projects for which I'd already done the legwork, playing steel guitar, and corresponding with similarly holed-up friends and family. I left this hidey-hole to go for long runs along the empty expanse of Route 9 and to take midday walks with Tina and our daughters, during which other walkers appeared in the distance but came no closer, like figures seen against the horizon on a postapocalyptic journey. Meanwhile, the students in the class were going to ground in their own pandemic retreats.

Most went home, though a couple moved into the eerily depopulated dorms the university kept open for the three hundred or so students remaining on campus. Stella, who had mixed feelings about returning to Korea, decided not to go back to Seoul until the end of the school year. Similarly, Luke decided that he would rather not rush back to Laurel, Montana, the railroad town outside Billings he had hoped to leave far behind him. Seeing his family and the natural beauty of Montana still appealed to him, but his hometown didn't. "It's a very dry, unwelcoming place," he told me later. "You're there, and you just—I just feel instantly depressed, if I'm being really honest. Like, I'll step off the plane and I know this week is going to be kind of a drag. There's just not much to do. And people can be very cold." He had been a high-school overachiever—honors, debate, cross-country, every teacher's pick to make it in the wider world—and one of only three in his class to attend college out of state. "It's a very small world; people live in somewhat of a bubble," he said. "I didn't enjoy it a whole lot, and I was picked on and stuff for coming here and everything. It's very taboo, almost, to leave Montana. You know, like, What are you going to learn there that you can't learn here? Who are those liberals out there to tell you what to do? The normal stuff. They don't want anyone coming into Montana, either. It's pretty awful."

Living on the mostly abandoned campus was grim and stark. He was relocated to a basement hall in which all but one of the other rooms were empty, and that one occupied by the RA. The only time he saw people was when he stood six feet apart from them in line at the dining hall, and everybody took their food back to their own room to eat. They had to leave all of their personal items behind when they stood in line for food, and once, two shouting dining hall employees pulled a guy out of line and sent him to resanitize because he had touched the volume button on his corded earphones. But, still, Luke thought that his classmates would feel bad if they saw that he had been allowed to stay at BC when they had been forced to go home, so when he attended class on Zoom he tried to set up the background so that we couldn't tell he was still at BC.

Susannah went back to Gorham, Maine, where, similarly to Luke, she was perceived as one of the few who had presumed to go Away. Her feeling about her hometown did not resemble Luke's animus toward his; in fact, she missed the small-town feel of knowing everyone when she walked into the diner that everybody went to, but she did feel marked out because she was one of perhaps ten kids in the graduating class of her public high school who went out of state to college and one of only three she knew of who went to a "fancy" college. (The others went to Northeastern and Bentley, also in Boston, the nearest major city and apparently the most exotic far-distant destination imaginable.) Like Luke, though less acutely, she felt the growing distance between herself and those who had stayed and were still caught up in the same familiar circle of partying and romances and locally circumscribed life plans that she'd left behind. She found herself less and less motivated to dive back into it. She told me, "I went home back to Maine and it was kind of like—well, part of it was nice: I love spending time with my family; I'm really close with them; it was nice seeing them all the time. But I was busy. I went to my local grocery store and I said, 'Give me an application,' and I started, I worked like twenty hours a week while taking classes. I was, like, I'm going to be home, I'm going to be making money."

Like both Stella and Luke, Susannah was one of the minority of students in Lit Core who felt acutely that the others in the room came from money and they didn't, so in at least one way, returning to Maine meant coming back to something that felt more like real life. "That's one thing about being at school," she said. "The financial pressures are definitely different for me than some of my friends." She meant that she didn't spend any effort on worrying about finding a primo hotel room in Cabo for spring break or whether it was time to ditch last year's knee-high $910 leather boots for this year's midcalf $960 leather boots. "Money is always tight with my family," she said. "So when I went back, I was 'I like to be able to control my own finances and stuff, and I'm going to have all this free time, and I'll be working.' And so I wasn't as bored as most people were at home."

At the other end of the financial spectrum, Wilson's father had a brainwave at the start of the pandemic. "My dad and my mom called me and they were like, Hey, we're going to go to Miami because they heard the heat kills coronavirus," he told me later. "So I flew to Miami. I was there, staying at a nice place, and then all of a sudden, like a week in, they closed the beaches. So my dad's like, 'All right, let's just go back home.'" Being back home on Long Island wore on Wilson, who described himself as a guy who needs to "go outside, play, do a sport, *do* something—that's how my body works. I needed something. Sitting inside was tough." It was especially tough on him because the pandemic had blown up his freshman hockey season, which had been going as well as it possibly could have gone. "We were the number-one team in the country, we were on a twelve-game winning streak, we had just beat Northeastern 10–1 a week before; we would probably have won the national championship that year. I was having a great year. It was awful." The owner of a local gym let Wilson and a friend work out there an hour a day, and he played a lot of golf. Though golf, like hockey, is meaningless static to me, I sympathized. I feel a similar urge to move around and cover ground, and I had fallen into the habit of running along Route 9, which was shunned by other runners and walkers, which meant that I didn't have to put up much with the early pandemic routine of being ordered to put on a mask by people so far away from me that they had to shout to make themselves heard.

The pandemic hit some students' families particularly hard and stretched them tight. For instance, Peter's parents worked in medical manufacturing, which made them essential workers, so he had to take on much of the load of taking care of his younger siblings, who were home from school. Only one student found an instant silver lining in the crisis. Dan was "absolutely thrilled" to go home and take an enforced break from the sick-making pressure of freshman year while BC retooled for online classes. He said, "Covid, honest to God, Covid to me felt like nothing short of a miracle." Most of them were just bored and frazzled and at loose ends, knocking around middle-class suburban houses with little energy or sense of direction. They had more time than ever to read and prepare for class, but they were unmotivated, distracted, and the prospect of class on Zoom wasn't very appealing. Moving online drastically narrowed the aperture through which interest, engagement, curiosity, and feeling could flow back and forth between student and subject matter, student and fellow students, student and teacher. It was going to be something less like having class in person and something more like watching imperfectly interactive TV.

So we got back to it on Zoom, and results were mixed at best. Some of the students showed up from their bedrooms—some, like Alice or Liz, actually in bed, though you couldn't quite make that out for sure—and had to position their laptop camera carefully to make sure Mister Tiger or that old One Direction poster they'd been meaning to retire stayed out of the frame. Others sat at the kitchen table, with a parent or sibling occasionally passing through the background to get to the fridge. Some were enveloped in grainy murk, others washed out by over-bright sun from a window behind them. Dan, an early adopter of Zoom-customizing tech, figured out how to set his background to the White House Situation Room, though the illusion wasn't perfect and parts of him would cut out and scramble as if he were periodically entering hyperspace. I opted out of the vogue for trying to craft attractive and suitably professorial Zoom backgrounds and instead put my laptop on a standing desk in my home office in the eaves, with a blank expanse of slanted white ceiling close behind me.

Everyone tried extra-hard to be accommodating and agreeable, and the students were touchingly relieved to get back to the regular routine of school, with a syllabus to get through and credits to earn and other such familiar business to lend shape and purpose to an existence that was otherwise both duller and more harrowing than before. For me, too, getting back to school helped mitigate the early pandemic feeling of being in a bad science fiction movie made in 1983 that had no special effects budget. The director had just slapped masks on extras and told some of them to cough.

But class on Zoom was fundamentally different, and not in a good way. I swiftly realized just how much my ability to manage a productive conversation depends on physical cues. I rely on reading faces and body language to know who's getting it, who's into it, who could use a nudge, whether we're ready to move on to the next thing or should gnaw on the current problem a little longer. And in modeling how to take an interest in something and channel that interest into rigor, I use the form of my physical attitude to help express the intellectual attitude I want the students to try out. How I carry myself in the actual room—how I use posture and gesture and other aspects of presence to convey my own thought process and confusion and pleasure and purpose and confidence in the group—does a lot of the work of showing how I carry myself as a student of literature.

Pick your cliché for discussing literature on Zoom—especially with thirty-five participants, which at that point still forced me to toggle between two screens. Slow-dancing in hazmat suits comes to mind. So does turning around an aircraft carrier, because it seems to take forever to do things online that in person could be done with a quick glance around the room, like determining who among the students whose hands are raised wants to respond to what another student just said. And it's not just that the tiny rectangles on the screen didn't convey enough information; they also conveyed bad information, false positives. Was that disinterest I was seeing? Skepticism? Pixelation? Or just the inherent physical and emotional flattening effect of the camera? I don't score boxing matches if I'm not ringside, because on TV it's much more difficult to gauge the effect of punches and even to tell which of them land truly flush. The screen flattens the human consequences of whatever's happening on it.

What happened on Zoom wasn't really a conversation. It was more like a play that's too stylized to fall into a naturalistic groove. I made a speech, then a student made a speech sort of in response to it, then another student made a speech, and so on—each separate from the others, though thematically related. Almost every student reported finding it harder to get into class discussions on Zoom, both in the broader sense of caring about them and in the narrow sense of jumping in to participate, and it didn't help that pauses or silences had lost almost all of their power to make human beings feel that they had to speak up. We still grappled dutifully with the problems I set for us, and we moved with minimal friction from one speech to the next, cordially covering the ground, but it felt more like talking about how to get from here to there than actually making a journey together.

.   .   .   .   .

We went back to trying to solve the puzzle of the narrator in *Oscar Wao*. To a degree that I never would have accepted in a regular in-person class, this meant that I ended up explaining my own solution. The explanation went something like this:

A good deal of Yunior's effort as narrator goes to maintaining what he regards as a regulation masculine front. He sums himself up as a familiar type, "a state school player" with all the requisite attributes: "I had my job and the gym and my boys and my novia and of course I had my slutties." But some of what he's telling us lets us see behind this mask. For example, he puffs up his manly credentials when he tells us that he didn't belong in Demarest, the Rutgers dorm where he roomed with Oscar, but he also steps partially outside himself to look at himself doing it: "Me, a guy who could bench 340 pounds, who used to call Demarest Homo Hall like it was nothing." He does something similar when he recognizes the Elvish language, Sindarin, from Tolkien's *Lord of the Rings* in a sign that Oscar puts on their dorm room's door. He says to the reader, "Please don't ask me how I knew this. Please." He's signaling that he has more ironic distance from his own identity than your standard-issue player should have and that he feels obliged to cover up this knowledge behind the facade of normalcy.

And we find out that, like Oscar, Yunior is also writing fiction in creative writing workshops at Rutgers. Yes, they're macho stories about drug deals and shootings, but it's still fiction—in fact, genre fiction, another thing he has in common with Oscar. So they're both aspiring writers, too. But, as Díaz pointed out in the Q and A at BC, one major difference between them is that Yunior gets to tell the story of Oscar's brief, wondrous life, and Oscar doesn't.

Yunior-the-narrator seems much more reflective, thoughtful, and sympathetic to Oscar than Yunior-the-character. Yunior-the-narrator can use diction, footnotes, asides, and other formal tools at his disposal to show how much he understands Oscar's situation as a misfit, how much he secretly shares with Oscar: both are aspiring writers; both are into genre fiction and comic books and anime; both are trying to figure out whether their history as members of the Dominican diaspora might be a curse or in some ways a blessing because it gives them great material to write about; both are serially falling in love; and both are oppressed by the felt need to conform. He can also use these formal devices to signal to the reader that his own normalcy is a pose, a necessary facade that he maintains to protect himself from the kind of sorrow and hurt routinely suffered by the unarmored Oscar.

But Yunior-the-character is a self-appointed drill sergeant whose efforts to shape Oscar into a more normal Dominican American male are exemplified by making him get up early in the morning to run. When Oscar resists this transformation and finally refuses to go any further, Yunior physically attacks him and allows others to bully him. Oscar gets his nickname, Oscar Wao, when the other guys in Yunior's circle realize that they can be more cruel to him because Yunior has withdrawn his protection. Yunior inadvertently gives the nickname to him when he observes to his buddies that Oscar "looked just like that fat homo Oscar Wilde." There's a flash of Yunior-the-narrator hidden in this moment. Stop and think about it: what does it say about Yunior's range of knowledge and experience, and about his aspirations as a writer, that he knows who Oscar Wilde is and what he looks like? Any such implications are covered up, though, by the aggressive intolerance for deviance suggested by "fat homo." And, since Yunior's friends have never even heard of Oscar Wilde, and mishear the name as Oscar Wao, the nickname is born, and everybody's too busy punishing Oscar for being a misfit to wonder whether Yunior might also be a secret misfit himself.

Step back and consider Yunior in relation to the figure of the dictator that suffuses the novel. A dictator controls not just the information available to his subjects but also what they think, how they act, what they write. It's not just the violent direct control of behavior through the exercise of police power that makes him a dictator; it's the way that his absolute power and example get into citizens' heads and cause them to police themselves and each other. In proposing dictatorship as a figure for masculinity, the novel's saying that it's not like somebody's there to beat you to death every time you do something that deviates from the norm. Rather, you beat *yourself* up with doubts and shame, and your friends and family police you back onto the straight and narrow by teasing you or urging you to change. In the theory classes that Díaz took at Rutgers, they would have called this relentless pressure "hegemonic masculinity," and the monstrously priapic head-of-state player Trujillo perfectly embodies the principle.

Remember Díaz's claim that the novel becomes more sinister if we ask what it means that Oscar doesn't get to tell his story. Oscar is silenced, and instead it's Yunior—who's afraid to be seen to step out of line, who's willing to police Oscar as well as himself—who gets to tell Oscar's story. This seems even more sinister when you consider that the theme of "paginas en blanco" reminds us that a dictatorship wants to cover things up, change history, leave things out, erase and revise the story. Even Yunior-the-narrator's apparently greater sympathy for Oscar becomes suspect in that light. "I would like to think it wasn't *too* bad," he says of the general cruelty to Oscar in which he participated. If that suggests self-knowledge or sympathy for Oscar, it also constitutes an oblique admission that he might be covering up the worst of it. Despite claiming to have become a more enlightened dude over time, Yunior consents to participating in the sacrificial silencing of his supposed friend Oscar to deflect the Sauron eye of dictatorial selfhood-policing authority from himself and maintain his own good standing as a regular guy.

.   .   .   .   .

Laying out my own solution to the puzzle of the novel's narrator was not even remotely the same thing as arriving together at a shared understanding. There's something clinical and peremptory about explaining such an analysis in a lecture or, in this case, a letter. No matter what qualifiers you put around the points you're making, no matter how much you invite questions and discussion about the interpretation you've outlined, you're in effect saying *Here's the approved reading of this novel; this is the answer, and you should be ready to be tested on it.* I never want to even appear to be saying that, but I felt that under the extraordinary circumstances imposed by Covid, I had no better choice. I just didn't think that Zoom was the place for thirty-five people to work out together a solution to the problem of the narrator in *Oscar Wao*, so I settled for content delivery. It felt especially distanced and pat because the subject matter had so much potential to make us uncomfortable.

We were much less of a community on Zoom, which meant that it never seemed like the right time to directly take on, for instance, Yunior's reliance on a rich assortment of what everyone in the room had been taught to regard as offensive words to describe ethnic and racial groups, sexual orientations, and human bodies. We talked about the book at length and in great detail, and we certainly talked about Yunior's diction, but we tiptoed around what would have been a legitimate and perhaps productive discussion of this aspect of it. Yunior relies on proscribed words to do a lot of work for him, and we chose—I chose, and the students gratefully went along with that choice—not to dig too deep into that particular rhetorical habit. I didn't ask them how they reacted as readers to those word choices, how those word choices opened a path into understanding the dictatorship of convention. Earlier in my career, when students were less touchy and I was younger and more inclined to say we're going to do what needs doing even if it makes everyone uncomfortable, I would have forced us to come straight at those proscribed words because they're extremely potent language that deserves interpretive attention. In recent years, though, I've found myself deciding that it's not worth the hassle and potential trouble that could come from outraged or offended students. That's not a good thing, but these are the outraged and offended times we live in. Still, if a student had given me a likely opening and we'd been in the same room, I probably would have risked a little ginger handling of radioactive word choices. On Zoom, it was a foregone conclusion that no such openings would come up, and I would let it go.

There's a larger point here about the college classroom that extends beyond Zoom. At its best, the community of inquiry you build in the classroom allows you to go places where the rest of the culture might fear to tread, which is why the attempted policing of classroom speech and content by everyone from wokeness-expunging state legislators to trigger-warning-happy sensitivity monitors does far more harm than good. I tend to believe the argument that the American people, left to their own devices, don't divide as neatly into Team Blue and Team Red as they're supposed to and can generally work out a rough, awkward compromise on most matters but that it's in the interest of professional fomenters of division from across the political spectrum to prevent them from doing that. Some subsets of those fomenters, the various attempted policers of the classroom, are trying to bring their culture war to a place that has so far been more exempt from it than you might think. People I know who aren't academics tend to assume that I'm constantly dealing with outrage and conflict, which dominate the picture of the college classroom purveyed by professional political operatives and the volunteer troll legions who tend their online ire mines. In the cartoon seen from the right, wave after wave of gibbering woke maniacs come at me (or, given what this cartoon assumes about the politics of the professoriate, follow me) from the left, calling for the defenestration or canonization of authors based on what they look like rather than what they wrote, trying to ban previously inoffensive but now microaggressive speech on ludicrously contrived grounds, furiously denying each other the right to imagine the inner lives of characters who are not demographically identical to writer or reader. In the cartoon seen from the left, especially those suspicious of the Catholic affiliation of the school at which I teach, hair-shirted Opus Dei creeps, foaming MAGA psychos, and William F. Buckley–tribute-band types come at me from the right, trying to enforce the holy trinity of Christ, the market, and Western civilization with a logic-free fervor that any wet-combed falangista of the 1930s would recognize as what he stands for, only a lot less nuanced and thoughtful.

But none of this actually happens much. Mostly, we just talk about the books, and most everybody is able to keep in mind that we're talking about what's being said on the page—not by me, not by us, and not by whatever demographic group the author can be made to stand for. We're talking about words conveying ideas, and for the most part, we stick to considering the what and the how of those ideas. And most of us in the room seem to be able to keep in mind that some of those words were written a long time ago, when different ideas and ways of talking were considered polite or acceptable, and that there's not much value in trying to figure out exactly how offended we should be if somebody were to come along today and write those exact same words. Are we crossing into the preserve of critical race theory or using hurtfully triggering words when we discuss how the narrator's diction conveys his worldview in *Oscar Wao*? I suppose you could see it in those ways if you squinted, but neither conventional template fits all that usefully over what we're doing.

Maybe I'll be proven overly optimistic by a complete disaster in my next class, but in my experience so far, people can handle this stuff—and it helps if you treat them as if they can handle it, and if you put in the work to make them feel that they're part of a community of inquiry rather than loners who must constantly decide whether it's time for intellectual fight or flight. Yes, it's true that these days students and their teachers get a fair amount of training, both in school and from life online, in not being able to handle things. That is, they're trained to spot an offense against identity—whatever that identity might be, from LGBTQ to Warrior for Christ—and melt down in outrage in response, to stop thinking and snap to the grid of their default ideological position at the slightest provocation. When they do it in class, they feel smart and principled and brave. When they do it online, they're rewarded with likes and dislikes, both of which count as attention, and other incentives so vanishingly slight that it makes me sad to even think about it. "Why the dislikes?" asks an online poster who just savaged another online poster, the nasty-to-plaintive display of fangs and then underbelly cueing more dislikes and likes in an endless cascade of poisonously reinforcing attention.

But I've found that such training in outrage does not necessarily push out all other training, nor does it satisfy most people who receive it. It's not really very rewarding to be outraged, as even a cursory look at our public culture will make clear. A lot of students seem relieved to put that routine aside and just concentrate on trying to figure out how the book works. Some of their relief may be institution-specific: Boston College students might on average lean a little farther away from hair-trigger outrage than students at, say, Evergreen State or Liberty University. But I don't think the BC part is as important as human nature—curiosity makes for a more belly-filling meal than outrage—or, I hope, the tone of shared inquiry, rather than confirmation-seeking or blowtorching the text and one another with critique, that I try to set in my classroom.

In a story in the *Washington Post* about high-school English teachers who decided to stop teaching *To Kill a Mockingbird*, a student who supported that decision said that the book "did not move her, because it wasn't written about her—or for her."[‡] I'm agnostic about the merits of *To Kill a Mockingbird* (and treating it as worth reading simply because it's "about race" will sooner or later get you into exactly the kind of trouble the teachers encountered), but the student's attitude cleanly misses much of what the study of literature is supposed to be about. If we want to take shelter in an echo chamber of like-minded voices that affirm our understanding of ourselves and the world, we have the rest of our ever-more-niched culture—split and split again into smaller and smaller fragments by political operatives and tech corporations for their own gain—to satisfy that urge. In a literature class, though, we should read things—unsettling novels, freaky poetry, undead sagas written long ago by people nothing like us but also surprisingly like us—*because* they're not written about us or for us. Finding a way to be moved by such books and to extract meaning from them makes us stronger readers, more capable thinkers.

So far, we've mostly found a way in my classes. Mostly we manage to treat each other like people of goodwill, and in class—especially once we've had a chance to get to know each other and build some kind of ongoing conversation—we can usually take on thorny, potentially nervous-making topics without melodrama. Even when there are several people in a class who share the attitude that being a thinking person means figuring out how to be outraged by a text's ideological shortcomings, I can try to make something useful out of that response. How is outrage cued by form? That is, how did the shape of the text generate the shape of your response? Is the text of more than one mind about that topic? Is it actually making your argument against itself, as well as giving you cause to make that argument? Instead of joining outraged students in beating up the text, and instead of jumping on a student's comment to declare that she has transgressed and must be corrected or shunned, it's my job to say that she's making a point, that this point is perhaps part of a larger conversation about *X* that's been going on for a while, and that it's our job to figure out what we can do with it. This can all be harder to do with grad students

‡ Hannah Natanson, "Students Hated 'To Kill a Mockingbird.' Their Teachers Tried to Dump It," *Washington Post*, Nov. 3, 2023, https://www.washingtonpost.com /education/2023/11/03/to-kill-a-mockingbird-book-ban-removal-washington/#.

since they tend to be more set in believing that being smart is about having a problem with what you're reading and hearing. Undergrads tend to be more flexible and game, more likely to take the text and the problem before us as given and go from there. But yank us out of the classroom and put us online, and suddenly there's a lot less community feeling (as the whole nation appears to be finding out about itself), and everybody's less game, the professor very much included.

Teaching can get to feel like playing a regular gig every Tuesday and Thursday. You show up and you slide into a groove and play your set and people drink and dance and you get paid and everybody goes home feeling like they had a night out. But you have to be awake to the possibility that something can happen that will suddenly raise the stakes: a touchy conversation, a student in extremis, whatever. In other words, you get comfortable but not so comfortable that you forget that things can get uncomfortable. You don't want to be taken by surprise when that happens. So you get comfortable with a situation that includes the possibility of things getting uncomfortable. A student might say something, or you might say something, that suddenly makes you aware of the constricting boundaries of the unspoken agreement between professor and students in a classroom filled with people who have enjoyed high-end schooling. The invisible curriculum and its scaffolding of norms and understandings become visible when they're in peril of being breached. That there was less chance of this happening on Zoom was just one of many reasons why class was less engaging and rewarding on Zoom.

10 True Stories on Zoom

We trudged onward through April on Zoom, and it was okay. But as I look back on the second half of that spring 2020 semester, I can see that it wasn't a pure experience of online teaching. Because we'd already had half a semester of classes in person, we'd had a chance to lay a foundation that would be very difficult to establish in a course that's online from the beginning. When we went online we already shared—to a greater or lesser degree that varied from person to person, of course—a sense of who was in the room, an awareness that together we were pursuing an inquiry, a bodily as well as an intellectual experience of being taken seriously when we spoke up. In the academic year that followed, 2020–21, I would teach only on Zoom, and that's now a lost teaching year for me. I did my best to deliver the goods, but the students from those classes and the class meetings themselves don't really register in memory, which has never happened to me before or since. By contrast, I vividly remember my spring 2020 Lit Core class, and now I can see that while community building mostly came to an end when we moved online, we were still able to take advantage of what we had already established in person.

Moving online during the pandemic afforded me insight into what I do as a teacher. In addition to conveying skills and content, I figure out who's in the room, where they're coming from, what they can do, and what they're interested in doing, and I try to strike a balance between helping them reach extant goals and showing them some new things to aspire to. It's easier to see that process operating in electives and graduate classes, especially in writing classes, where students are more likely to have already defined objectives for themselves, but it happens even in a required freshman literature class. Over time, I've come to appreciate more deeply the importance of the one-on-one teaching that happens in office hours, hanging around before and after class, on email, and in my responses to drafts and papers, but even in meetings of the full class, the one-on-one dynamics move beneath the surface of the collaborative effort. I'm trying to help each student find a way to go from where they are to where they want to get to, and often that means introducing them to destinations they may not have had in mind before they signed up for the class.

Most of that was much harder to do on Zoom, but it wasn't impossible. Some one-on-one aspects of teaching actually grew in importance when we moved online, like conversations during office hours, which I took to holding at all times of the day and evening, whenever students wanted to talk. I still do that in addition to in-person office hours, another permanent change as a result of the pandemic. And of course the pandemic also generated added incentive for all to make sure that meaningful teaching and learning did continue to happen. Students and their bill-paying parents started asking, reasonably enough, whether online college was worth the high price they'd paid for college in person. I'd say no: it's better than nothing but not as good as in-person college, and it should cost less. (I had a daughter at Boston College at the time, and another in high school who would end up there, so I was also a BC parent. But since employees pay just room and board, not tuition, and BC had announced prorated room and board rebates, the question of value for your college dollar didn't matter to me anywhere near as much as it did to those paying full tuition for online education.)

Next up was our turn to nonfiction. The students found Joan Didion's and Hunter S. Thompson's depictions of the counterculture of the 1960s and early 1970s interesting in the way that they would have found Chaucer's depiction of medieval pilgrimages interesting if we were reading *The Canterbury Tales*. Boomers never seem to quite get around to accepting that much of what they care about—like saving the world by doing whatever feels good, determining whether Duane Allman or Jerry Garcia was the better guitar player, or literary theory—registers as ancient history to eighteen-year-olds in the twenty-first century, but why shouldn't it? Yes, the period Didion and Thompson describe happened in living memory—during the barely sentient early years of my own postboomer lifetime, in fact. But at this point that period's much closer to the Great Depression than it is to the present, and by the end of this decade it will be equidistant from both the Gilded Age and the present. One of the many, many things literature can do is to open wormholes into bygone historical moments and their signature forms not just of public discourse but also of inner life, and that period-bridging time travel is effected by literary style just as much as by subject matter.

.   .   .   .   .

"The center was not holding. It was a country of bankruptcy notices and public-auction announcements and commonplace reports of casual killings and misplaced children and abandoned homes and vandals who misspelled even the four-letter words they scrawled. It was a country in which families routinely disappeared, trailing bad checks and repossession papers. Adolescents drifted from city to torn city, sloughing off both the past and future as snakes shed their skins, children who were never taught and would never now learn the games that had held the society together. People were missing. Children were missing. Parents were missing."

So begins Didion's essay "Slouching Towards Bethlehem," which originally appeared in the *Saturday Evening Post* in 1967. She goes on to say that the country in question was "the United States of America in the cold late spring of 1967," when it was becoming clear that at some point "we had aborted ourselves and butchered the job," and that she went to San Francisco to tell this story because that was where "the social hemorrhaging was showing up." There, in the Haight-Ashbury district, "the missing children were gathering and calling themselves 'hippies.'"

Didion, a strong stylist, gave us a lot of form to notice. Structurally, the essay's broken into dozens of fragments of varying sizes. Many of them are anecdotal descriptions of her encounters with hippies and those who sought to understand or exploit or corral them, but some of the fragments are chunks of writing drawn from pamphlets and fliers and other sources she found on the street. She uses the first person with virtuosic subtlety, one of the formal features that make the essay a classic of New Journalism, the style of nonfiction using novelistic techniques of scene, dialogue, and point of view that flourished in response to the upheavals of the 1960s. We spent some time trying to decide whether the phrase she uses to describe declining an offer to take acid, "I say I'm unstable," suggests shrewd reportorial good manners or an important piece of information about our narrator. We also spent some time tracing the resonances in her essay of "The Second Coming," the apocalyptic poem by William Butler Yeats from which the essay's title is drawn and to which its first sentence refers. To accomplish that task, we already had in our shared toolbox a technical term, *intertextuality*—the principle that when one text borrows from another, it's inviting us to put the two texts together and treat them as one for the purposes of interpretation. This tool comes in handy on all sorts of interpretive occasions, from hip-hop samples to episodes of *The Simpsons*. And, starting with those misspelled four-letter words alluded to in the opening paragraph, there's also a thread running through the essay in which Didion repeatedly shows us that she has to explain the hippies because they don't have sufficient command of language or logic to explain themselves. The best they can do to describe an acid trip, the signature rite of their recently discovered tribe that the curious reader of the *Saturday Evening Post* would find most mystifying and in need of explaining, is "Wow."

As we often did, we started with the opening paragraph, which gave us one more formal trait to gnaw on. It overuses the verb *to be*: the center was not holding, it was a country of this and it was a country of that, people were missing, children were missing, parents were missing, and so on. Verbs establish the relationships between nouns, so relying so heavily on *to be* blunts and obscures those relationships. Things just seem to be ... happening. Didion, a writer of such bracing purposefulness and clarity that reading her paragraphs is like dipping into one ice-cold pond after another, surely knew that overusing *to be* muddies cause and effect.

Dwelling on all those *to be* constructions helped us see how she lays out the problem and her own response to it. The opacity of the opening conveys the confusion of the conventional middle American reader the *Saturday Evening Post* imagined itself to address. *Hey, I followed the rules. How come my kids aren't following the rules?* That conventional reader, whom the essay not only addresses but also defines as a character the reader will play, can see the problem but not the cause—obscured at first by all those uses of *to be*—because that reader is part of the cause: the adults who run the country and enjoy its prosperity and other benefits screwed it up by failing to pass along to their children community-preserving values or a sense of belonging or even the basics of a shared language of citizenship. Over the course of the essay, as we spend time with Didion spending time with those initially perplexing but ultimately edifying hippies, the scales will fall from the reader's eyes. It makes sense, then, that the only glimmer of clarity imparted by verbs other than *to be* in the essay's famous opening comes courtesy of the adolescents who bewilder and panic their elders by drifting from city to city and sloughing off their past and future. The essay's going to be all about trying to understand that drifting and sloughing.

The students did a solid job on "Slouching Towards Bethlehem." We were far enough into the semester that they had little trouble picking up Didion's stylistic signals and parsing them, and her account of a massive national failure of those running the show to look out for their fellow Americans resonated with pandemic anxieties in the cold late spring of 2020. But when we looked back on the semester in interviews in 2021 and after, the essay had left little lasting impression on them. "Oh, yeah, the one about the hippies" was about it for most of them. This was in stark contrast to aspiring writers in the advanced nonfiction writing classes I also teach, who snap to attention when confronted by Didion's cool, detached, masterfully controlled prose. They want to figure out how she generates so much momentum and such ice-bath clarity with just a few well-chosen words. How does she *do* that? The main reason that "Slouching Towards Bethlehem" didn't have a similar effect on Lit Core students was probably that, like Miles Davis opening for AC/DC, it served as setup and foil for the much louder, cruder, ruder, infinitely less restrained crowd favorite that followed. In the end, "Slouching Towards Bethlehem" was relegated to being the one in which the narrator *doesn't* do a lot of drugs and go on a road trip to Vegas.

Remember how much the hardworking and achievement-obsessed Dan loved Hunter S. Thompson's *Fear and Loathing in Las Vegas*? He regarded discovering it as the highlight of his semester, and that response typified a striking tendency I observed among Lit Core students. The straighter the arrow, the more dutiful and Calvinistic and disciplined the young achiever, the more likely it was that Thompson would stagger into his or her well-ordered mind and detonate a suicide vest packed with not only excess and depravity but also the shrapnel of joy. Tyler, the relentlessly healthy-minded optimist and a cappella singer committed to getting the most out of every experience and to playing the role of universally sympathetic middleman in his parents' divorce, also loved *Fear and Loathing*. So did Luke, the debate champion and cross-country runner from Montana, who was inspired by the pandemic to switch from planning a future in international relations to planning to work for a company that was 3D-printing a spaceship (and eventually went into socially responsible investment). Jenny, a serious and diligent young woman bound for law school who had pulled together with her mother and siblings to forge a difficult way forward after her father's sudden death the year before she came to BC, said *Fear and Loathing* was her favorite among the books we read.

I guess it makes a certain sense that I don't share Dan's, Tyler's, Luke's, or Jenny's enthusiasm for Thompson, since I don't share their astronaut rigor. I teach *Fear and Loathing*, also a classic of New Journalism, because it makes such a good pair with Didion's "Slouching Towards Bethlehem" and because at least in this book I can appreciate Thompson as a stylist in his own right. Being a maximalist overwriter takes discipline, which in his body of work he too often lacks, but in this one short book he's on his rococo game from start to finish. That makes it very easy for students to see form when we read Thompson, and pairing his hot, intimate version of the waning counterculture with Didion's coolly distanced treatment of the waxing counterculture encourages them to see how different forms can express different meanings. But a little Thompson goes a long way with me, and I'm still surprised that so many students love his writing. I'm surprised that more of them aren't more put off by his barrage of now-esoteric references to Bishop Pike and Sonny Barger, by how he can justify any nastiness on his part as sticking it to the Man, by what a 1960s-vintage jerk he enthusiastically describes himself to be. Also, though I am not interested in being outraged by what I read in books and usually find it tedious when others take writers to task for their failure to be ideologically unimpeachable, we do live in an age in which such outrage and ideological taking-to-task rank high among conventional responses to literature, so I'm surprised that more students don't object to Thompson's winking racist-not-racist double-talk and his considerably less ironic contempt for the few female characters who appear in the book.

I think Dan was right to put his finger on the appeal to clean-living achievers of Thompson's determined effort to self-medicate the pain of being human by making a beast of himself. He wallows in hedonism, impulsiveness, law-breaking, poor judgment, and other dimensions of an across-the-board failure to act like a person with a career and a future to consider. Yet, as you read on, that wallowing begins to look like some kind of alternative antiastronaut rigor—not a free fall into failure so much as a purposeful descent into the lower depths to tap a motherlode of meaning not available to those who take the conventional high road. So achievers could perhaps sort of recognize themselves in the funhouse mirror of his book, if you accepted, say, sucking pure adrenochrome off the head of a paper match as the downward-aspiring equivalent of dutifully applying oneself to upward-aspiring activities like SAT prep courses or captaining the lacrosse team.

The adrenochrome episode, recounted in a chapter titled "A Terrible Experience with Extremely Dangerous Drugs," isn't nonfiction, really. Adrenochrome doesn't have any of the effects he ascribes to it, so that scene's either about a different drug or Thompson just made it up (none of which has stopped adrenochrome from making a comeback as a key element of the QAnon baby-harvesting conspiracy mythos). As a narrator, he's similar to Yunior in *Oscar Wao* in that he's unreliable and wants you to know it. When Thompson's not obviously making things up, he makes no bones about cartoonishly exaggerating to the point that it qualifies as making things up. *Fear and Loathing* is sometimes described as a novel, but that's kind of by default; it's more of an intentionally delusional memoir. But Thompson is also like Yunior in the seriousness of purpose with which he sets out to exemplify, not just identify and depict, what's wrong with the world through which he moves. Thompson's body of work features again and again his arrival at a revelation: horrified and repelled by

America, he makes a beast of himself only to realize that his depravity makes him a typical American and not a misfit at all. It's as if a werewolf, crashing through the window of a house to steal a baby, finds itself interrupting mom and dad just as they sit down at the dining room table to eat the baby themselves. Thompson's a fairly standard-issue period bro (a brush with the law led to the air force, not college, or else he'd be an antediluvian laxbro) who got weird by drinking the Kool-Aid of the counterculture, but he's still recognizably that bro: all about sports, getting blasted and cranking tunes, worshipping motorcycles and guns, kicking back with drinks by the pool to groove on the conjoined realizations of how fucked up he is and how fucked up everything is. He discovers the horribleness at the heart of America in his own heart, not just out there in Vegas.

The definitive historical image in *Fear and Loathing*, of the counterculture as a wave that broke and receded, comes at the end of Thompson's idyllic memory-riff on living in San Francisco in "the middle sixties"—being introduced to acid at the Fillmore, riding his 650 BSA Lightning at one hundred miles an hour across the Bay Bridge, partaking of "a fantastic universal sense that whatever we were doing was right, that we were winning." By the time he heads to Las Vegas at the start of the book ("We were somewhere around Barstow on the edge of the desert when the drugs began to take hold"), any expectation that "our energy would simply *prevail*" has given way to profound disappointment. "We had all the momentum; we were riding the crest of a high and beautiful wave. . . . So now, less than five years later, you can go up on a steep hill in Las Vegas and look West, and with the right kind of eyes you can almost *see* the high-water mark—that place where the wave finally broke and rolled back." Put Thompson's survey of the wreckage left in the wake of that receding wave together with Didion's account of the developing wave and the self-destructive heedlessness of postwar America that generated it in the first place, and you've got a story of decline and fall told on a grand scale by two distinctive voices representing two distinctive sensibilities in soaring counterpoint.

·　　·　　·　　·　　·

As the economy tanked during the Covid shutdown, students' postcollege prospects looked grimmer than they had in January. Graduating seniors were even more freaked out by the pandemic than freshmen were. Not only had the big finish of their college careers disappeared in a cloud of acrid smoke, but so had many of the entry-level jobs for which they were hoping to compete. Seniors sent me wry, fatalistic updates from their old bedrooms, in which they were now holed up without much prospect of moving on to what they had previously imagined as exciting new chapters in their lives as independent adults. To borrow Wharton's language, they were feeling less like entrepreneurs, warriors, or hunters and more like water plants than ever.

The students in Lit Core were feeling pretty water-planty themselves. Previously unconsidered and now rapidly expanding areas of concern over which they had little control occupied their thoughts: whether they or their loved ones would catch this new plague and die a lingering death or suffer long-term debility, whether the pandemic would ever end and normal life would ever return, whether the experience of college they had shaped their young lives around securing for themselves would be ruined for them. But the pandemic had also spawned at least one new worry over which they did have more control: what impression they conveyed to others in class on Zoom. That meant, among other things, making sure that the rest of us didn't see or hear what they didn't want us to see or hear. There was a lot going on in and around those tiny Zoom rectangles.

Like many students in the class, Marguerite returned home to a bedroom that had not been updated to reflect its occupant's recent entry into adulthood. Except for the twin bed that had long ago replaced the crib, the room had never really been redone since she'd moved into it as a toddler. "The walls were bright yellow, I had green curtains with a white swirly pattern on them, and a dresser decorated with fairies in a garden," she told me, "and there was a stuffed bunny named Bunini on the bed." To prevent anyone from seeing her room on Zoom, she would prop her laptop on a chair and sit with her back to her open window. All we could see was Marguerite with her window and the sky behind her.

Charlotte sat at one end of the dining room table during class, and her mother sat at the other, teaching sixth grade history. Charlotte used AirPods, but her mother didn't, so Charlotte could hear her mother's class in the background of her own. Charlotte had attended the school at which her mother teaches, so nostalgic echoes of her own middle-school years trickled in around her AirPods to blend with her college classes. Mother and daughter sat just far enough apart that with judicious use of the mute button Charlotte could participate in my class without the rest of us hearing her mother or her mother's students.

Arthur attended class in the TV room, and it was his mother who didn't want us to see the wrong things. "My mom would be insistent on making sure everything looked clean," he told me, "because she did not want people in my classes to judge us." Books and remotes were usually piled on the coffee table, and blankets and pillows were strewn on the couch and recliner, where both Arthur and his father loved to fall asleep, but she would always remove all this clutter before his classes. "If I took a class without these being cleaned, she would get pretty mad at me. She wanted me to keep up the appearance of living in a tidy household on Zoom."

Elizabeth didn't want us to see or hear her older sister, who sat off camera in pajamas or sweats and made sarcastic comments about what students in the class were saying. Sometimes her sister talked over them, offering her own, supposedly far superior responses to my questions. "It was really mean, but I promise she is actually a very kind person," Elizabeth told me. Having had her senior year and her final track season blown up by Covid, her sister, a student at a different college, had grown bitter and morose. "She never looked presentable, and she actually challenged herself to see how long she could go without leaving our house," Elizabeth said. "I think she went three or four weeks." During those early days of Zoom, Elizabeth was always worried that she might somehow become unmuted and allow her sister's mockery to be heard by all.

Liz often attended Lit Core on Zoom from bed after sleeping in. Class started at noon, which meant she had been lying there all morning, and if she had to rush out to the kitchen for life-giving coffee, she would turn the volume of her laptop all the way up so as not to miss anything before rushing back and getting into bed once more with coffee cup in hand. A diligent student who prides herself on her work ethic, she didn't want us to know that she had sunk to such levels of sloth during the pandemic. "That was definitely the worst that I did," she told me, "and I am embarrassed to admit it." The worst? Have I mentioned that these were basically good kids?

Stella, who had stayed on campus, didn't want us to see that for the first few classes on Zoom, she was wearing the same oversized red Hollister sweatpants and old Forensics & Debate high-school hoodie, so she would aim her camera angle so that only her face was visible. "During the regular day-to-day of in-person classes, I would often wear something more on the uncomfortable but fashionable side—either a floral dress paired with ankle boots, or just a nice sweater and jeans at least," but that all went to hell during the pandemic. As she described that period in an email to me, "it felt apocalyptic and surreal" to be left on campus after everybody else took off, leaving "clothes strewn outside of dorms along with full-length mirrors and blankets. The familiar chatter of students walking the dorm hallways, the ever-present, ever-pervasive scent of weed in the morning, the bathroom conversations with the girls were gone just like that." For a week after everyone left, she stared at her phone all night, drifting off to sleep just before dawn. "All sense of normality had vanished. And though my experience being on campus for the rest of the semester was very different from the experiences of those students who went home, I think what was shared between all of us was this need to establish routine, a sense of normality for ourselves." As the semester went on and the need for the reimposition of order grew stronger, she straightened out her sleeping schedule, ate lunch outside in front of Gasson Hall at the center of campus, and started putting on makeup and getting dressed for Zoom classes, trying to act like a human being again.

David didn't want to reveal "anything that may give my professor or peers any indication of what kind of person I am in my home," a person similar to "but not quite the same as the one who shows up to class." Before class he would pick up stray clothes and organize his desk, and he would also cover his weight rack with a towel and hide his pull-up bar and yoga mat. It sickened him to think that others might believe that he was "shoving my lifestyle in their face." He was a trim, well-presented guy, so it would have come as no surprise to us that he worked out, and with gyms closed, he must naturally be doing it at home, but somehow he couldn't stand the thought of our seeing evidence of this easily imagined fact. He knew that nobody was closely examining his Zoom background, but still he constantly checked it to "make sure there was nothing to be talked about. The easiest solution would be to turn off the camera and give nothing at all," but—against the policy recommendation of the university—I had asked my students to keep their cameras on. Teaching tiny people in tiny rectangles was hard enough; teaching blacked-out rectangles would have been somewhere between even harder and hopeless.

Colleen's "main worry was anyone seeing or hearing my father yelling and cursing at me in the background of my Zoom. He would stay home on days when he was too intoxicated or depressed to get out of bed and go to work, which left me confined in my small childhood bedroom, as I did not wish to be around him in our apartment. When I was on Zoom with my door closed, I would ignore him, and this only made him yell louder. I was dreading the moment he would barge in and start cursing, but thankfully it never came." This was the father, you will recall, who wore the BC cap his upwardly mobile daughter had given him to show how proud he was of her, even if his tough-guy reserve prevented him from saying so. While he raged or sulked outside her door, Colleen sat in front of her laptop at her "perfect desk saved from a garage sale" with her twenty-pound cat, Fred, in her lap, surrounded by decor unchanged since she'd picked it out for her thirteenth birthday: walls painted her favorite light blue, quilted headboard, coordinating turtle canvases from TJ Maxx. On a shelf above were arrayed things she hadn't had the heart to get rid of: a green wicker chair too big for a dollhouse but too small for her American Girl dolls, an angel on a religious plate that had fallen over too many times, a plastic mini Child of Prague with a broken hand she got from family in Ireland, a record from her great aunt's closet by a band she didn't recognize but thought looked cool, a piece of driftwood from the one time she visited Montauk, a small silver basket with two plastic doves she had carried as a flower girl for her cousin, a Venetian mask from that cousin's honeymoon, a very dead corsage from her great aunt's jubilee. And there was a teddy bear named Teddy, who, of course, she wasn't ever going to get rid of. Fred the cat, who loved attention, thought she was talking to him when she spoke up in class. She tried to control his tail with her hands to keep it from showing up on camera and had to get up from time to time and briefly go off-camera when he jumped down from her lap and scratched at the door to be let out. "I'm in my teenage bedroom," she would constantly remind herself, "and everyone else on Zoom kind of is too."

.   .   .   .   .

Cutting Annie Proulx's long novel *Accordion Crimes* from the syllabus when the pandemic shortened our semester created a hole that I filled with a couple of pairs of reliably teachable short stories: Nathaniel Hawthorne's "My Kinsman Major Molineux" and Jack London's "South of the Slot," both about outsiders in the city; and Flannery O'Connor's "A Good Man Is Hard to Find" and Vladimir Nabokov's "Cloud, Castle, Lake," both about strange catastrophic journeys.

Allie, the TA, picked the second pair and taught the class in which we discussed them. When I have a TA, I let that TA run at least one class. It's a welcome change of pace for all, it allows a TA to get a taste of running the show, and it gives me one more thing to talk about in my letter of recommendation. I wasn't doing Allie any favors, though, by giving her one of the final classes of the semester. Everybody was pretty much done with the semester after *Fear and Loathing in Las Vegas*, and we skated through the short stories on our way to a finish line that couldn't come fast enough to satisfy most of us in that weird and uncertain spring.

Allie had teaching experience, having taught composition at BC and also English to language students at high schools and dodgy institutions of higher learning in Eastern Europe. But she hadn't yet taught a literature course, and she had only led class in person. The night before she led the discussion in Lit Core, she wrote in her journal, *I'm a little worried about how it will go because I'm afraid they'll be very quiet. It's the end of the semester and they're tired. The stories seem not as easy as when I chose them, which I think is normal, and it'll be done via Zoom.* Her class session went well, especially because Stella and Dave and Dan and Tyler and Marguerite and some of the other most talkative and community-minded students saw that she was in a vulnerable situation and made an extra effort to pitch in and make sure that it did. Still, afterward, she wrote in her journal, *Seeing all those spaced out faces fills me with dread.* She had to lecture much more than she'd planned to, explaining the two stories rather than leading the group in plumbing their intricacies, and she realized that even preparing good questions and improvising good follow-up questions could not guarantee a lively exchange on Zoom. She told me, "It makes so much sense to me to understand Zoom as corporate conferencing software, because it does feel like, Oh, I put someone on to report, and now they're telling me about our quarterly earnings or whatever it is that people at companies talk about. Zoom was built for them, and not for a collaborative conversation." She cited "the lack of social cues" and "the temptation to do something else" when attending class on Zoom as crucial conversation killers.

She moved on from the MA program at BC to a PhD program at another university, where over the long haul of the pandemic, she was forced to become adept at remote teaching. I felt a little guilty when she described the approach she eventually came up with. She used lots of breakout groups, Google docs, forum posts, peer review, some lecturing— "pretty much anything other than trying to do a close reading all together, which is of course impossible on Zoom." That "of course" stung a little because it reminded me that when the crisis arrived and forced us to reconsider our habits and change our ways, I'd just kept on trying to do the same old thing, even though it was now nearly impossible to do it well.

We read and discussed the two pairs of short stories after we were done with Didion and Thompson, a shift that slightly undermined the original design of the Lit Core syllabus, which had the tandem of Didion and Thompson running the anchor leg of the semester. The idea had been that we would cap off our inquiry by extending it from fiction into nonfiction, from literature into the news, from make-believe realms of the imagination into the believe-it-or-else realities of everyday life. Didion and Thompson also modeled one of many ways to apply the lessons of the semester: go out into the world, seek out interesting experiences, and impose form and meaning on them by writing about them.

The rise of Donald Trump had made the move from literature to life feel a lot easier to explain and more urgent to make. From the very first day of class, when we'd spent some time close-reading the resonant three-word sentences "Call me Ishmael" and "Build the wall," he'd been a handy recurring reference point. It also helped make the case for a required literature course to have a sitting president whose presence in the White House and omnipresence in the culture could not possibly be explained by political science, economics, or any other discipline with pretensions to quantitative precision. Any model that featured rational actors voting their interests didn't begin to suffice, and those who study literature and culture might well pick up where other disciplines ran out of analytical steam. Trump was a Mickey Spillane character who put Bill Clinton (a

Barry Hannah character), Ronald Reagan (a Philip K. Dick character), and all other contenders in the shade as a virtuoso unreliable narrator. As a historical phenomenon, he was all about what he meant. And *how* he did what he did and said what he said—the pounding repetition of keywords (disgusting disgusting disgusting, bad bad bad, disgraceful disgraceful disgraceful), the ALL-CAPS SHOUTING and seventeenth-century Capitalizatioune and Spellinge on Twitter, the endless perfect examples of verbal irony ("Believe me, it's not a problem, believe me")—cried out for the application of our interpretive tools to get at its meaning.

(I want to make clear that when I bring up Donald Trump now and again in this book, which isn't all that surprising when one considers that he was a potent wielder of form and meaning who was in fact president of the United States in the spring of 2020, it has almost nothing to do with whether I think Trump had bad or good policy ideas or belonged to a party I prefer, or any such everyday political considerations, which didn't mean much to him anyway. In my long-standing view, he's a one-of-a-kind blight whose single-issue commitment to feeling important at all costs and reverse-Midas gift for destroying everything he touches put him in a special category that transcends the mundane business of electoral politics and the endless, tedious culture wars on which advantage-seeking political operatives encourage Americans to squander their time and energy. To confirm the "long-standing" part, I can present as evidence a seminar paper about Trump's public image titled "The Uncleane Beast as Model Citizen," which I wrote in graduate school in 1989. He was a registered Republican at the time, but he would eventually switch to the Democratic Party, then back to the Republican. When I recently looked at that paper, dot-matrix-printed in Apple's old New York font, I noted mention on page 2 of the possibility of his ending up in the White House, which he was already floating as a subject for public discussion in New York tabloids in the late 1980s. I felt like a character in a horror movie discovering a dark prophecy in an ancient scroll written in an arcane crabbèd script that he found in a crypt.)

This move from literature to life via Trump came straight from the basic humanities playbook. If you're looking for lessons in how to live, you have to work on your chops so that you can get meaning out of all kinds of texts in which those lessons might be found. If you're looking for lessons in chopsmanship, then you need some kind of application to the problem of how to live to impart the necessary urgency of a meaningful answer to the So what? question. Getting to be the most powerful human on earth by repeating three-syllable phrases that sound like the titles of non-green-lighted Steven Seagal movies—*Build the Wall, Lock Her Up, Drain the Swamp*, and in another few months you could add *Stop the Steal* to the list—seemed like a pretty significant so-what.

11 Outcomes

There was no big finish at the end of the semester because that's not what happens at the end of a semester, especially on Zoom. In writing-workshop courses, I tell the students I'll be looking for their byline in the future, and I urge them to keep me posted on their exploits. In American Studies courses, I urge students to drop me a line if they run across a good book or movie that would fit on the syllabus. But on the last day of Lit Core, I just say that they know how to find me, and I'll look forward to seeing them around campus, and I'll be glad to have them in other classes I teach; and I often do see them again. Because I said it on Zoom in the spring of 2020, I have no memory of the moment. I clicked End Meeting for All and that was it. A week later, they turned in their take-home finals, and I marked up those finals and their final round of papers and returned them. One principal feature of any given semester, especially when nobody in the room is a second-semester senior, is that there will be another semester after it.

Still, we were done, which meant it was time to consider consequences. Did the students in Lit Core get what they came for? Did they get what I wanted them to get out of it? At semester's end, were they ready—or readier than they had been in January—to swim in the sea of language in our stormy times? It could take advanced close-reading skills to parse the super-compressed meanings of dueling slogans like "black lives matter" and "blue lives matter" and "all lives matter" or the familiar sequence of what Anthony Fauci said about the Covid pandemic, what the president's free-form Twitter poem said about what Fauci said, what Fauci said and didn't say about what the president said, and how all manner of commentators glossed the meaning of what they said. Were the students more confident and less skeptical about the work of interpretation and more prepared for meaningful employment, citizenship, difficulty, and joy because they had arrived at a deeper and more articulate understanding of the struggles of Dybek's neighborhood kids navigating the passage to the wider world, Wharton's warrior-water plant, or Díaz's doomed nerd idealist and his toxic amanuensis?

I think so. I hope so. Covid certainly didn't help. Lit Core online was less efficient, energetic, fun, humane, and rewarding than it was in person. We got less done, I was a much less effective teacher, and there was less sense of community and more of a sense of just getting through it. The move to Zoom stopped and reversed the semester-long process of gradually turning over to the students more and more responsibility for directing and initiating our discussions, so I did too much of the thinking out loud in class down the homestretch. But the essence of the class and why it matters didn't change. The coming-together of a community of inquiry around the work of deep-diving into literature in search of meaning, the building of analytical skills in class discussions and in writing and revising papers, the routine of putting tools in the kit and testing their use, the mechanics of trial and error and reinforced practice—that all still happened. So did some useful thinking about the lessons on how to live that the books we'd read might have to offer. Reading through their papers and take-home finals as I did my grading at the end of the semester, I could see that students were making interpretive arguments about meaning founded on literary evidence better than they had in January. They also knew something they hadn't before about realism and magical realism, diaspora and immigrant literature, journalism and counterculture, selfhood and social order, money and identity, narration and diction, character systems and intertextuality, ideas and language, the risks and rewards of being a misfit.

For me, what matters most about Lit Core is our encounter with literature as equipment for living, both in the sense of honing interpretive skills on what we read and in the sense of finding in it ideas about how to live. That encounter is very much still in progress when the semester ends, because much of what happens in the classroom begins to reveal its full meaning in retrospect and at a distance. But the end of the semester is the time for what administrators call outcomes assessment: the students had evaluations to fill out, and I had grades to assign. Inadequate as these methods may be, that's how the institutions of academia keep score.

.   .   .   .   .

The process of judging the quality of one's own and colleagues' teaching is (or should be) plagued at every step by doubts, and that should go double for student evaluations. I don't have a problem with the principle that students can tell us something meaningful about their teachers. Of course they can, and I'd be very interested in the results of exit interviews of students in my classes conducted by competent investigators, which is one of many reasons I decided to write this book. But the way student evaluations are done in college—within the frame of the grading relationship, anonymously and online, by putting apparently precise number values on a bunch of variables that really call for well-considered words—leaves us with an instrument that's a lot cruder and more misleading than it looks.*

Almost thirty years ago, in a dark-paneled, tobacco-cured bar near the college on a hill where I had my first academic job, a sharp young psychology professor who was obviously going places explained to me how student evaluations worked. He emphasized that they were assessments of how satisfying students found a course, which was not the same thing as how good a teacher they thought you were or how good a course they thought it was, and that they were measurably affected by factors like the size of the class (smaller is better), what time of day it met (later is better),

---

* See Len Gutkin's essay in *The Chronicle of Higher Education* summarizing research on student evaluations, with links to relevant studies: "The Review: Course Evaluations Are Garbage Science," Dec. 4, 2023, https://www.chronicle.com/newsletter/the-review/2023 -12-04.

the instructor's race and gender (white men do better), the grade the student was expecting in the class (higher is better), and the intangible but significant matter of how much they liked the professor as a person. In my experience, a class feels extra-satisfying to a student who thought at first that it was going to be a difficult experience leading to a bad grade but by the end of the semester feels that it has gone pretty well, was enjoyable, and might well result in a decent grade.

Now, it so happens that I am a man of Sicilian and Catalan parentage who teaches mostly not-huge, discussion-based classes that meet in the afternoon or evening—because I try to save early mornings for writing, and when my kids were little I got in the habit of making sure I was around in the morning to help get them out the door to school. Also, although I may seem a bit forbidding at the beginning of the semester, mostly because I am at pains to make clear from the outset the expectations of the course and establish our seriousness about pursuing a purposeful inquiry, as the course goes on, I reveal myself as more fuzzy bunny than monster. If at first I seem like a stern by-the-book officer, in other words, I turn out to be the kind who does his best to leave nobody behind, even those who screw up. I do require students to participate in class but am happy to meet with them one-on-one to scheme up the most comfortable ways for them to do that. I am understanding about illnesses, the ongoing attrition among the grandparents of college-age students, the workload in other courses, and the tidal wave of anxiety sweeping through the ranks of young people raised by smartphones. I have never once in all my years of teaching refused to work out an extension on a paper. Though I try to make clear that we're up to something serious, I want students to have a good time in class and try to model that for them, and even to be a little funny (on purpose, I mean). And I try to show them at every class meeting that I'm interested in what they're thinking, not in making them think whatever I'm thinking, and that the main work of the class is to put tools in their tool kit to help them generate their own ideas and turn them into sound arguments. I don't teach a set of ideas; I teach some ways of coming at things, and I encourage students to bring their own ideas to that work. My tendency to cluster grades in the B-minus-to-A-minus range and to save a couple of important assignments for the end of the semester, which helps me get a sense of where students finish in relation to where they started, also tends to give students confidence that they can get what they consider a decent grade in the class. When they fill out evaluations—after the final class meeting but before they receive from me their graded final assignments and their final grade for the course—most of them can still plausibly tell themselves that if they finish strong they'll do well.

This all has the side effect of tending to produce more positive student evaluations, and I have had occasion to wonder if I have let that side effect influence the development of my teaching habits. I honestly don't know the answer. On the one hand, if there's a rating system, even one you think has near-zero value, you do prefer to get higher ratings. On the other hand, I don't think student evaluations are all that useful. They can usually tell you whether an instructor is doing an acceptable or an unacceptable job, which you almost certainly already knew, but their utility falls off rapidly from there. At the university where I teach, evaluations consist mostly of numerical ratings from one to five (five being the highest), and English professors tend to get a lot of fours and fives, but in effect there are only two meaningful "numbers": one that means okay and the other that means not-okay. So a binary system of ones and fives would work just as well, as would zeros and ones, or green and red signal flags waved from a distant clock tower.

The written comments are mostly rote and telegraphic, not much more expressive than *ruled* or *sucked*, but from time to time, I've come across one that was of lasting use to me. Long ago, when I was just starting out as a teacher, a student noted that class was easier to follow when I looked directly at the students and not over their heads, and that stayed with me. Another one back then wrote, "He called us by our names, and I appreciated that," and that also stayed with me. I think it's telling that the comments that have stuck with me were written by hand in the era before evaluations moved online. I don't think those who put stock in student evaluations have fully grasped that moving them online turned them into yet another survey you fill out while playing the kind of character you play online, who tends to be shallower, meaner, more emptily glib, more of a hate-watcher or uncritical stan, and more willing to dash off any old thing that will provide a momentary spurt of anonymous auto-pleasure. The same online role-playing that gave us Boaty McBoatface (the name that won by a wide margin in an online poll in 2016 to name a new polar

research ship in the UK) and the charnel house of cretinous grandstand-
ing meanness that is the comments section after *Boston Globe* articles
tends to produce comments not much more useful than "The Rise of Silas
Lapham? Really? Wow. Just wow. LOL LMAO."

Even so, I have to grant that written comments have made me a better
teacher. Take "Get rid of notes!"—a comment a student wrote in pencil on
a paper evaluation of one of the first classes I ever taught, a survey of
American literature from colonial times to the Civil War that I taught at
Wesleyan University in the early 1990s while I was finishing my dissertation nearby at Yale. It was a lecture class, big enough that I used a lapel
microphone, and it met in a hall with tiered banks of connected desks that
rose up in concentric half-rings from the well at the bottom in which I
stood. The subject was nowhere near a specialty of mine, and I barely got
through the semester by drawing liberally on what I'd observed professors
do in similar survey courses I had taken as an undergraduate and TA'd as
a grad student. It didn't help my still-formative sense of professorial
authority that I'd been an undergrad at Wesleyan and had, in fact, fallen
asleep in lectures in the very room in which I was now lecturing. So "Get
rid of notes!" initially seemed crazy, even cruel, to me. What was I supposed to do, freestyle off the top of my head by drawing on my imaginary
deep command of the field and nonexistent extensive experience as a
lecturer?

But I came to see that "Get rid of notes!" was sound craft advice, offered
with generous intent. The student was saying that things had gone best
that semester when I had departed from my prepared remarks and just
explained and listened, citing passages in the book and analyzing them
and encouraging students to join in. Indeed, over time I've become more
and more comfortable coming to class with no more than the chart of the
tune on which we're going to jam: a well-marked-up book, an idea of what
I want us to accomplish, and the most minimal of notes—typically just a
page or two of lined paper on which I've listed by hand the page numbers
of some passages that we should wrestle with together and some rough
reminders of points I want to make sure we get to. On a good day, I glance
at my notes once or twice in passing, just to make sure we're getting
to everything. Whatever we might lose in preprogrammed structure and
coverage, which isn't that much, we gain back severalfold in students'

authentic involvement in doing the work of the class and in the way that I'm forced to listen to them and not just talk at them.

I don't do much lecturing anymore, but I think about "Get rid of notes!" from time to time—especially one day late in the fall semester of 2021, my first semester back to fully in-person classes after a lost year on Zoom. That was a great semester. Students and their professors were so thrilled to be back in person that everyone charged into class with extra vigor and goodwill. I was teaching Studies in Narrative, the gateway course that sophomores take once they've decided to major or minor in English. It was a particularly excellent group, game and funny and earnest and committed and kind to each other, and they had the kind of dream chemistry that gets meaningful contributions out of everyone in the room and makes it a pleasure to toss them a problem to pounce on. Late in the semester, well into our discussions of Italo Calvino's elegant but abstruse *Invisible Cities*, I somehow misplaced my notes for the day's class. I didn't notice they were missing until I got to the classroom, opened up the manila folder in which I carried the current business of that course, and couldn't find them. I had prepared the week's classes over the previous weekend, as I often do, and I'd been caught up in something else until just before class time—a writing deadline, probably—so I didn't have my plan for that day's class frontloaded in·my head. Normally, I'd reload it as I looked over my notes again on the lectern in front of me just before we started. But I couldn't find them.

So I told the class that I couldn't find my notes and said we better figure out what we should talk about, and we did, and it was one of the best class sessions I've ever taught, crackling with energy and discovery. I really didn't know what we were going to do, where we were going to go, and I found out along with everybody else. A lively student named Anna was uncharacteristically quiet for the first half hour or so, furiously scribbling something in her notebook with furrowed brow; then she raised her hand to say that she'd come up with a chart that might help explain the structure of the book. I had her put it on the board, and we spent much of the rest of the class period talking about Anna's Chart™, which really did help us explain the structure of the book to ourselves. Afterward, a student came up and told me, "This is why I want to major in English." So, yeah, to that now-fiftyish (I hope, if you're still with us) person who took that survey class at Wesleyan and wrote something thoughtful on her or his evaluation form, I heard you and I still hear you. Note to self: Get rid of notes.

And how did students' evaluations of Lit Core in spring 2020 look? Fine, but not particularly informative. Twenty-three of the thirty-three students who completed the course took the time to fill out evaluations, which are optional. On the whole, they thought the course was sufficiently organized and challenging, I was sufficiently enthusiastic and respectful and prepared and able to stimulate interest in the subject matter, and so on. One of the very few numerical items that I do pay attention to is how much effort students thought the course required of them. As a general rule, I want more than half to say that my course required more effort than similar courses, and that item came out just about right: 60 percent said that it required more effort, about a third said it required the same effort, and just one respondent said that it required less effort. I used to assign a lot more reading than I do now, so I've certainly come down over the years to meet my students' expectations halfway, but I want to keep the work-load in the sweet spot where I think it's too little and they think it's a lot but still manageable.

The written comments in response to the prompt *What are the strengths of the course?* were pleasant enough to read, though not brimming with actionable information. I suppose I should be happy to be assured that I'm "intellectual," though I'm not sure what that means; and I certainly appreciated this one: "Expectations were clear from the beginning, and Professor Rotella often shared his reasoning behind decisions. The mixture of discussion and lecture heavily favored discussion, and Professor Rotella used his lecture time efficiently and productively." That looks like a solid A-minus to me, and I'll take it. And in the end, I was most pleased to see several versions of this one: "It was very helpful in how to make connections between the way the works were written and what their meaning was." Form expresses meaning! Mission accomplished.

The written comments in response to the prompt *How could the instructor improve the course?* were all over the place, which is par for the course. One person wanted me to lecture more, another felt that the class "could perhaps be more discussion-oriented." A couple of students mentioned that it's hard to speak up in a discussion when there are so many people in the room, which is certainly true, and a couple of others wanted more split classes and small-group work, which amounts to the same valid point. A couple found the amount of reading overwhelming, and another one wanted me to slow down the pace of the course, not to reduce the amount of reading but so that we could take more time to know each book more deeply (which sounds like Arun, who is on the record as stating that he likes to take it slow in grooving on a book). One wrote, "Too much focus on literary interpretation and connecting form to theme. There is more to literature than drawing form-theme connections. I wish we would have covered a wider array of readings. Also, too much writing." There was a substantive point in there for me to think on: even if *form expresses meaning* is our analytical mantra, can I be more explicit about other ways of responding to literature beyond connecting form to theme?

None of these responses struck me as wildly unfair, and it's probable that at some point in the semester, I agreed with each of them—except the complaints about too much reading or writing. Lit Core sections should be smaller, and I wish there were enough TAs and available rooms that everyone who teaches Lit Core could split the class in half whenever he or she wanted to. And I always have to strike a balance between going deep on each text and reading a variety of works, as well as balancing interpretively connecting form to meaning with other responses to literature—emotional, for instance, or as a gateway to history, or as a repository of ideas—that can lead to and from interpretation. I can always adjust those balances, and it's good for me to be reminded to keep revisiting them. As I mentioned before, one permanent change that came out of this first pandemic semester was that I adopted as a regular feature of almost all undergrad classes the brief weekly writing exercise based closely on the reading. It's a low-stakes, high-frequency way to diversify class participation so that it doesn't always require putting up your hand and speaking in front of everyone. This also allows me to replace midterms and finals with a checkup that's more timely, sensitive to week-to-week completion of the reading, and likely to lead to better conversations in class.

There was also a question on the evaluation asking if the student would recommend this class to others. Twenty-one of the respondents said yes, one abstained from answering that question, and one said, "I would not because it is time consuming and not interesting to me." Of course, there were another ten students in the class who didn't fill out evaluations, and that group would be likely to include some of the least-engaged students, so there may well have been more no votes that went uncounted.

.   .   .   .   .

Because I write about boxing and spend time in the fight world, I score rounds from ringside and I vote every fall as an elector of the International Boxing Hall of Fame, but those are just about the only forms of evaluation I perform willingly. Mostly, I find evaluation to be a burden that only gets in the way of appreciating or understanding things. Yet as a professor, I have to assess and rate and rank all the time. It comes as a nasty surprise to most people who go into the school business—and it certainly came as one to me—just how much of your time you have to spend on evaluating other people's work. Marking up and grading papers, refereeing other scholars' book and article manuscripts, assessing and arguing tenure and promotion cases, passing judgment on book proposals, ranking applicants for fellowships and grants, writing letters of recommendation for students and colleagues, deciding on graduate admissions, deciding who gets awards and prizes, reviewing—when a backlog of all this stuff you tend to put off comes down on you, it can seem as if you're really in the evaluation business and just trying to squeeze in some teaching and writing on the side. Nobody I know loves this aspect of being an academic, and nobody really trains you to do it well, but it's a significant part of the job. And you should try to do it well—because you owe it to people who put in the work and expect to be judged fairly; because you want to be treated well by others when the positions are reversed; and because as a matter of policy and principle, you should try to do things well.

Grading student work is the form of evaluation that raises the fewest doubts for me. Compared to the much iffier process of evaluating other professors' work—a process made all the more fraught by the opacities and head fakes and ulterior motives and high career stakes and conflicting notions of rigor that frequently pervade it—grading is pretty straightforward. A B paper looks like a B paper, an A paper looks like an A paper, and there's not that much mystery in the distinction. If you ask students to grade their own work, they usually come up with something that resembles your own judgment, though, if anything, they grade themselves more harshly. My nonacademic friends who imagine the classroom devastated by constant culture war also tend to picture an unending stream of distraught students and enraged parents questioning every B-plus, but, again, that hasn't been my experience. On the rare occasion that a student wants me to explain a grade, I'm happy to explain it, and that's usually the end of it. *Look, we'd both be thrilled if you'd written an A paper, but you wrote a B-minus paper, and let me explain what makes it a B-minus paper, so you can do better next time.*

When I read a student's paper, I line-edit and comment as I go along. In the margins, I'll note well-made points, good moves, ideas that inspire further thinking; and I will also try to tighten language and sharpen the focus of the argument, suggest where it could do more with an idea, and point out where it could use more or better evidence or analysis or explanation. When I write a comment at the end, I start by saying something about what the paper does well: gets at a main theme of the story, connects form to meaning, identifies a problem and sets itself up to answer it. If there's some quality of the paper I can reasonably use a word like *strong*, *sophisticated*, or *insightful* to describe, I use that word to positively reinforce effort and effectiveness. Then I point out some ways in which the paper could more fully develop the possibilities of its argument: reducing repetition and eliminating filler like plot description to make room for more meaty analysis, setting up the main points more forcefully in the introduction, unburying and moving up the excellent points now buried deep in paragraphs that should be reorganized around them.

A typical summary assessment might go something like this: *This paper is strongest where you get in close to the imagery and diction of the novel and use that evidence to support a compelling reading of the problem that Lily Bart poses for high society. There are some obstacles, though, to the full development of this argument. As you will see from going through my mark-up and marginal comments, there are some mechanical matters to attend to (see comments on sentence structure and punctuation on pages 2, 4, 5 for details). Also, there's too much plot description in the long paragraph on page 2: remember, you can assume that I have read the text, so you can dispense with plot description and stick to analysis. I have suggested in my mark-up on p. 2 how you could convert that paragraph to analytical rather than descriptive purposes. But the main obstacle is that*

you wrote your way into your best version of your argument in the last
third of the paper (see my note at the bottom of p. 4). As a result, the paper
would be more effective in delivering that argument if you were to move
that best version of it to the beginning and start where you now end, as we
discussed in our in-class writing workshop in April. That would give the
paper the best chance to do full justice to your insightful reading of the
novel. The comments are not only an attempt to understand what the
paper set out to do, assess how well the paper did it, and show how it could
do it more effectively; they're also an explanation for the grade I give to
the paper. The lower the grade, the more I tend to write, both to justify the
grade and to make sure I offer a clear picture of how the paper could have
earned—or could still earn, if there's a chance to rewrite it—a better one.

The vast majority of the grades I assign fall between B-minus and
A-minus, though there are some Cs, the very occasional D or F, and the
also-occasional straight A, which I reserve for exemplary work that nails
not just the assignment but also the course's larger purposes. There has
certainly been grade inflation in college and in high school over the years,
and in my lifetime I've seen that progress to the point that I now keep a
box of tissues in my office to hand to students who can't stop themselves
from weeping when they come in to discuss the first B they have ever
gotten on a paper in their lives. But to some extent, I think the concentra-
tion of grades in the B-minus-to-A-minus range is also consistent with the
nature of college these days. It's hard to get into schools like the one at
which I teach; the students who do get in tend to have devoted a great deal
of their young lives to becoming professional about school, and most of
them know how to do a solid job.

It would be a little easier for me if I felt free to use the full range of
grades, but unless everybody else chose to do that as well, it would make
me such an outlier among faculty that I would spend all my time explaining Cs to anguished students who don't get them from anyone else. Until
college teachers across the nation decide collectively to take a step back all
at once to using the full grade range, which I would urge us to do, I can
work with the reduced range available. I would be happier still to get rid
of grades entirely and substitute a paragraph that sums up how a student
did on a paper or in a course, but, again, assigning a letter grade is the
norm, and I don't want to spend all my time explaining why I have broken

with it. I just don't feel particularly oppressed by having to assign letter grades or by the fact that they tend to cluster in the B-minus-to-A-minus range, even though it's obviously a flawed system for evaluating student work. A grade is like a salary—not the only or even the main reason you do the work but one tangible way to indicate that you have done it—and it strikes me as no terrible thing that most students who put in the effort to do well in a course make just about the same as the others. They're not *that* far apart.

A lot of professors I know do agonize over grades, and I feel a little insensitive that I don't, but I don't. That's in part because I don't think grades are very important. They're useful to the extent that they reflect a student's current capacity and willingness to meet expectations and demonstrate command of the ideas and methods of the course, but they're at best a crude measure of accomplishment and ability. As a snapshot of where the work is at the point it happened to be turned in, they aren't always a reliable measure of where students are going. I've had to give Cs and Fs to inspired thinkers who just couldn't get it together to deliver the goods, Bs to students who were full of ideas and work ethic and clearly destined for success but just weren't putting all the pieces together yet, and A-minuses to students who were probably hitting their peak and already coasting and didn't seem likely to have much more to say for themselves. Grades can't tell us how smart anybody is, and sometimes I find myself obliged to remind college students of that. Also, while I'm all for taking school seriously, they do well to bear in mind that they're not trying to get into college anymore, and there's no committee of life-course-determining Norns to hold a B against them.

Maybe I also don't regard Bs as traumatic because, unlike many of my peers in the professoriate, I haven't been a straight-A student since I was a little kid. In elementary school, I was a showoff achiever in every subject, a getter of 103s on tests, a leading student musician, and, before puberty came along to reshape the pecking order in my grade, I was also a star of the games we played—an arms-raised scorer of many baskets and goals and runs in gym class, a winner of ribbons in swim and track meets, the kind of dead-pull hitter whose arrival at the plate would cause the other team's outfielders to shift way back into deep left field to chase the booming moon shot sure to come off my bat. In middle school, I started dropping off in math and science, stopped practicing the violin, and turned into an irksome defender, a shifty passer, still a dead-pull hitter but now the kind who steered low line drives within inches of the third base line and settled for a single or perhaps at best a double, as long as I didn't have to slide into second base. In high school, I got wildly uneven grades and switched to self-taught guitar and skulked around in a down jacket and got high. In college, I did much better in my classes—in part because I stopped getting high and was able to avoid most of my academic weaknesses and concentrate on my strengths—but got used to receiving A-minuses on what I thought of as my best papers, along with a comment that usually went something like "This was a good paper, but it didn't have much to do with the course." Similarly, I received a few entirely deserved less-than-great semester grades in grad school classes because I didn't always demonstrate close engagement with the ideas and methods of the courses I took. I didn't talk much in class, and when obliged to choose between writing about what interested me and writing about something directly connected to the essence of a course, I went for the former. (The paper I mentioned earlier that I wrote about Donald Trump, which I wrote for a course on consumer culture, would be a good example of that.)

Maybe I'm also fine with handing out Bs in large numbers because I don't have a problem with being the equivalent of a lifelong B student in subjects beyond school that I love and that sustain me, like music, basketball, and running. A B can mean a lot of things: you have talent, but you aren't yet in full command of it; you don't have an overload of talent, but you're getting something meaningful out of what you've got; you'd do better if you tried harder; you're competently assimilating and imitating the work of others, but you're not yet making the material your own; you're trying hard and you've got original ideas, but you need to bring your chops up to a level at which you can execute those ideas in ways that do justice to them; you raise interesting possibilities, but the work's not well aligned with what's being taught; and a dozen other possibilities. I respect the unassuming, unprepossessing B, a modest but versatile workhorse of a grade.

As it happened, in Lit Core in the spring of 2020, I ended up awarding the highest letter grades I'd ever given for a course. Dan was right about what would happen when the university loosened up its rules on the pass-fail option in response to the coming of the pandemic, even though he need not have worried that it would somehow negatively affect his own GPA. Just about everybody who felt they had no realistic shot at a grade better than B-plus took the pass-fail option, so what remained were mostly A-minuses, some As, some B-pluses, and a whole lot of Passes. I don't have a problem with that. The actual grades just aren't that important to me—not as important as, for instance, the way that Budhardin's elephant continues to haunt students who took the class.

.   .   .   .   .

I knew that there was a lot more going on in students' heads than could be captured by grades, evaluations, or other standard measures of outcomes—which is a big part of why I decided to ask them what was, in fact, going on in their heads and ended up writing this book. One thing I've learned as both student and teacher is that you can't always predict what effect teaching will have on learning. In the classroom, output can flow from input in eccentric bends and leaps, and often the models offered by teachers or fellow students, rather than the content of the subject matter, make the most lasting impression.

You never know who's going to get what from a class, and it can take a while to find out—as I can attest, since I'm still extracting the juice from things that happened in classrooms half a century and more ago. The excitement of discovering a craft worth doing well and setting out to do it well can persist long after a grade attached to that work has ceased to matter at all. So can the example set by a teacher or a fellow student. Modeling—what you do in the classroom and write in response to written work, how you carry yourself and how you ask others to carry themselves—typically has a deeper and more enduring effect on your students than the books you assign. The way you identify and address a problem worth solving or respond to someone else's thinking will probably last long after Oscar Wao's and Lily Bart's misfit sorrows have faded from students' memories. That's the long game of education, and in school, we play the long game for keeps.

When I think about what I have learned from my teachers, subject matter rarely comes first to mind. I remember them primarily for how they carried themselves, how they modeled the process of teaching and learning. Each appears in memory as a characteristic stance, an attitude toward the universe. They have given me much, much more than I returned to them as their student. There are, of course, a few cautionary examples among them of what not to do, which can also provide valuable lessons, but for the most part, I've been blessed with teachers so good and so generous that I feel both unending gratitude and a little shame when I think of how much I owe them. I will say in my own defense that, as it turned out, even at my dreamiest and most detached I was in fact paying attention and learning my lessons, though it could take a while—okay, decades—for some of those lessons to sink in, and not always or even often in the way that the teacher might have intended.

Most of what I remember of Miss Tengan, my first- and second-grade teacher, is her gentle but firm no-nonsense air, which encouraged the variously foaming and dreamy-detached maniacs under her tutelage to fit ourselves into the scheduled activities of the day like so many bottles of 190-proof spirits into the cardboard-slotted interior of a liquor store box. I retain a couple of vivid images of her in my mind—little blip-movies rather than still photographs. In one, she has the boys in our class lined up in front of the urinals in the bathroom next to our classroom, and she's going over some basic procedures likely to encourage getting our pee in the urinals and not all over the bathroom or each other or ourselves. Don't unzip until you're right in front of the target, look at what you're doing and not all around at whatever else might be going on in the bathroom (like, say, Bobby McDermut climbing over the partitions between stalls and making faces at those sitting on the toilet below), shake and zip *before* moving on. An understatedly put-together woman with interesting cheekbones who has been obliged to perform a distasteful duty to curb the excesses of runty males who can't resist spraying their scent-marker everywhere, she's holding her exasperation in check, rising above the annoyance to turn this sorry occasion into another opportunity to impress on her charges sound habits leading to success—or at least heading off abject failure—in school and in life.

I also see her standing at the front of the room, the kids quietly lined up behind her, everybody ready to go outside. They're all looking at me. I've been entirely lost in reading my *Man from U.N.C.L.E.* book, *The Calcutta*

Affair, a fat pale-orange Big Little Book with large print, lots of pictures, and Cold War espionage, so I completely missed it when the rest of the class heard and obeyed her request to stop doing what they were doing and line up for recess. To this day, I can see the way two contrary impulses register in Miss Tengan's posture and face. The set of her slim shoulders under her jacket and the tilt of her head on her graceful neck convey a certain impatience for this head-in-the-clouds to snap out of it and get in line. But on her face is a look of conditional approval, flat in the mouth but livelier in the eyes, because this kind of intense reading is good wherever and whenever it happens. That's true even if such reading involves this dumbass book, on the cover of which there's a crude drawing in bright colors of Napoleon Solo and Ilya Kuryakin carrying elaborately silencered automatic pistols that the book says they will soon return to their shoulder holsters—which, even at the age of seven, I realized made no sense, given that the silencered gun wouldn't fit in the holster. The way Miss Tengan looked in that moment expresses how I feel when a student mostly ignores the assignment but turns in a good paper.

The enthusiasms of Mr. Lubway, my fifth-grade teacher, left me cold. Alone among all the teachers at the Lab School, a private institution in a condition of moderate grooviness after having been struck amidships but not holed below the waterline by the 1960s, he had his class recite the Pledge of Allegiance every morning. He explained that he had come to value the rituals of American liberty while living for a time under a repressive regime in Poland, but I didn't like standing and murmuring in near-unison, which felt like bending the knee. At some point early in the year, I started sitting out "under God" or replacing it with "under the sky," which I still do on those rare occasions when I find myself reciting the pledge. Mr. Lubway also loved Gilbert and Sullivan, and he made us memorize songs with way too many words that came out in a tongue-twisting spate that resembled the playing of an overbusy guitar noodler taking endless choruses of wailing solo. The centerpiece of the year was mounting a play about a farcical war between pirates and orphans, a pastiche written by a previous class of Mr. Lubway's that grafted an original plot and lyrics onto Gilbert and Sullivan tunes. In addition to hating Gilbert and Sullivan, I hated being in plays. I got through this one—in which I played a pirate with few solo lines but a lot of onstage group business to execute with the other pirates—by promising myself that this was it, the last time. After this one, I would be willing to work backstage or play an instrument in the pit or contribute in some other capacity to a production, but I would refuse to go onstage to pretend to be somebody who wasn't me, no matter what anybody threatened to do to me. I stuck to this resolve and have stuck to it to this day. (Yes, I know, teaching is kind of like going onstage, but the character I play is me.)

I picture Mr. Lubway banging on the old upright piano in our classroom with his longish silver hair flopping and regimental mustache aquiver, urging us on with a florid passion that seemed so self-exposing, so dangerous to reveal, that it embarrassed me for his sake. I vividly recall recognizing within myself a deep urge to distrust and resist everything this guy cared so much about, yet I memorized the songs, I acted in the play, I got with the program. I learned enduring lessons that year about how to be a pro and do your part in getting things done right, even if they're not your thing. I despised his enthusiasms, but his wholehearted confidence in them, his conviction that what he wanted us to do was worth doing well and that the experience would be of value, carried all before it. If you do a difficult thing, you're a person who has done a difficult thing. There's inherent value in that.

And, conversely, there's inherent value for a teacher in recognizing that a particular student is *not* going to do a difficult or even a fairly easy thing, no matter how hard you try to reach that student. I can still see versions of a certain look on the faces of Mrs. Matchett, my math teacher throughout middle school, and Mme. Pillet, my French teacher throughout high school. It's the look of a good professional teacher who's used to succeeding, a decent person warmly committed to her subject and her students, realizing that despite year after year of effort on her part, this particular student is not going to come around on her watch. Neither of them gave up altogether on me, but each visibly concluded that it was time to cut her losses and expend more energy on students who would put more into their own educations than I was willing to put into mine at that stage of my school career. I can't fully explain why I resisted them and their subjects, but I did, and in the fullness of time, I learned a valuable lesson from them about a student's and a teacher's respective responsibilities in the transaction between them. As a teacher you owe it to every student to try to reach them, but sometimes you don't reach them, even after years of trying, and you don't shortchange the other students to keep chasing after one who refuses to ante up. Sometimes a student is simply you-proof at that stage in his or her schooling, as I was in the cases of both Mrs. Matchett and Mme. Pillet.

With some teachers and subjects, it's just the opposite. You walk into that classroom, and you become an optimal, even ideal version of yourself in a way that stays with you forever. This kind of quiet exaltation happened to me more and more routinely, and less and less by haphazard lightning-strike luck, as I got older and better at taking an interest in things. Mr. Hoffenkamp, with whom I took a high-school English class called "The Hero as Seeker," in which we read Saint-Exupéry's *Night Flight* and watched *The Hustler* ("Do you like to gamble, Eddie? Gamble money on pool games?"), set a tone of patient confidence in the layered complexity of the work and in the ability of the community of inquiry to get to the bottom of it. "I'm not sure what's going on in this story, but there's plenty to figure out," his manner seemed to say, "and together we'll figure it out, and we'll take as long as we need to. We've got all semester." Ms. McCampbell, my high school's Shakespeare specialist, conveyed a similar confidence in her students, but hers managed to seem much more personal. She was glad you could make it to class that day because we were discussing *Twelfth Night*, in which she found deep interpretive joy, and she was looking forward to talking about it with you, and she seemed so sure that you'd rise to the occasion that you didn't want to let her down. Joseph Siry, whose architecture courses I took in college, would stray in front of the screen and into the projected image of the building on which he was lecturing, eyes closed. The image of the house or church or sky-scraper under consideration would ripple across his long, stark form as he sought the right descriptive turn of phrase or analytical formulation—the very image of the thinker inhabiting the object of his thought, and vice versa. His example, like those of Mr. Hoffenkamp and Ms. McCampbell, comes back to me when I'm reminding myself to put good work on the syllabus, to trust that work and the students, and to put aside concerns about whether they will be able to get into it. They will find a way, and I'll help them by letting them know I'm sure they'll find a way and by making a show of finding my own way into it.

I was only occasionally persuaded by the stylized takes on American film and literature and music of Joe Reed, another teacher I encountered in college, but I enjoyed watching him turn his own raw reaction into a brief for understanding the work of art under scrutiny as a machine for producing that reaction. He *loved* this, *hated* that, was perpetually affronted or beguiled by the presumption or shrewdness or blindness of the work. That's where he started. As I type this, I can hear his singsong delivery: "*Moo*vies come from *moo*vies, and they have a be*gin*ning, middle, and *end*, but *not* neces*sa*rily in that *or*der." I heard in his tone a kind of delighted fury at being pushed around by art, and he also managed to simultaneously convey both interpretive certainty and an admission that he was winging it, spitballing, putting together his analytical reaction this way this time but maybe some other way the next, as the spirit and contingency moved him. As Joe Reed practiced it, interpretation was more poetry than science; it was literature, akin to the object it beheld. I didn't have to buy his particular interpretations to take away that lesson from his classroom.

I've had many more teachers I could tell you about—certainly more than I can get to in this chapter or even a whole book on the subject. The historian Jon Butler, for instance, deftly jiu-jitsu'd his critique-maddened grad students by making it a rule of his seminar that first we had to figure out what was going on in the book before anybody could have an opinion about what might be wrong with it. The classicist Andrew Szegedy-Maszak, the first professor I ever had who made everybody speak up in his seminar, changed my life by forcing me to ante up in class. Mary Danielewski, the only trainer or coach with whom I've ever done business in an otherwise strictly DIY athletic life, taught me how to deadlift and squat properly when I was recovering from a stress fracture and couldn't run. She was admirably flexible—adjusting, for example, to the fact that I am immune to encouragement and prefer to just do the damn thing and skip the cheerleading—and she made a specialty of usefully vivid descriptions: try to drive the soles of your feet through the floor, load the weight on the way down, don't Gollum. Kevin Barry, my steel guitar teacher, is a rare bird, a superlatively talented expert who models not only technical virtuosity but also a joyous attitude toward even the most elementary aspects of his craft. He meets you where you are in a way that makes you want to work harder to get closer to where he is. He'll say, "You hear how nicely that phrase falls over the F-sharp minor with a flat five? Let's do that ten more times. I'll play the chord and you play around with the scale and try to be as musical as you can with it, and let's just hear how cool that is." There has been great value to me as a fellow teacher in watching Kevin and Mary put up with my B-studentness, especially when I take forever to grasp something so obvious to them that it's difficult for them to imagine that others might not see it.

Thinking about models of teaching and learning made me want to check in with Rich Slotkin, the distinguished scholar of American violence and the frontier. He has been my rabbi, as they say in Chicago politics and the NYPD, in the school business since I attended a reading he gave on campus when I was an undergraduate at Wesleyan. He was a professor of American Studies, but he was reading from a novel-in-progress, and somewhere deep inside, below the level of conscious awareness, I noted that being a professor was a good day job for a writer and that the arrangement seemed to agree with him. My first impression of him was of a big bearded guy with a commanding voice, though as I got to know him, I came to hear his voice as more interested in getting things right than commanding. I also came to realize that if he shaved off the facial hair and trimmed his thicket of 1980s Chuck Norris hair, he would be revealed as a banty little guy with an outsize presence. I took several classes with him and have continued to seek him out for guidance over the years. He's in his eighties and retired now, and we still keep in touch from time to time. Part of what makes Slotkin an excellent correspondent is that he's satisfyingly in-character. Years ago, when I was getting ready to fly across the country for a campus interview, I received an email from him that concluded with the line "Now go and smite Amalek, and spare not his camel or his ass."

When I asked Slotkin if he had anything to tell me about the devious-cruising paths a teacher's influence can take, he told me a story from his days as a student at Brooklyn College in the 1950s. "I took the Big Shakespeare Lecture with Professor Grebanier, who was famous enough to figure in a Woody Allen joke," he said. "He was pompous and self-important—and, worse than that, he had named names in the 1950s when the Brooklyn faculty was being purged of 'subversives,' so my parents, who were alums, despised him. Nevertheless, he was a fabulous lecturer, a showman who even made his obnoxious manner an effective tool for getting the point across and making it memorable. I learned more about lecturing from him than from smarter, better, more scholarly profs I had later on." More than sixty years later, Slotkin could still hear Grebanier's "plummy and self-satisfied voice and tone" and could list the lessons he took away from Grebanier's approach to lecturing as stage performance: "Enjoy yourself, and pleasure communicates itself. You aren't doing a data dump; you're performing the way you deal with your subject, the way you analyze, appreciate, respond. And you change the act with each class, depending on what play or novel or film you're dealing with, and what mode of analysis you want to demonstrate. One model per class, and don't do it all at once. So if you did ironic distance last time, try passionate engagement this time, and by the end of the term you will have conveyed a repertoire of responses. How much of that I understood at the time I couldn't say, but that was the takeaway over time."

For all his self-absorption, Grebanier not only taught Slotkin invaluable lessons about teaching and learning, he also inspired him simply by noticing him. "My personal connection with him was minimal, and I had no more than one or two conversations with him about my work," Slotkin said. "But it's exciting to be taught by a first-class mind or even a mere academic celebrity, even if you don't buy their line or aren't even interested in the subject. If such a prof then pays you the tribute of taking you seriously, the validation is real and important." You never know who's going to learn what from whom. Styles, as I may have noted once or twice, make fights.

.   .   .   .   .

When I first drafted this final chapter of the book in the spring of 2023, I was on leave, writing full-time and looking ahead to the fall, when I'd be teaching a workshop on magazine writing and a different version of Lit Core that's all about the literature and culture of Boston. I would be in fiftieth grade. Meanwhile, the students who took Lit Core with me in spring 2020 were mostly about to graduate. Several were going on to professional school or graduate school. Some, especially those in the School of Management, were going on to jobs in finance, banking, accounting, and so on. Susannah, who double-majored in information systems and philosophy, got into the Emerging Leader program at Fidelity, which rotates graduates with "liberal arts" (read: something other than business) degrees through different divisions of the company so that they can find their best fit. She knew that moving up in the world of finance might put even more distance between her and the peers she grew up with in Gorham, Maine, but she hadn't ruled out returning there someday and becoming a teacher after she'd made her corporate bones. Colleen was on track toward her dream job, going into her final year of a five-year masters program at BC's school of education that would accredit her to become a teacher specializing in special education students with moderate support needs. Teachers have to speak up in class, and she was ready for that. Phil was already playing pro hockey, and Wilson would soon be joining him. Dan, always a perfectionist, had been holding out for just the right job in finance but was coming around to realizing that he might have to settle at some point for just any old business job to start with, and he had resolved to find one, possibly in a place offering both plenty of investment firms and reasonable facsimiles of his ideal Tahitian beach. (His plans change a lot, though. In late 2024, he had an offer from the IRS to become a criminal investigator, a T-Man, but the offer evaporated in the wake of Trump's victory. By the start of 2025, when this book was in copyedit, he was thinking about moving to Southern California to become a firefighter.) Stella was back in Seoul, at Korea University. She and her mother couldn't afford the cost of Boston College, in the end, and she had to transfer. She was majoring in English, getting ready to write a thesis, and had recruited me to advise it long-distance. The department was balking at giving her credit for this thesis, but she was going to write it anyway because she thought it would be a good and useful thing to do. She will go far in this world. Eli had been heavily involved with theater at BC; he might yet continue along that path. No doubt his parents were still giving him a hard time about it. I hoped and trusted that as these and all the other veterans of section 20 of Lit Core in spring 2020 went about their business in the world, they would be noticing form and looking to connect it to meaning, recognizing patterns and considering the narrator, and thinking from time to time of that elephant.

Because most of what happens in the classroom begins to reveal its full meaning in retrospect and at a distance, I don't really know and will never know exactly what happened in Lit Core in the spring of 2020. The students know what happened—or they will know in the fullness of time. An education is something that you go and get and carry away with you, something you *take* from your teachers and your peers and the books you read, not something that is handed to you or that you can earn simply by being a good boy or girl. Some students know this intuitively on the day they show up at college; some come to it partially and by stages and have to overcome their own skepticism and hesitation to get there; some never do quite get all the way there. Teaching feels like an honor, a thrilling craft joy, a reason to have faith in one's fellow humans, because it consists of saying *Here's what I've got; come and get it*, and—to a greater or lesser extent, to the best of their abilities and depending on conditions, not every time but often enough—students come at you and gently remove it or rip it from your hands and kind of hold it at arm's length and say to themselves, *Yeah, I think I can maybe find a use for this*, and then they go off into the world to do something with it.

Afterword: A Note on Sources and Choices

In the fall of 2021, I started interviewing the students who had been in my Lit Core class in the spring of 2020. Most of them were juniors by then, and a couple had transferred to other schools. Some didn't respond right away, and four didn't respond at all, but in the end, I interviewed twenty-nine of the thirty-three students who took the class, plus Allie, the teaching assistant. The interviews lasted about an hour, and I recorded them. In several cases, I went back for second and third interviews; in some cases, an interview led to an extended email correspondence; and I got to know some interviewees much better because they took more classes with me.

I'm drawing on those interviews and follow-up conversations when I attribute words and ideas to students in this book, in quotation marks or out of them, though in a few cases I'm drawing on my own memory of what that student said in class or on notes I jotted down at the time. Beyond the usual selecting and trimming, I have not revised what students said, following the standards of quotation I employ when writing for fact-checked magazines. There's one minor but frequent exception to this policy, however. In addition to removing *ums* and *uhs*, which is standard practice, I have similarly removed many repetitions of the word *like* where it functions as a variant of *um*—that is, aural filler that can like really like get in the way, like, when you're like reading what like somebody like said.

When I characterize students' thinking, either individually or as a group, I'm similarly drawing on their own recall of what they thought and felt. Obviously, the same goes for my recall of my own thoughts and words. You will have noticed, however, that at times I tell you something on the order of "Then somebody said something like this." That's because I have resisted the urge to make our memories sharper than they are. I am enthusiastically in favor of nonfiction using novelistic techniques to tell a story, but I don't trust nonfiction that in the name of telling a good story invents or imagines dialogue or thought processes for its characters without admitting that that's what it's doing. Down that road lies "based on true events" and "for narrative convenience I have combined characters and reordered events and otherwise made shit up" and other such abuses of the truth claim of nonfiction, and that's not our destination. This book is a reported essay, not *The Crown* or *Fear and Loathing in Las Vegas*. So I have tried always to be straight with you about what we remember and what we sort of remember and what definitely or probably happened. That's in keeping with one of this book's main themes: when you're in class and in the groove—or bored out of your mind and staring out the window at the rain—it may feel as if you're temporarily removed from time into the eternal present of school, but the way a class may persist or fade or mutate in memory forms just a part of how time relentlessly impinges on the experience of learning and teaching.

It would have been convenient for me if there was a video record of every class meeting from the semester I'm writing about, but there isn't—because I want it that way as a matter of principle. Boston College does have a system for recording classes, but I opt out of it because I think it's important that students and teachers should be able to speak freely in a classroom. We're there to try things out, experiment, iterate, make mistakes, and in the course of doing that, we may end up saying things that could conceivably be edited in ways that could put any of us in a difficult position. So there's no video of my classes, and usually I'm very happy about that, though there were times as I wrote this book that I half-wished I'd forgotten to opt out for just that one semester.

I've changed the names of the students in this book. I started out intending to use everyone's real name, and I asked students' permission to do that, and they all said it was okay with them—except Elizabeth, who liked the idea of a pseudonym "if it could be something cool." (My apologies, not-Elizabeth, if you don't regard the name Elizabeth as cool, but it struck me as an appropriate substitute for your real name, especially because your real name is a longer version of the real name of the student I call Liz.) In the end, I decided to change them anyway, for at least three reasons. First, in interviews, the students were remarkably forthcoming about themselves and their families, and I thought it my duty to temper their youthful willingness to tell all. Second, and more important, even though they had chosen to talk with me on the record once the course was over, they hadn't signed up to be in a book back when they signed up for my section of Lit Core as freshmen. Third, I decided that what happens in class deserves some added protection. Just as I don't allow anyone to record what happens in my classroom, I felt that my desire to use real names ran afoul of my commitment to the principle that people have a right to say whatever they want to say in class without having to consider whether it's going on some kind of permanent record attached to their name. So I changed the students' names, and I tried to come up with substitutes similar in tone and source to the original. For example, if I were changing my own name I might go with Vito or Stefano, and if there had been a Brittany in the class, I might have gone with Bethany or Brooke, but I also could have gone with Madison. I didn't change other details of their lives, which struck me as too specific in their resonance to mess with.

In person or on Zoom, Lit Core was school, and I've spent pretty much my whole life in school. I started preschool at Ancona Montessori on the South Side of Chicago at the age of two, and I've been either a student or a teacher or both ever since, except for the two years in New York between college and grad school when I worked for the Academy for Educational Development and New York City's Board of Education. So I'm a school lifer, and the classroom is home turf, but I recognize that this doesn't necessarily make me the perfect person to write about teaching literature. Anytime anyone tells you anything about school, as I have been doing in this book, you should get second opinions. If fellow teachers of literature read this book, I'm sure that at least some of them will say that I'm doing it all wrong because I'm not a real literature person (my degrees are in the interdisciplinary field of American Studies), or I'm insufficiently committed to or critical of the Great Books, or I'm an elitist because I teach at an expensive school with a large endowment that has an insufficiently diverse student body, or I teach at an insufficiently elite school, or I have inadequately theorized this or that, and so on. Most of those limiting factors are worth mentioning, as is the fact that I'm not very interested in literary criticism as a field and don't think that it makes progress like a science. It's more like literature: interpretations change over time, but they don't necessarily improve on each other or advance toward some goal of more perfect knowledge. I try to keep up with what's going on in blues, country music, boxing, city life, the study of neighborhood, the work of many different writers and other artists, and other things that interest me, and I am deeply interested in how meaning flows through all sorts of written and other artifacts, but I don't keep up with the debates and priorities of the field of literary studies. I also find critique wildly overrated by academics and fellow travelers. As far as I'm concerned, there should be less critique and more explaining, less ripping things to shreds and more *making* things, which in Lit Core means making interpretive arguments that hold up.

You will have noticed that there's no big musical number or car chase to cap off the semester. School is not TV. There may well be arc in the story of the fifteen-week encounter between students and teacher—in fact, I'm committed to the principle that there is—but it's usually not the kind of steep and neatly defined three-act arc that fits the Hollywood bill, since it can take extremely subtle shape and extend for years and years beyond the limits of the semester. I know that's true, since I'm still digesting things I learned in classrooms a long time ago. Nobody made an impassioned Zoom speech during the final class session of Lit Core in spring 2020 in which they revealed that they were in love with another student or that they were a spy or a space alien. As far as I know, nobody resolved to write the next Great American Novel or, more likely, the Great American Video Game—though the students are still young, and either could yet happen. Still, when I look back at that semester, I can make out the slow, steady pulse of discovery and transformation and reflection in our community of inquiry, and it manifested in all sorts of ways, from students facing their fear of speaking in class to skeptics coming around to the idea of interpretation as equipment for living. And the always-shifting larger relationship of school to the world around it revealed itself in a thousand and one ways, not least in many different versions of the attempt to connect how characters live in books to how we live out here in the world where we buy and sell and eat and breathe. When breathing in proximity to others became a problem and we had to abandon the classroom, it forced us to consider just what we could lose and how much it means to us.

Much of what matters most about the classroom can be lost or taken away. The last pandemic and the next one, the impulses to move everything in life online and turn teachers into contingent workers, the widening divides between haves and have-nots and between red and blue, the way that those divides make school contested ground in fierce debates about things that don't have much to do with schooling, the current vogues for dismissing the humanities as a waste of time and for classing teachers with journalists as enemies of the people—these encroach on the classroom in general and on the literature classroom in particular. I take the threat of those encroachments as a reminder to explain and cherish and stand up for what we do there.

Acknowledgments

I could not have written the book I wanted to write without the generous participation of the students who took Lit Core with me in the eventful spring of 2020. In interviews, follow-ups, and continuing correspondence, they have given freely of their thoughts and stories and inner lives, and I thank each and every one of them from the bottom of my heart. Without their fulsome contributions and refreshing candor, I would have had to settle for just my own point of view, which wouldn't have been enough to do the job properly. I'm responsible for how the book came out and the arguments it makes, of course, but their enthusiasm and openness and articulate skepticism enabled me to write it at all. Students, thinking and learning, provide the engine of this book and of any class I regard as worth teaching.

My second great debt here is to my own teachers, a train of models extending back more than half a century from Kevin Barry, the endlessly patient maestro with whom I take lap steel guitar lessons, to Rose Bello, my no-nonsense kindergarten teacher at the University of Chicago's Laboratory Schools. I have been ridiculously lucky in the quality of the teachers I've had over the years—especially teachers of literature, like Hal Hoffenkamp, Darlene McCampbell, and Rich Slotkin. These teachers and my gratitude for all I owe them come to mind often as I make my way through a class period, a semester, a life. They're kind of like the forebears invoked in the Viking death prayer originally recorded by the tenth-century traveler Ibn Fadlan and rendered as stirring pulp dialogue in *The Thirteenth Warrior*: "Lo, there do I see my father. Lo, there do I see my mother and my sisters and my brothers. Lo, there do I see the line of my people, back to the beginning. Lo, they do call to me, they bid me take my place among them in the halls of Valhalla, where the brave may live forever."

I've learned a lot of craft lessons from colleagues and students in the English Department and American Studies and journalism programs of Boston College, where the work of teaching and learning is taken seriously. In working on this book, I've also profited from advice, sources, ideas, readings, and encouragement offered by Dayton Haskin, Garnette Cadogan, George Justice, James Parker, Phil Deloria, Wolde-Ab Isaac, Emma Horrigan, Susan Rabiner, Alex Star, Eric Schmidt; my brothers, Sebastian and Sal Jr.; and my late father, Salvatore G. Rotella. This book began life as an essay I wrote for David Rowell, my friend and longtime editor at the dear departed *Washington Post Magazine*. He has supported the project every step of the way with characteristic acumen, sensitivity, and a much appreciated willingness to tell me when enough is enough. I have also drawn on another previously published essay, "On Teaching: A Stance, An Attitude," which appeared in *Raritan*, edited by Jackson Lears.

Kate Marshall, Jeff Anderson, Joe Abbott, Kevin Barrett Kane, and their hardworking colleagues at the University of California Press brought the book into existence with professional dispatch and friendly good humor. Leonard Cassuto, Mark Edmundson, and Michael Roth contributed generous and insightful readings of the manuscript.

I have learned a great deal from my family about what happens in the classroom and what it means. My daughters, Ling-li and Yuan, were undergraduates when I was working on this book, and seeing school through their eyes helped draw me to this subject and give it life. My wife, Tina Klein, encouraged me to write this book and marked up a draft with characteristic clarity-inducing rigor. My ongoing conversation with her about teaching and learning has been particularly valuable for me because we're so different in classroom attitude and temperament.

At this writing, my mother, Pilar Vives Rotella, has been a professional teacher for seven decades and is still going at the age of ninety-one. She has tapered down to teaching a couple of continuing ed courses from a high of something approaching twenty (!?) college courses a year in her heroic prime, when she was somehow also writing her dissertation, living through the upheavals of the late 1960s on the South Side of Chicago, becoming an American, and raising three young sons who demanded that she teach herself to pitch so that we could concentrate on smashing the hell out of the ball and tearing around the jacket-bases on the way to the inevitable titanic collision at the Cubs-cap home plate. This book is dedicated to her as a modest token of thanks for all that I have learned and continue to learn from her example.

Reading List

Junot Díaz, *The Brief Wondrous Life of Oscar Wao* (New York: Riverhead, 2007).

Joan Didion, "Slouching Towards Bethlehem," in *Slouching Towards Bethlehem* (New York: Farrar, Straus and Giroux, 1968).

Stuart Dybek, *Childhood and Other Neighborhoods* (1980; Chicago: University of Chicago Press, 2003).

Nathaniel Hawthorne, "My Kinsman Major Molineux," in *The Snow-Image and Other Twice-Told Tales* (1832; Boston: Ticknor, Reed, and Fields, 1852).

Jack London, "South of the Slot," in *The Strength of the Strong* (1909; New York: Macmillan, 1914).

Vladimir Nabokov, "Cloud, Castle, Lake," *The Atlantic*, June 1941.

Flannery O'Connor, "A Good Man Is Hard to Find," in *A Good Man Is Hard to Find* (1953; New York: Harcourt, Brace, 1955).

Annie Proulx, *Accordion Crimes* (New York: Scribner, 1996).

Peter Schakel and Jack Ridl, *Approaching Literature in the 21st Century* (New York: Bedford/St. Martin's, 2004).

Hunter Thompson, *Fear and Loathing in Las Vegas* (1971; New York: Harper, 2005).

Edith Wharton, *The House of Mirth* (1905; New York: Random House, 1999).

Index

Founded in 1893,
UNIVERSITY OF CALIFORNIA PRESS
publishes bold, progressive books and journals
on topics in the arts, humanities, social sciences,
and natural sciences—with a focus on social
justice issues—that inspire thought and action
among readers worldwide.

The UC PRESS FOUNDATION
raises funds to uphold the press's vital role
as an independent, nonprofit publisher, and
receives philanthropic support from a wide
range of individuals and institutions—and from
committed readers like you. To learn more, visit
ucpress.edu/supportus.